Structured Relapse Prevention

Structured Relapse Prevention

An Outpatient Counselling Approach
2nd edition

MARILYN A. HERIE, PHD, RSW, AND LYN WATKIN-MEREK, BSCN

camh

Centre for Addiction and Mental Health
Centre de toxicomanie et de santé mentale

Library and Archives Canada Cataloguing in Publication

Herie, Marilyn, 1963–
Structured relapse prevention: an outpatient counselling
approach / Marilyn A. Herie and Lyn Watkin-Merek. — 2nd ed.

First ed. written by Helen M. Annis, Marilyn A. Herie and
Lyn Watkin-Merek
Includes bibliographical references.
ISBN: 978-0-88868-517-9 (PRINT)
ISBN: 978-0-88868-912-2 (PDF)
ISBN: 978-0-88868-913-9 (HTML)
ISBN: 978-0-88868-914-6 (ePUB)

1. Substance abuse—Relapse—Prevention. 2. Alcoholism—Relapse—
Prevention. 3. Drug abuse—Relapse—Prevention. 4. Alcoholism
counselling. 5. Drug abuse counselling. I. Watkin-Merek, Lyn, 1955–
II. Centre for Addiction and Mental Health III. Title.

HV4998.H47   2006 362.29'186   C2006-900073-5

Printed in Canada

This publication may be available in other formats. For information about alternate formats or other CAMH publications, or to place an order, please contact Sales and Distribution:

Toll-free: 1 800 661-1111
Toronto: 416 595-6059
E-mail: publications@camh.ca
Online store: http://store.camh.ca

Website: www.camh.ca

This book was produced by the following:
Development: Andrew Johnson, CAMH
Editorial: Nick Gamble, CAMH; Elizabeth D'Anjou
Design: Mara Korkola, CAMH
Typesetting: Jean Lightfoot Peters
Print production: Christine Harris, CAMH

3096 / 03-2015 / P7167

Preface

We are pleased that you have decided to offer Structured Relapse Prevention (SRP) as a treatment option for your clients. Since the original edition of this manual was published in 1996, there have been many changes in how outpatient substance use treatment is conceptualized and delivered. Over the past decade, we have seen:

- an increased emphasis on culturally competent clinical interventions and relationships, and on tailoring approaches to meet the needs of diverse client populations
- a greater appreciation (and application) of harm reduction approaches, particularly for clients who are unwilling or unable to access mainstream substance use services
- more widespread recognition of the importance of meeting the needs of clients with concurrent mental health and substance issues, which has led to the development of community partnerships and the integration of services at both system and program levels
- the development and dissemination of "best practice" principles and guidelines in substance use treatment, which has encouraged practitioners and programs to re-examine service delivery, screening and assessment, and clinical interventions.

All of these developments have one thing in common: enhancing clinical practice so it meets the unique needs of every client who accesses substance use treatment services.

In revising the content of this treatment manual, we have retained the elements that clinicians have told us are helpful. These include the essential structure of the approach—which is research-based and consistent with best-practice principles—and the session-by-session outlines and clinical tools. We have also added some new elements:

- a section outlining a version of SRP adapted for clients with concurrent disorders
- updated clinical background articles
- web-based clinical screening and feedback resources for clients and clinicians
- a CD containing copies of tools, questionnaires, forms and exercises that can be printed and used in clinical settings.

The material in this manual was originally developed as part of CAMH's OPTIONS project. OPTIONS (Outpatient Treatment In ONtario Services) was designed to increase clients' access to cost-effective outpatient treatment by developing and making available treatment protocols and training packages. An important feature of the OPTIONS project was its commitment to consulting with and actively involving community service providers to apply research-based knowledge consistent with client's needs. The SRP model was field tested and used by outpatient counsellors and by probation and parole officers in Ontario, and was guided by an external advisory committee drawn from a variety of service settings.

ACKNOWLEDGMENTS

The original SRP manual, which provided the foundation for this revision, benefited enormously from the time and expertise of many readers in the field. We wish to acknowledge the clinical team at PineGate Addiction Service in Sudbury for their help in tailoring the original materials: Richard Audet, Sheila Crighton, Patricia Dryden, Sylvie Giroux, Michele Glover, Nancy Huneault, Donald Moore, Guy Racine, John Scott, Iris Vandeligt and Gianni Vigna.

To ensure that SRP fit the probation and parole context, 10 probation officers from six offices in Western Ontario tried out the original materials with their clients. We gratefully acknowledge their advice and feedback: Des Donovan, Cayuga; Burns MacLeod, Woodstock; Gail Mitchell and John MacKay, London; Katie Bosveld, Windsor; Debbie Gibson and Robin North, Guelph; and Judy Gingrich, Rosemary MacKenzie and Susan Cox, Kitchener.

Thanks also to the advisory committee that guided the creation of the first edition in the early 1990s: Linda Bell, Bellwood Health Services, Toronto; Bill Dufton, Ministry of the Solicitor General and Correctional Services; Carole Hea, Occupational Health and Safety, University of Waterloo; Thomas Hills, community; Nancy Huneault, PineGate Addiction Service, Sudbury; Stephen Kennedy, former Director, Addictions Assessment and Referral Service of Ottawa-Carleton; Carol Lever, Ontario Substance Abuse Bureau, Ministry of Health; Peter McKenna, Addiction Assessment Centre, Brockville; Brian McLatchie, Pinewood Centre, Oshawa; Sharon Mulligan, Smith Clinic Outpatient Services, St. Joseph's General Hospital, Thunder Bay; Ian Stewart, Halton Alcohol and Drug Assessment, Prevention and Treatment Services, Halton; Beverly Thompson, Westover Treatment Centre, Thamesville; and Tim Uuksulainen, Ministry of the Solicitor General and Correctional Services.

We would like to acknowledge the CAMH therapists and managers who reviewed this second edition: Eva Ingber, Raj Sohi, Tania Saccoccio, Tim Godden, Susan LaFontaine, Patti Socca, Deborah Goldenberg, Phyllis Wong and Shannon Costigan. We give a special acknowledgement to Andrea Tsanos, Advanced Practice Clinician, for her expertise and practice wisdom. Andrea's contribution is such that she has collaborated with us as a co-author on Part IV of this manual, Adaptations for Clients with Concurrent Disorders. Finally, we are deeply indebted to Dr. Helen Annis, who developed and led the clinical research on the SRP intervention and was the first author of the 1996 edition of this book, and to Dr. Garth Martin, who led the dissemination research of SRP during the 1990s, and was instrumental in helping to put this manual into the hands of clinicians across Ontario and beyond.

Contents

Part III: Coping Skills Exercises

Part IV: SRP for Clients with Concurrent Disorders

Appendix A: Additional Sample Forms

Appendix B: Clinical Background Articles

PART I:
About SRP

Introduction

What Is Structured Relapse Prevention?

Structured Relapse Prevention (SRP) is an approach to outpatient counselling that uses cognitive-behavioural treatment to help clients learn the coping skills they need to deal effectively with day-to-day substance use triggers and risk situations. It was developed starting in the late 1980s at the Addiction Research Foundation, one of the founding organizations of the Centre for Addiction and Mental Health (CAMH). SRP has been used as a stand-alone, outpatient intervention of eight to 12 sessions, as an aftercare component to inpatient treatment, and as a set of tools to be used as needed when working with clients who are ambivalent about changing their substance use. SRP has also been used with individuals or groups in a variety of service contexts, including substance use treatment services, employee assistance programs, probation and parole settings, and mental health settings.

About This Manual

This manual provides all of the clinical tools you will need to implement SRP treatment with groups and individual clients. Although the manual presents a set of structured session-by-session guidelines and tools, it can be adapted to fit the needs of your own clients and groups. Some clients will benefit from the complete treatment program outlined here, while others will be best served by using selected clinical tools in a less formal way.

The structure of the manual is as follows:

Part I includes this introduction, an overview of the approach, some background material on how SRP relates to the five stages of change, and a summary of some empirical studies on its effectiveness.

Part II gives a detailed, session-by-session guide to the SRP approach. It is divided into five sections, corresponding to the phases, or "components," of SRP counselling:

Assessment, Motivational Interviewing, Individualized Treatment Planning, Initiation of Change and Maintenance of Change.

The descriptions of the SRP treatment components contain all of the clinical materials you will need, including forms for client homework assignments and questionnaires, all of which can be copied for your clinical use (or printed from the CD that accompanies this manual). In addition, Therapist Checklists are included for each of the components: brief, point-form lists of the materials you will need, the topics for discussion during the session, the related clinical tools, and the homework assigned at the end of the session. While the Therapist Checklists are meant to provide you with suggested guidelines for doing SRP, as has been mentioned, the program can be adapted in whatever ways best fit your setting and your clients' needs.

Part III provides a series of exercises to help clients develop and improve coping skills; you are free to copy or print these, too, for clinical use. You and your client can identify the areas of coping that would be most relevant and helpful to work on in treatment, using a simple checklist provided as part of the Individualized Treatment Planning component in Part II.

Part IV contains a new feature of this edition of the manual: an adapted version of the SRP guidelines specifically for clients with concurrent mental health and substance use problems ("concurrent disorders"). This "CD-adapted" section contains general suggestions for screening and assessing clients with concurrent disorders, hints for running SRP groups with this population, revised versions of the Therapist Checklists, and adaptations of many of the clinical tools, including several of the most crucial Coping Skills Exercises.

Appendix A offers some supplementary administrative forms you may find useful (sample clinical notes and a chart audit checklist).

Appendix B reproduces three clinical articles containing background information useful for working with SRP clients:

Tupker, E. & Sagorsky, L. (2004). Motivational Interviewing. In S. Harrison & V. Carver (Eds.), *Alcohol & Drug Problems: A Practical Guide for Counsellors* (3rd ed.; pp. 23–44). Toronto: Centre for Addiction and Mental Health.

Herie, M. & Watkin-Merek, L. (2004). Relapse prevention. In S. Harrison & V. Carver (Eds.), *Alcohol & Drug Problems: A Practical Guide for Counsellors* (3rd ed.; pp. 143–168). Toronto: Centre for Addiction and Mental Health.

Martino, S., Carroll, K., Kostas, D., Perkins, J. & Rounsaville, B. (2002). Dual diagnosis motivational interviewing: A modification of motivational interviewing for substance-abusing patients with psychotic disorders. *Journal of Substance Abuse Treatment, 23*(4), 297–308.

At certain points in this manual, you will be advised to read one of the articles. In addition, you may want to review the articles periodically throughout your SRP work, since they include useful insights that may address some of the challenges your clients may be facing.

As you will see, there are many resources and tools in this manual! Although you may want to review the book from beginning to end the first time you use it, it is designed to be a "toolkit" of resources and client exercises. We have tried to make it as practical and user-friendly as possible, and we hope that you and your clients find it useful.

Who Are SRP Clients?

SRP counselling is designed for people who have a moderate to severe substance use problem and are willing to work, on an outpatient basis, with a counsellor toward changing their use of alcohol or other drugs.

SRP clients are men and women of various ages and backgrounds. They have different problems and needs, and they begin treatment at different stages of readiness.

A few sample profiles of clients who have been through SRP at CAMH are presented below.

Client Profile: John

"John," a 28-year-old business manager, started SRP counselling to address his alcohol and cocaine use. John was encouraged to seek treatment by his family physician, who was concerned when John presented in his office with complaints of lack of energy and depressed mood. John found that his cocaine use was always triggered after a drinking occasion. He also noticed that his substance use was having a negative effect on his relationship and his productivity at work. When he first started attending Motivational Interviewing sessions before his SRP group began, John said that he wanted to quit using cocaine, but just to cut down on his drinking. John's counsellor worked with John's stated goals, and helped him to weigh the costs and benefits of quitting cocaine use and cutting down alcohol consumption. As John began attending the Initiation phase sessions of SRP, he began to notice that even small amounts of alcohol placed him at high risk of cocaine use. Midway through his SRP treatment sessions, he changed his goal to abstinence from all substances. John told his counsellor that it had been important to him to come to this decision on his own.

Client Profile: Kumar

"Kumar," age 35, was mandated to treatment as a condition of bail after he was arrested and charged with assault. One evening, after being out with friends at a bar, he had come home and gotten into an argument with his partner. He became aggressive and pushed her against a wall. She called emergency services, and Kumar was arrested and charged. In the beginning Kumar was resistant to the idea of coming in for treatment, and he repeatedly stated, "But I'm not an alcoholic!" Kumar typically drank eight beers on Friday nights after work, and three or four beers on two other days during the week. After a few group SRP sessions, he began to identify some of the negative consequences of his drinking. Kumar decided that cutting down on his drinking would be his best option. Although his counsellor expressed some concerns about his goal given his aggressive behaviour and involvement with the legal system, the counsellor and Kumar

---

agreed to look at a harm reduction plan for reduced drinking. Kumar's goal was to not drink at the bar alone or with friends, but to have one or two drinks on a Saturday, and only if it did not interfere with his being able to participate in family activities. At the end of treatment Kumar reported being able to keep to his goal, and had begun attending anger management counselling.

Client Profile: Dianna

"Dianna," a 25-year-old self-employed personal shopper and SRP client, was encouraged by concerned family members to seek treatment for her heavy use of alcohol. She reported drinking five to eight glasses of wine, five days per week. She said that her drinking often led to blackouts and high-risk sexual behaviour. Also, Dianna had sustained a life-threatening injury as a result of falling while intoxicated, which had left her with permanent health consequences. Dianna promised her family that she would be abstinent from alcohol for a period of six months. During her 11 weeks in SRP treatment, Dianna began seeing many benefits to not drinking, including a new relationship with a partner who did not use substances. However, even after three months of abstinence, Dianna was expressing ambivalence about abstinence as a long-term goal. She and her counsellor agreed to follow up her SRP treatment with biweekly sessions to address her ambivalence, and to continue to work on relapse prevention.

"John," "Kumar" and "Dianna" are just three out of hundreds of clients at CAMH who have benefited from SRP. With the help of their therapists and SRP program aids, these clients identified their problems and triggers to use; they set clear goals, learned new coping strategies and changed their substance use behaviour.

How Does SRP Work?

SRP is a flexible program, designed to accommodate clients' different needs and treatment goals.

SRP counselling focuses on engaging the client to:
• assess his or her goals and commitment to change
• design an individually tailored treatment plan
• identify his or her strengths and resources
• learn to anticipate triggers to alcohol or other drug use, and develop alternative ways of coping
• develop confidence by practising coping skills in real-life risk situations
• make connections between alcohol and other drug use and other life situations
• ultimately, take over the therapist's role by anticipating risk situations and pre-planning coping strategies.

What Does SRP Include?

A complete program involving SRP typically includes:
- a full clinical assessment with personalized feedback
- one or more Motivational Interviewing appointments prior to SRP counselling
- engaging the client in developing an individually tailored treatment plan consisting of:
  - a treatment contract
  - a personal hierarchy of triggers to alcohol or other drug use, to be worked on in treatment through homework assignments
  - client goal setting and self-monitoring.
- eight to 12 counselling sessions (individual or group)
- Initiation of Change homework assignments
- Maintenance of Change homework assignments.

Program Overview

There are five major components of SRP counselling:
- Assessment
- Motivational interviewing
- Individualized treatment planning
- Initiation of change counselling
- Maintenance of change counselling.

A summary of each of these components, and, in the case of the last two, a description of the tools used, is given below.

ASSESSMENT

Counselling begins with a full clinical assessment, with a focus on the following areas of the client's situation:
- psychosocial functioning
- history of alcohol and other drug use, and of related problems and consequences
- reasons for and commitment to change
- coping strengths and weaknesses.

This assessment is complemented by a detailed exploration of the client's most problematic triggers to alcohol or other drug use over the year prior to entering treatment. (Triggers may involve internal mood states as well as environmental and social situations that affect clients.) The Inventory of Drug-Taking Situations (IDTS-8) assessment tool (provided in this manual) should be included as part of the Assessment phase.

MOTIVATIONAL INTERVIEWING

Personalized feedback of the assessment results takes place within the context of the Motivational Interviewing phase, which helps the client reach, and then begin to act on, a decision to change his or her alcohol or other drug use. Motivational Interviewing focuses on exploring the client's expressed reasons for changing his or her alcohol or other drug use, on the perceived pros and cons associated with such a change, and on the strength of his or her commitment to change, supplemented by a discussion of the client's triggers for use and his or her coping strengths.

The client *must* reach an explicit decision to try to work toward changing his or her substance use before proceeding to SRP counselling.

INDIVIDUALIZED TREATMENT PLANNING

Following the Assessment and Motivational Interviewing components, each client is engaged in developing an individually tailored treatment plan. The steps include:
• an orientation to SRP counselling, with the client agreeing to sign a treatment contract
• a review by the client of specific recent triggers to alcohol or drug use, with the client deciding on a personal hierarchy of risk areas to be worked on in treatment through a series of homework assignments
• goal setting by the client and self-monitoring of triggers.

INITIATION OF CHANGE

The actual SRP counselling consists of two phases—Initiation and Maintenance—which comprise the final two components of the approach. The Initiation phase focuses on counselling strategies known to be powerful in initiating a change in behaviour, while the Maintenance phase concentrates on strategies with greater potential for the long-term maintenance of this change (i.e., relapse prevention).

Powerful initiation aids include avoidance of risk situations for alcohol or other drug use; coercion (e.g., a legal mandate); hospitalization or residential treatment; protective medications (e.g., Antabuse); the involvement of a partner or other responsible person; and a relatively directive role by the therapist.

Four counselling sessions are typically involved in the initiation phase of SRP counselling. If both group and individual sessions are available, clients should be encouraged to choose their preferred treatment situation.

MAINTENANCE OF CHANGE

In the Maintenance, or relapse prevention, phase, performance aids used in the Initiation phase are gradually withdrawn as the focus shifts to the client's own coping strategies. The strategies are designed to help the client develop confidence and self-efficacy in being able to confront and successfully cope with triggers to alcohol or other drug use. Planned homework assignments, involving gradual exposure to increasingly more difficult drug use triggers, encourage clients to anticipate their identified high-risk situations and to practise new coping strategies between counselling appointments. Four to eight counselling sessions are typically involved in this phase.

Monitoring Tools

Both phases of SRP counselling make use of a number of client monitoring forms. These forms record weekly homework assignments (i.e., anticipated triggers, proposed coping responses, actual coping used and outcomes) and document weekly goal setting, daily recording of urges and temptations, level of confidence experienced, details of any lapse or relapse that occurs and specific coping exercises.

The Situational Confidence Questionnaire (SCQ-8) is administered periodically over the course of treatment to monitor the client's growth in confidence in coping with substance-use triggers across each of eight risk areas for relapse.

These treatment monitoring tools can help focus further homework assignments on areas in which the client reports a continuing lack of confidence in dealing with specific types of substance use triggers. An attempt is made to raise the client's confidence and self-efficacy in all areas of identified risk before he or she is discharged from treatment.

SRP and the Five Stages of Change

The five phases of SRP counselling can be matched to the five stages of change: precontemplation, contemplation, preparation, action and maintenance.

SRP Counselling Phase	Stage of Change
1. Assessment	Precontemplation
2. Motivational Interviewing	Contemplation
3. Individualized Treatment Planning	Preparation
4. Initiation of Change Counselling	Action
5. Maintenance of Change Counselling	Maintenance

Empirical Support for SRP

Results of clinical trials of SRP counselling have shown excellent treatment process and treatment outcome results, which are summarized below.

For a discussion of some of the empirical findings, as well as a more complete examination of the theoretical and conceptual issues related to relapse prevention, see "Relapse Prevention" by Herie and Watkin-Merek (2004), reproduced in Appendix B.

TREATMENT PROCESS

- Most homework assignments (83 per cent) are successfully completed by clients. Homework assignments that are generated by the client are more likely to be completed successfully (90 per cent) than those generated by the therapist (73 per cent).
- Although homework assignments involve entry into risk situations for substance use, most clients successfully adhere to their treatment goals. Typically, any lapses occur outside of the conduct of homework assignments.
- Negative mood states and interpersonal conflict increase the likelihood that a lapse will lead to a serious relapse.

TREATMENT OUTCOME

- In the year following SRP treatment, most clients dramatically reduce their substance use (e.g., in one study, alcohol consumption was reduced to about one-eighth of the pre-treatment levels).
- Group SRP counselling can be just as effective as Individual SRP counselling.
- Clients with well-differentiated Inventory of Drug-Taking Situations profiles (i.e., those who can identify a hierarchy of risk situations) do better in SRP counselling than clients with undifferentiated profiles.
- Clients with good outcomes show high confidence levels and make use of coping strategies when faced with high-risk situations.
- The greater the number and variety of coping strategies used by a client, the lower the likelihood of relapse.

Results from client satisfaction surveys indicate that 95 per cent of clients rate the program as effective in helping them deal with their problems.

PART II:
Session-by-Session Guide

Phase 1: Assessment

People enter the Structured Relapse Prevention (SRP) program for different reasons and with different goals in mind. They also begin treatment at various stages of readiness.

To get a clear picture of each client's problems, needs and motivation to change, SRP counselling begins with a full clinical assessment, which is complemented by a detailed exploration of the client's main triggers to alcohol and/or other drug use over the year before treatment started.

Description	Clinical Tools
Assessment involves a standardized set of procedures designed to: <ul><li>establish baseline information on alcohol and/or other drug dependence</li><li>assess the client's readiness for SRP counselling</li><li>serve as treatment planning tools for SRP counselling by identifying: –the client's high-risk situations for alcohol and/or other drug use –the client's coping strengths and weaknessess</li><li>assess the client's high-risk situations for alcohol and/or other drug use</li><li>identify the client's coping strengths and weaknesses.</li></ul>	<ul><li>Alcohol Dependence Scale (ADS) . . . . p. 15</li><li>Drug Abuse Screening Test (DAST) . . . . p. 18</li><li>Personalized Alcohol Use Feedback Online Tool (*optional*) . . . . p. 20</li><li>Commitment to Change Algorithm (Alcohol or Drugs) . . . . p. 22</li><li>Inventory of Drug-Taking Situations (IDTS-8) . . . . p. 24</li><li>Assessment Summary Form . . . . p. 29</li></ul>

Assessment

THERAPIST COMPLETES WITH CLIENT

☐ Commitment to Change Algorithm: Alcohol

and/or

☐ Commitment to Change Algorithm: Drugs

CLIENT COMPLETES

☐ Alcohol Dependence Scale (ADS)

☐ Drug Abuse Screening Test (DAST)

☐ Personalized Alcohol Use Feedback Online Tool (*optional*) (Available at http://notes.camh.net/efeed.nsf/feedback. If the client cannot access this tool online, the therapist can print out the questions, complete them with the client in a paper and pencil format, then enter the data online and bring back the personalized feedback for discussion at the next session.)

☐ Inventory of Drug-Taking Situations (IDTS-8)

THERAPIST COMPLETES

☐ Assessment Summary Form

Client Name: _____

Alcohol Dependence Scale (ADS)

Instructions

1. Carefully read each question and the possible answers provided. Answer each question by circling the ONE choice that is most true for you.
2. The word "drinking" in a question refers to "drinking of alcoholic beverages."
3. Take as much time as you need. Work carefully, and try to finish as soon as possible. Please answer ALL questions.

If you have difficulty with a question or have any problems, please ask the questionnaire administrator.

These questions refer to the past 12 months.

1. How much did you drink the last time you drank?
   a. Enough to get high or less   b. Enough to get drunk
   c. Enough to pass out

2. Do you often have hangovers on Sunday or Monday mornings?
   a. No   b. Yes

3. Have you had the "shakes" when sobering up (hands tremble, shake inside)?
   a. No   b. Sometimes   c. Almost every time I drink

4. Do you get physically sick (e.g., vomit, stomach cramps) as a result of drinking?
   a. No   b. Sometimes   c. Almost every time I drink

5. Do you have the "DTs" (delirium tremens)—that is, seen, felt or heard things not really there; felt very anxious, restless and over-excited?
   a. No   b. Sometimes   c. Several times

6. When you drink, do you stumble about, stagger, and weave?
   a. No   b. Sometimes   c. Often

7. As a result of drinking, have you felt overly hot and sweaty (feverish)?
   a. No   b. Once   c. Several times

8. As a result of drinking, have you seen things that were not really there?
   a. No   b. Once   c. Several times

9. Do you panic because you fear you may not have a drink when you need it?
   a. No   b. Yes

10. Have you had blackouts ("loss of memory" without passing out) as a result of drinking?
    a. No, never   b. Sometimes   c. Often
    d. Almost every time I drink

11. Do you carry a bottle with you or keep one close at hand?
    a. No   b. Some of the time   c. Most of the time

12. After a period of abstinence (not drinking), do you end up drinking heavily again?

    a. No   b. Sometimes   c. Almost every time I drink

13. In the past 12 months, have you passed out as a result of drinking?

    a. No   b. Once   c. More than once

14. Have you had a convulsion (fit) following a period of drinking?

    a. No   b. Yes   c. Several times

15. Do you drink throughout the day?

    a. No   b. Yes

16. After drinking heavily, has your thinking been fuzzy or unclear?

    a. No   b. Yes, but only for a few hours
    c. Yes, for one or two days   d. Yes, for many days

17. As a result of drinking, have you felt your heart beating rapidly?

    a. No   b. Yes   c. Several times

18. Do you almost constantly think about drinking and alcohol?

    a. No   b. Yes

19. As a result of drinking, have you heard "things" that were not really there?

    a. No   b. Yes   c. Several times

20. Have you had weird and frightening sensations when drinking?

    a. No   b. Once or twice   c. Often

21. As a result of drinking, have you "felt things" crawling on you that were not really there (e.g., bugs, spiders)?

    a. No   b. Yes   c. Several times

22. With respect to blackouts (loss of memory):

    a. Have never had a blackout
    b. Have had blackouts that last less than an hour
    c. Have had blackouts that last for several hours
    d. Have had blackouts that last a day or more

23. Have you tried to cut down your drinking and failed?

    a. No   b. Once   c. Several times

24. Do you gulp drinks (drink quickly)?

    a. No   b. Yes

25. After taking one or two drinks, can you usually stop?

    a. Yes   b. No

Authors: H.A. Skinner, J.L. Horn, K. Wanberg and F.M. Faster. Addiction Research Foundation, Toronto, Ont., Canada © 1984

ALCOHOL DEPENDENCE SCALE (ADS)

Scoring

For each question, score:

a = 0   b = 1   c = 2   d = 3

The total of scores for all questions yields the final score.

DEGREE OF DEPENDENCE ON ALCOHOL

0	No evidence of dependence
1–13	Low level of dependence (1st quartile)
14–21	Moderate level of dependence (2nd quartile)
22–30	Substantial level of dependence (3rd quartile)
31–51	Severe level of dependence (4th quartile)

Client Name: _____

Drug Abuse Screening Test (DAST)

The following questions concern information about your potential involvement with drugs, *not including alcoholic beverages*, during the past 12 months. Carefully read each statement and decide if your answer is "No" or "Yes." Then, fill in the appropriate box beside the question.

When the words "drug abuse" are used, they mean the use of prescribed or over-the-counter drugs in excess of the directions and any non-medical use of drugs. The various drug classes may include: cannabis (e.g., marijuana, hash), solvents, tranquillizers (e.g., Valium), barbiturates, cocaine, stimulants (e.g., speed), hallucinogens (e.g., LSD) or narcotics (e.g., heroin). Remember, the questions *do not include alcoholic beverages*.

Please answer every question. If you have difficulty with a statement, then choose the response that is mostly right.

These questions refer to the past 12 months.	Yes	No
1. Have you used drugs other than those required for medical reasons?	☐	☐
2. Have you abused prescription drugs?	☐	☐
3. Do you abuse more than one drug at a time?	☐	☐
4. Can you get through the week without using drugs?	☐	☐
5. Are you always able to stop using drugs when you want to?	☐	☐
6. Have you had "blackouts" or "flashbacks" as a result of drug use?	☐	☐
7. Do you ever feel bad or guilty about your drug use?	☐	☐
8. Does your spouse (or parents) ever complain about your involvement with drugs?	☐	☐
9. Has drug abuse created problems between you and your spouse or your parents?	☐	☐
10. Have you lost friends because of your use of drugs?	☐	☐
11. Have you neglected your family because of your use of drugs?	☐	☐
12. Have you been in trouble at work because of drug abuse?	☐	☐
13. Have you lost a job because of drug abuse?	☐	☐
14. Have you gotten into fights when under the influence of drugs?	☐	☐
15. Have you engaged in illegal activities in order to obtain drugs?	☐	☐
16. Have you been arrested for possession of illegal drugs?	☐	☐
17. Have you ever experienced withdrawal symptoms (felt sick) when you stopped taking drugs?	☐	☐
18. Have you had medical problems as a result of your drug use (e.g., memory loss, hepatitis, convulsions, bleeding, etc.)?	☐	☐
19. Have you gone to anyone for help for a drug problem?	☐	☐
20. Have you been involved in a treatment program specifically related to drug use?	☐	☐

Author: H.A. Skinner, Ph.D. Addiction Research Foundation, Toronto, Ont., Canada © 1982

DRUG ABUSE SCREENING TEST (DAST)

Scoring

1 point for every YES response to Question 1–3, 6–20

1 point for a NO response to Question 4 and 5

DEGREE OF PROBLEM RELATED TO DRUG ABUSE

0	NONE reported
1–5	LOW level
6–10	MODERATE level
11–15	SUBSTANTIAL level
16–20	SEVERE level

About the Personalized Alcohol Use Feedback Online Tool

A number of online tools have been developed to provide clients (and the general public) with personalized information about the health risks, costs and consequences of their alcohol use. Clients who are not yet prepared to acknowledge the existence of an alcohol problem, or those who are still unsure about the need for treatment, can benefit from seeing objective, neutral feedback that is relevant to their situations.

Of course, not all clients (or therapists) have ready access to an Internet-accessible computer and a printer. In such cases, the therapist can print out the online questions in advance of the session (or ask a contact who does have Internet access to do so), ask the client to complete it, enter the data, and return with the printout of personalized feedback at the next session.

The following two online tools have been particularly helpful to us in the early stages of engaging with clients and using motivational strategies to promote change:

- **The Centre for Addiction and Mental Health (CAMH)**
  Personalized Alcohol Use Feedback
  http://notes.camh.net/efeed.nsf/feedback

- **The Alcohol Help Center Check Your Drinking (CYD) Survey**
  http://www.alcoholhelpcenter.net/cyd/

Each of these online self-assessment tools provides excellent motivational feedback to clients—for example, information about how their alcohol consumption compares with that of other Canadians of their age and sex; an estimate of the amount they spend on alcohol in a year; an approximation of the number of extra calories they consumed; information about possible health risks associated with their level of use; alcohol-related consequences; and an idea of the likelihood that their drinking is reaching levels that may be considered problematic. This information is presented in easy-to-understand graphs, charts and text, and can be printed out for future reference.

A handout is provided on the following page that takes clients through the process of accessing the CAMH online tool, and provides a screen shot from it.

ONLINE QUESTIONNAIRE

How Does Your Drinking Affect You?

The Centre for Addiction and Mental Health has a short, confidential online questionnaire that you can fill out, and then get back a personal report about some areas where alcohol might be affecting you.

To try it out, type this address in the window of your web browser: http://notes.camh.net/efeed.nsf/feedback

The computer screen will look like this:

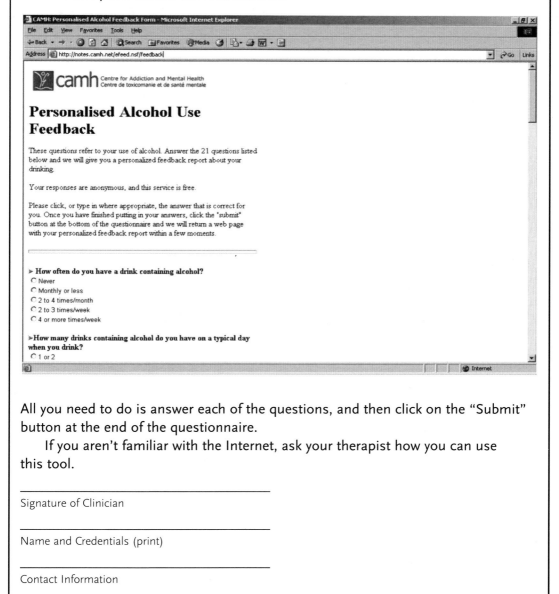

All you need to do is answer each of the questions, and then click on the "Submit" button at the end of the questionnaire.

If you aren't familiar with the Internet, ask your therapist how you can use this tool.

Signature of Clinician

Name and Credentials (print)

Contact Information

Commitment to Change Algorithm

ALCOHOL

This interview is used to classify the client according to one of five stages of change. Ask the following questions in sequence, and end the interview when the client's stage has been identified.

- Did you drink during the last 30 days? Circle:

  YES   or   **NO**

- Are you considering quitting or drinking moderately* within the next 30 days? Circle:

  YES   or   **NO**

  Code PRECONTEMPLATION

- Were you continuously abstinent for more than the last 30 days or did you drink moderately* for more than the last 30 days? Circle:

  YES   or   **NO**

  - Did you follow through on at least one quit attempt** or one attempt to drink moderately* during the last 30 days? Circle:

    YES   or   **NO**

    Code PREPARATION   **Code CONTEMPLATION**

- Were you continuously abstinent for more than the last 30 days or did you drink moderately* for more than the last 30 days? Circle:

  YES   or   **NO**

  Code MAINTENANCE   **Code ACTION**

The client's stage is: _____.

STAGES OF CHANGE

PRECONTEMPLATION—The client engaged in drinking during the last 30 days, and is not considering quitting or adopting moderate drinking upper limits* within the next 30 days.

CONTEMPLATION—The client engaged in drinking during the last 30 days but is considering quitting or adopting moderate drinking upper limits* within the next 30 days.

PREPARATION—The client engaged in drinking during the last 30 days but followed through on at least one quit attempt or one attempt to adopt moderate drinking upper limits* during the last 30 days.

ACTION—The client was continuously abstinent during the last 30 days or successfully adhered to moderate drinking upper limits* during the last 30 days.

MAINTENANCE—The client was continuously abstinent for more than 60 days or successfully adhered to moderate drinking upper limits* for more than 30 days.

* "Moderate drinking" refers to drinking within the following upper limits:
- do not drink daily
- drink no more than 4 drinks on any day (if male); drink no more than three drinks on any day (if female)
- drink no more than 14 drinks in any week (if male); drink no more than 9 drinks in any week (if female)
- one drink = 1 1/2 oz. (43 mL) spirits
    3 oz. (85 mL) fortified wine
    5 oz. (142 mL) table wine
    12 oz. (341 mL) regular beer
** "Quit attempt" refers to successful abstinence as defined by the client (e.g., in relation to time, place, persons or situations).

Commitment to Change Algorithm

DRUGS

This interview is used to classify the client according to one of five stages of change. Ask the following questions in sequence, and end the interview when the client's stage has been identified. Conduct the interview only for the client's primary drug of abuse.

- Did you use _____ during the last 30 days? Circle:

  YES   or   **NO**

- Are you considering quitting _____ within the next 30 days? Circle:

  YES   or   **NO**
                          ↓
                  Code PRECONTEMPLATION

- Were you continuously abstinent from _____ during the last 30 days? Circle:

  YES   or   **NO**
                          ↓
              - Did you follow through on at least one quit attempt* of _____ during the last 30 days? Circle:

                YES   or   **NO**
                  ↓   ↓
              Code PREPARATION   **Code CONTEMPLATION**

- Were you continuously abstinent of _____ for more than the last 30 days? Circle:

  YES   or   **NO**
    ↓   ↓
  Code MAINTENANCE   **Code ACTION**

The client's stage is: _____.

STAGES OF CHANGE

PRECONTEMPLATION—The client engaged in drug use during the last 30 days and is not considering quitting within the next 30 days.

CONTEMPLATION—The client engaged in drug use during the last 30 days but is considering quitting within the next 30 days.

PREPARATION—The client engaged in drug use during the last 30 days but followed through on at least one quit attempt* during the last 30 days.

ACTION—The client was continuously abstinent during the last 30 days.

MAINTENANCE—The client was continuously abstinent for more than 30 days.

* "Quit attempt" is defined as a minimum of 11 days of continual abstinence.

About the IDTS-8

This eight-item version of the Inventory of Drug-Taking Situations, known as the IDTS-8, is based on a longer (50-item) self-report questionnaire developed by Annis and Martin (1985) to provide a profile of the situations in which a client used drugs over the past year. Following a classification system based on the work of Alan Marlatt and his associates (Marlatt & Gordon, 1980; 1985), the original questionnaire assessed eight categories of drug-use situations, divided into two major classes:

PERSONAL STATES

In these situations, the drug use involves a response to an event that is primarily psychological or physical in nature. The situations are grouped into the following five categories:
• unpleasant emotions (10 items)
• physical discomfort (five items)
• pleasant emotions (five items)
• testing personal control (five items)
• urges and temptations to use (five items).

SITUATIONS INVOLVING OTHER PEOPLE

In these situations, a significant influence from another person is involved. The situations are grouped into the following three categories:
• conflict with others (10 items)
• social pressure to use (five items)
• pleasant times with others (five items).

The client is awarded subscores in each of these eight categories, and taken together the scores represent his or her drug-taking risk.

In the abbreviated version presented here, clients identify and rank the three categories of situations out of the eight that provide the highest risk for them, and then, for each of the situations, note the degree of problematic substance use they engage in.

You may want to administer a separate IDTS-8 for each substance a client identifies as problematic.

REFERENCES

Annis, H.M. & Martin, G. (1985). *Inventory of Drug-Taking Situations* (4th ed.). Toronto: Addiction Research Foundation.

Marlatt, G.A. & Gordon, J.R. (1980). Determinants of relapse: Implications for the maintenance of behavior change. In P. Davidson and S. Davidson (Eds.), *Behavioral Medicine: Changing Health Lifestyles*. New York: Brunner/Mazel.

Marlatt, G.A. & Gordon, J.R. (1985). *Relapse Prevention: Maintenance Strategies in the Treatment of Addictive Behaviors*. New York: Guilford Press.

Name: _____ Date: _____

Inventory of Drug-Taking Situations (IDTS-8)

Is this your PRIMARY substance of abuse?	☐
or	
your SECONDARY substance of abuse? (check one box)	☐

IDENTIFYING CAUSES

The first step in trying to change your substance use habits and patterns is to identify the reasons that led to your use of alcohol or other drugs. Below are eight typical causes ("trigger situations").

Think of your drinking or other drug use **over the past year**, and circle any that apply to you.

1. *unpleasant emotions* (e.g., when I was angry, frustrated, bored, sad or anxious)

2. *physical discomfort* (e.g., when I was feeling ill or in pain)

3. *pleasant emotions* (e.g., when I was enjoying myself or just feeling happy)

4. *testing personal control* (e.g., when I started to believe I could handle alcohol or drugs)

5. *urges and temptations* (e.g., when I walked by a pub or saw something that reminded me of drinking or drug use)

6. *conflict with others* (e.g., when I had an argument or was not getting along with someone)

7. *social pressures* (e.g., when someone offered alcohol or drugs)

8. *pleasant times with others* (e.g., when I was out with friends or at a party).

In terms of how often I drink or use drugs in each of the above situations, I would rank the "trigger situations" that I have circled above as follows:

1st (most frequent): _____

2nd (in frequency): _____

3rd (in frequency): _____

(Depending on time available at this session, the next exercise might be a take-home assignment.)

AREAS OF RISK

Think about your drinking or other substance use in the last 12 months in each of the following situations. If you NEVER drank heavily or used other drugs in that situation, you would circle "0." If you ALMOST ALWAYS drank heavily or used other drugs in that situation, you would circle "100%." If your answer falls somewhere in between, place an **X** along the line so that it shows about how close to 0% or 100% you think is appropriate. In the example below, the **X** shows that the person drank heavily or used other drugs a little less than half the time in a particular risk situation.

EXAMPLE

In the last 12 months I drank heavily or used other substances:

0%	25%	**X** 50%	75%	100%	=	48%
Never				Almost always		

In the last 12 months I drank heavily or used other substances when I was experiencing:

1. *Unpleasant emotions*

0%	25%	50%	75%	100%	=	%
Never				Almost always		

2. *Physical discomfort*

0%	25%	50%	75%	100%	=	%
Never				Almost always		

3. *Pleasant emotions*

0%	25%	50%	75%	100%	=	%
Never				Almost always		

4. *Testing personal control*

0%	25%	50%	75%	100%	=	%
Never				Almost always		

5. *Urges and temptations*

0%	25%	50%	75%	100%	=	%
Never				Almost always		

6. *Conflict with others*

0%	25%	50%	75%	100%	=	%
Never				Almost always		

7. *Social pressures*

0%	25%	50%	75%	100%	=	%
Never				Almost always		

8. *Pleasant times with others*

0%	25%	50%	75%	100%	=	%
Never				Almost always		

Adapted from: H.M. Annis and G. Martin, Inventory of Drug-Taking Situations *(4th ed.). Toronto: Addiction Research Foundation* © *1985*

THERAPIST CHECKLIST

Troubleshooting for Undifferentiated IDTS-8 Profiles

Developing a hierarchy of risk situations is central to the SRP approach. Therefore it is important to troubleshoot response patterns on the IDTS-8 that are undifferentiated (i.e., patterns with uniformly low identified risk or patterns of consistently high risk across all risk situations). The following suggestions can help you to determine whether clients do, in fact, experience certain types of situations as a greater risk for substance use.

BEFORE THE COUNSELLING SESSION

Response Checks

☐ literacy level   ⟶   Could the client read the question?

☐ understanding   ⟶   Did the client understand what was asked?

☐ attitude   ⟶   Did the client take the task seriously?

              ⟶   Did the client take care in responding?

              ⟶   Is the client aware that his or her answers will be important in developing a treatment plan?

• If the answer to any of the above is No, the IDTS should be readministered.

• If the answer to all of the above is Yes, proceed to the next checks.

Incentive Checks

☐ Is there any reason the client might want to present as "good" or "bad" on the IDTS?

FLAT, LOW PROFILE: Is there a reason the client might want to minimize his or her substance use problem? (e.g., coercion from courts, spouse or employer)

FLAT, HIGH PROFILE: Is there a reason the client might want to exaggerate his or her problem? (e.g., to draw attention, to cry for help)

• If the answer to any of the above is Yes, the IDTS should be readministered after an appropriate exploration of the issue.

• If the answer to all of the above is No, proceed to the next checks.

Readiness for Change Check

☐ Is the client at the precontemplative or contemplative stage only?

Awareness of Triggers Check

☐ Is the client aware of the types of cues that trigger his or her substance use?

- If the client is not aware of triggers to use, ask the client to complete Daily Diaries (see page 49). When the client has a better appreciation of his or her triggers, readminister the IDTS-8.
- If the client is aware of triggers to use, proceed with the final check.

Resistance to Focus on Triggers Check

☐ Is the client not willing to view his or her drug problem in terms of current situational triggers to use? (E.g., is the client expecting an alternative approach, such as a medical prescription, exploration of childhood experiences or psychodynamic approach)

- If this is the case, try having the client discuss a recent substance use incident, with a focus on antecedents (both mood states and environmental events). Ask the client to complete Daily Diaries.
- If the client begins to accept the relevance of triggers to use, readminister the IDTS-8.
- If the client is willing to view his or her drug problem in terms of current situational triggers, then this may be a valid flat (undifferentiated) IDTS profile. Proceed with asking client to complete Daily Diaries to try to establish currently important triggers to use.

Assessment Summary Form

BACKGROUND

Name: _____ File no.: _____

Home phone: (_____) _____ Bus. phone: (_____) _____

Postal address: _____

_____

Age: _____ Sex: _____ Marital status: _____

Highest level of education reached: _____

_____

Occupation: _____

Current employment status: _____

Current legal status: _____

Primary drug for which client is seeking treatment: _____

Secondary drug(s), if any: _____

Other notable presenting characteristics: _____

ALCOHOL USE

Number of years of problem drinking: _____

Has the client undergone past alcohol treatment? ☐ Yes ☐ No

If Yes, describe treatment: _____

ADS Score

☐ None ☐ Low ☐ Moderate ☐ Substantial ☐ Severe

Has the client encountered alcohol use consequences? ☐ Yes ☐ No

If Yes, describe consequences: _____

_____

Summary of Personalized Alcohol Use Feedback

_____

_____

_____

_____

Alcohol Use Goal

☐ Abstinence ☐ Reduction ☐ Undecided ☐ No change ☐ Not applicable

OTHER DRUG USE

Number of years of problem substance use: _____

Has the client undergone past drug treatment?   ☐ Yes   ☐ No

If Yes, describe treatment: _____

DAST Score

☐ None   ☐ Low   ☐ Moderate   ☐ Substantial   ☐ Severe

Has the client encountered drug use consquences?   ☐ Yes   ☐ No

If Yes, describe consequences: _____

Summary of Drug Use History

_____

Drug Use Goal

☐ Abstinence   ☐ Reduction   ☐ Undecided   ☐ No change   ☐ Not applicable

Areas of Risk Summary (from IDTS-8)

_____

_____

_____

Other Issues

_____

_____

_____

_____

_____

_____

_____

_____

_____

_____

_____

_____

_____

NOTE: If the client identifies other mental health issues, you may want to use the SRP tools adapted for use with concurrent disorders; see Part IV of this manual (page 121).

Phase 2: Motivational Interviewing

Therapists use Motivational Interviewing to provide feedback on the assessment results and to help a client reach a decision to change his or her alcohol or other drug use.

It is important for clients to reach an explicit decision—to state their definite intent—to try to work toward changing their use of alcohol or other drugs before proceeding to SRP counselling.

The basic principles of this component of the SRP approach include the following:

- Labels are de-emphasized: acceptance of the "alcoholism" or "drug addict" label is not necessary for change to occur.
- Personal choice is emphasized regarding future use of alcohol and other drugs.
- The therapist conducts an objective evaluation but focuses on eliciting the client's own concerns.
- The therapist presents objective assessment feedback in a clear but low-key fashion, without imposing conclusions on the client.
- Resistance is seen as an interpersonal behaviour pattern influenced by the therapist's behaviour.
- Resistance is met with reflection.

Treatment goals are negotiated between the client and therapist based on assessment feedback data and acceptability of treatment goals to the client; the client's involvement in and acceptance of goals is treated as vital.

NOTE: For more details, see "Motivational Interviewing" by Tupker and Sagorsky (2004), reproduced in Appendix B.

Description	Clinical Tools
The client receives feedback on the Assessment phase findings, with a focus on exploring the client's: • reasons for change in alcohol or other drug use • pros and cons of change • strength of commitment for change • coping strengths • triggers for use (exploration of IDTS-8 profile, if undifferentiated).	• Client's completed IDTS-8 • Decisional Balance Assignment . . . . p. 34 • Feedback about Goal Setting and Commitment to Change . . . . p. 35

THERAPIST CHECKLIST

Motivational Interviewing

BEFORE THE COUNSELLING SESSION

Review the client's results from the Assessment phase, including the IDTS-8 (p. 24) and the Assessment Summary Form (p. 29). Note whether the IDTS-8 is undifferentiated.

DURING THE COUNSELLING SESSION

☐ Discuss assessment findings with the client.

☐ Engage the client in a discussion of his or her reasons for wanting to change alcohol or other drug use.

☐ Have the client weigh the pros and cons of change, using the Decisional Balance Assignment.

☐ Discuss coping strengths and weaknesses with the client.

☐ Review the client's problematic triggers to alcohol or other drug use, and have the client suggest some interim coping alternatives.

☐ If the client's IDTS-8 profile is undifferentiated, explore possible reasons for this (see Therapist Checklist: Troubleshooting for Undifferentiated IDTS-8 Profiles [p. 27]).

☐ Work together with the client to complete the Feedback about Goal Setting and Commitment to Change form, and follow up with a discussion. (Note that clients should take the completed form away with them.)

NOTE: Motivational Interviewing may require only one session or it may need several sessions. This checklist is intended only as a guide to areas of discussion that may help clients strengthen their commitment to change.

Decisional Balance Assignment

One of the first steps toward successfully changing your substance use is reaching a clear decision that you want to change.

In this exercise, you will think about and record some of the important advantages and disadvantages of changing or continuing your drinking or other drug use. You will stack up what you have to lose against what you have to gain.

Fill in the table below. When you are finished, review your answers and weigh your reasons for change. Which way does your decisional balance tip?

Changing Your Current Drinking or Other Drug Use

What's good about it?	What's not so good about it?

Continuing Your Current Drinking or Other Drug Use

What's good about it?	What's not so good about it?

Name: _____   Date: _____

Feedback about Goal Setting and Commitment to Change

Thank you for attending this appointment to talk about some of the things that have been going on in your life. The purpose of this treatment process is to work with you to come up with helpful solutions that fit your personal goals and priorities.

You are asked to complete this form because some people find that written feedback and information can help them make decisions about behaviour change, look at different treatment options or just reflect on how substance use issues affect their lives.

SETTING GOALS FOR CHANGE

1. What is your goal for the substance you most often use?

   Substance: _____

   ☐ Not using at all ☐ Cutting down ☐ Continuing to use ☐ Undecided

2. What is your goal for the substance you use the next most often?

   Substance: _____

   ☐ Not using at all ☐ Cutting down ☐ Continuing to use ☐ Undecided

3. What is your goal for any other substance(s) you use sometimes?

   Substance(s): _____

   ☐ Not using at all ☐ Cutting down ☐ Continuing to use ☐ Undecided

A Note about Risk

How or whether you use substances is your own personal decision. However, if you continue to use alcohol or other drugs, you will expose yourself to increased risks, especially if you:

- *are pregnant*
- *have mental health issues*
- *use prescription drugs (medication)*
- *have diabetes*
- *have a seizure disorder*
- *have an active peptic ulcer or gastritis*
- *have active hepatitis*
- *are under a legal order to abstain*
- *have advanced coronary heart disease*
- *have cancer*
- *have cirrhosis of the liver*
- *are at risk of negative social consequences (such as fighting with a partner).*

TO CHANGE OR NOT TO CHANGE?

What would you like to change in your life?

Change can be hard—even making a decision to change may take a long time for some people. Change is also a process. It generally doesn't happen all at once, but in stages.

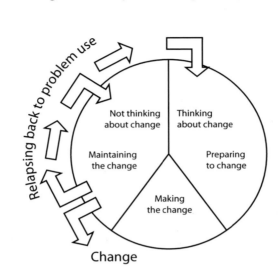

Where are you in the change process?

The questions on the next page may help you to get a better picture of:

- how important changing is to you
- how confident you feel
- how ready are you to quit or cut down your use of substances.

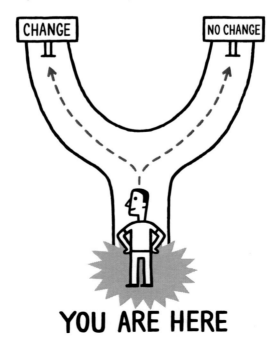

THE READINESS RULER

People usually have several things they would like to change in their lives. Your substance use may be only one of the things you hope to change. Your **motivation** to change your substance use can vary, depending on other things that are happening.

On each of the rulers below, circle the number (from 0 to 10) that best fits with how you are feeling right now.

1. How **important** is it to you to reduce or quit using alcohol or other drugs?

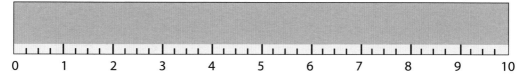

2. How **confident** are you that you will not use alcohol or other drugs?

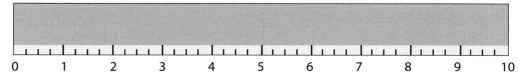

3. How **realistic** is it that you will stay away from alcohol and other drugs in the long term?

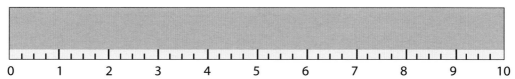

SOME QUESTIONS TO THINK ABOUT

- Why are you at your current score and not at zero?
- What would it take for you to move to a higher score?
- What has made this change important to you so far—why are you not at zero?)
- What would it take to make this change even more important to you?
- What support would you need to make a change, if you chose to do so?
  This exercise can also be used to explore readiness to change other behaviours, such as taking prescribed medication, looking for a job or finding stable housing. Feel free to discuss any of the information on this form with me.

_____

Signature of Clinician

_____

Name and Credentials (print)

_____

Contact Information

Phase 3: Individualized Treatment Planning

Following the Assessment and Motivational Interviewing components of SRP, an Individualized Treatment Plan is developed for each client. The client is fully involved in this stage—and other stages—of treatment.

Description	Clinical Tools
The following steps are used to engage the client in the development of an individually tailored treatment plan: <ul><li>orientation to SRP counselling and signing of treatment contract</li><li>review of IDTS-8 results; exploration of specific recent triggers for alcohol or other drug use</li><li>development of a personal hierarchy of risk areas that the client wishes to work on through weekly assignments</li><li>client goal setting and self-monitoring.</li></ul>	<ul><li>Treatment Contract: Individual Counselling . . . . p. 41</li><li>Treatment Contract: Group Counselling . . . . p. 43</li><li>Identifying Problem Substance Use Situations . . . . p. 45</li><li>Coping Skills Checklist . . . . p. 48</li><li>Daily Diary . . . . p. 49</li></ul>

Individualized Treatment Planning

BEFORE THE COUNSELLING SESSION

☐ Photocopy the client's completed IDTS-8.

Bring the following blank forms:

    ☐ Treatment Contract: Individual Counselling

      or

    ☐ Treatment Contract: Group Counselling

    ☐ Identifying Problem Substance Use Situations

    ☐ Coping Skills Checklist

    ☐ Daily Diary.

DURING THE COUNSELLING SESSION

☐ Provide an orientation to SRP counselling.

☐ Have the client sign a Treatment Contract.

☐ Provide the client with a copy of his or her completed IDTS-8 (if this has not already been done), and engage the client in a discussion of common triggers to use.

☐ Have the client complete the first section of Identifying Problem Substance Use Situations.

☐ Have the client complete the Coping Skills Checklist.

☐ Explain the rationale for self-monitoring.

☐ Have the client set a goal for the coming week.

CLIENT HOMEWORK

☐ Fill out the remainder of Identifying Problem Substance Use Situations.

☐ Complete a Daily Diary for the week.

Name: _____ Date: _____

Treatment Contract: Individual Counselling

My therapist has discussed with me my goals related to my substance use and my reasons for wanting to change my pattern of substance use. The Structured Relapse Prevention (SRP) counselling program has also been explained to me.

I have reached the decision that I want to work hard toward changing my alcohol or other drug use by entering SRP counselling. I understand that, in order to remain in SRP counselling, I must comply fully with the terms outlined below.

I agree to the following:

ATTENDANCE

I will be **on time** for all treatment sessions. If I am ill, or if an emergency arises, I will telephone my therapist to cancel and reschedule my appointment.

SUBSTANCE USE

I will remain fully committed to discussing and learning about my use of alcohol or other drugs. If I change my substance use goal, I will discuss the change openly with my therapist.

PARTICIPATION

I agree to participate fully in the treatment process. This includes:
- completing self-monitoring and homework exercises
- treating other clients and staff, and agency property, with respect.

CONFIDENTIALITY

I understand that my treatment progress will be documented. I understand that my therapist will write notes in my chart reflecting what is said during counselling sessions.

I understand that staff will maintain complete confidentiality, except where they are required by law to do otherwise. I understand that these specific exceptions to client confidentiality include:
- clinical consultation as needed with other members of the therapeutic team
- court subpoena or summons
- information regarding particular infectious diseases
- medical information in the case of an emergency (released to the attending physician)
- suspected child abuse or neglect
- threat to harm myself or others
- threat to the welfare of a child
- risk of driving when impaired.

I understand that there may be occasions when treatment sessions will be observed by authorized staff, students or community health care professionals (either in person or through a one-way mirror) for the purposes of training, treatment planning and program development. All guidelines of staff confidentiality will apply in these cases.

I have discussed these terms of agreement with my therapist and I agree to follow them.

_____   _____
Signed   Witness

_____
Date

Name: _____ Date: _____

Treatment Contract: Group Counselling

My therapist has discussed with me my goals related to my substance use and my reasons for wanting to change my pattern of substance use. The Structured Relapse Prevention (SRP) counselling program has also been explained to me.

I have reached the decision that I want to work hard toward changing my alcohol or other drug use by entering SRP counselling. I understand that, in order to remain in SRP counselling, I must comply fully with the terms outlined below.

I agree to the following:

ATTENDANCE

I will be **on time** for all treatment sessions. If I am ill, or if an emergency arises, I will telephone my therapist to cancel and reschedule my appointment.

SUBSTANCE USE

I will remain fully committed to discussing and learning about my use of alcohol or other drugs. If I change my substance use goal, I will discuss the change openly with my therapist.

PARTICIPATION

I agree to participate fully in the treatment process. This includes:
• listening to what others in the group have to say; letting them talk without interruption; being attentive; sitting in the group
• respecting the opinions, decisions, etc., of other group members and staff; refraining from racist, sexist or otherwise inappropriate behaviour
• disclosing information about myself; giving constructive feedback to other group members and listening to others' feedback about myself
• completing daily self-monitoring and homework exercises
• treating other clients and staff, and agency property, with respect.

CONFIDENTIALITY

I agree to maintain complete confidentiality with regard to discussions between clients before, during or after group or individual treatment sessions.

I understand that my treatment progress will be documented. I understand that my therapist will write notes in my chart reflecting what is said during counselling sessions.

I understand that staff will maintain complete confidentiality, except where required by law to do otherwise. I understand that these specific exceptions to client confidentiality include:

- clinical consultation as needed with other members of the therapeutic team
- court subpoena or summons
- medical information in the case of an emergency (released to the attending physician)
- suspected child abuse or neglect
- threat to harm myself or others
- threat to the welfare of a child
- risk of driving when impaired.

I understand that there may be occasions when treatment sessions will be observed by authorized staff, students or community health care professionals (either in person or through a one-way mirror) for the purposes of training, treatment planning and program development. All guidelines of staff confidentiality will apply in these cases.

I have discussed these terms of agreement with my therapist and I agree to follow them.

_____   _____
Signed   Witness

_____
Date

Name: _____ Date: _____

Identifying Problem Substance Use Situations

Complete Part 1 with your therapist after reviewing your assessment results on the Inventory of Drug-Taking Situations (IDTS-8).

You can complete Part 2 either during the session with your therapist or as a homework assignment. If you complete it at home, bring it with you to your next appointment.

PART 1

What situations have tended to trigger your substance use over the past year? (Check any that apply.)

☐ unpleasant emotions
(e.g., when angry, frustrated, bored, sad or anxious)

☐ physical discomfort
(e.g., when feeling ill or in pain)

☐ pleasant emotions
(e.g., when enjoying yourself or just feeling happy)

☐ testing personal control
(e.g., when you started to believe you could handle alcohol or other drugs)

☐ urges and temptations to use
(e.g., when walking by a pub or after seeing something that reminded you of drinking or other drug use)

☐ conflict with others
(e.g., after an argument or when not getting along well with someone)

☐ social pressure to use
(e.g., when someone offered you alcohol or other drugs)

☐ pleasant times with others
(e.g., when out with friends or at a party)

Now rank the situations you checked above that are **most often** linked to problem drinking or other drug use:

Rank 1 (most frequently a problem): _____

Rank 2 (next most frequent): _____

Rank 3 (next most frequent): _____

PART 2

Your therapist has helped you identify general types of situations that have tended to trigger your problem drinking or other drug use over the past year. Now, think about the situations you have ranked 1, 2 and 3, and write down examples of specific incidents of problem drinking or other drug use.

Rank 1 Situation

Think carefully about the particular drinking or other drug use experience you wish to describe, and then answer the questions below in as much detail as possible.

BEFORE USING

• Where were you? _____

• Was anyone else present? _____

• Were others drinking or using other drugs? _____

• How were you feeling? _____

• What were you thinking? _____

• Describe what happened that triggered your use: _____

_____

• How do you think you might handle a similar incident without using? _____

_____

_____

_____

Rank 2 Situation

Think carefully about the particular drinking or other drug use experience you wish to describe, then answer the questions below in as much detail as possible.

BEFORE USING

• Where were you? _____

• Was anyone else present? _____

• Were others drinking or using other drugs? _____

• How were you feeling? _____

• What were you thinking? _____

• Describe what happened that triggered your use: _____

_____

• How do you think you might handle a similar incident without using? _____

_____

_____

_____

Rank 3 Situation

Think carefully about the particular drinking or other drug use experience you wish to describe, then answer the questions below in as much detail as possible.

BEFORE USING

• Where were you? _____

• Was anyone else present? _____

• Were others drinking or using other drugs?_____

• How were you feeling? _____

• What were you thinking? _____

• Describe what happened that triggered your use: _____

_____

• How do you think you might handle a similar incident without using?_____

_____

_____

_____

Adapted from: H.M. Annis and G. Martin, Inventory of Drug-Taking Situations *(4th ed.). Toronto: Addiction Research Foundation © 1985*

Name: _____ Date: _____

Coping Skills Checklist

The following list contains a number of areas where you might want to develop more skills for coping with triggers and cravings for alcohol or other drugs. Please check off the **five** areas that you would most like to work on during the next few weeks.

Your therapist will provide you with homework exercises that address the specific areas you choose.

- ☐ Coping with cravings
- ☐ Early coping strategies (for the first few weeks of your treatment)
- ☐ Increasing social support
- ☐ Refusing alcohol and other drugs
- ☐ Coping with physical discomfort
- ☐ Problem solving
- ☐ Spirituality
- ☐ Assertiveness
- ☐ Anger management
- ☐ Coping with boredom
- ☐ Relaxation
- ☐ Coping with unpleasant feelings and memories of trauma
- ☐ Coping with flashbacks and unpleasant emotions
- ☐ Coping with anxiety
- ☐ Coping with loss
- ☐ Healthy relationships
- ☐ Sexual relationships and dating
- ☐ Money issues

Name: _____ Date: _____

Daily Diary

By monitoring the risky situations that you encounter, and any urges and temptations that you feel to drink or use other drugs, you can develop better coping strategies and alternative behaviours. Keeping track of any drinking or other drug use that does occur helps you to get an overall picture of how well you are doing. The simple exercise of daily monitoring can, in itself, help you to achieve your goals.

For each day this week:

Describe the most risky situation (urges, temptations and cravings) that you experienced during the day. Write down where you were; what time of day it was; who (if anyone) you were with; what you were doing, thinking and feeling; and what happened.	Describe what you did to cope in this situation (e.g., went for a walk, left the situation, thought of the negative consequences of using).	If you did use any alcohol or other drugs, record what and how much.
MONDAY		
TUESDAY		
WEDNESDAY		
THURSDAY		
FRIDAY		
SATURDAY		
SUNDAY		

Phase 4: Initiation of Change

This phase of the SRP program focuses on counselling strategies that help initiate a change in behaviour. (The next phase, Maintenance of Change, concentrates on strategies to help maintain change over the long term.) The Initiation of Change phase usually involves four counselling sessions.

Powerful strategies for initiating a change in a client's behaviour include:
- avoidance of risk situations
- hospitalization or other residential care
- protective drugs
- coercion
- involvement of spouse, or other family members or friends
- directive role of therapist.

Description	Clinical Tools
• The client and therapist together prepare a weekly plan of anticipated risk situations and coping alternatives. The focus is on avoidance and seeking support from others. • The therapist helps the client conduct a functional analysis of a recent episode of drinking or other drug use.	• Weekly Planning Form: Initiation of Change . . . . p. 56 • Daily Diary . . . . p. 58 • Situational Confidence Questionnaire (SCQ-8) . . . . p. 59 • Cope Alert Card . . . . p. 61 • ABC Analysis Chart . . . . p. 62 • Coping Skills Exercises . . . . pp. 79–120

THERAPIST CHECKLIST

Counselling Session 1: Initiation of Change

The counselling sessions in this Initiation of Change phase focus on avoiding alcohol and other drug use situations, and on seeking support from reliable friends and family members.

BEFORE THE COUNSELLING SESSION

☐ Review the client's answers on the Coping Skills Checklist.

Bring the following blank forms:

☐ Weekly Planning Form: Initiation of Change

☐ Daily Diary

☐ SCQ-8

☐ ABC Analysis Chart

DURING THE COUNSELLING SESSION

☐ Review the client's completed homework forms (Identifying Problem Substance Use Situations and the Daily Diary) and discuss any problems that have arisen.

☐ Discuss the basics of functional analysis, i.e., the "ABCs" of drinking and other drug use.

☐ Work with the client to conduct a functional analysis of a recent episode of alcohol or other drug use.

☐ Discuss anticipated risk situations for the coming week and possible coping alternatives.

☐ Complete the Weekly Planning Form: Initiation of Change with the client.

☐ Have the client complete the SCQ-8.

CLIENT HOMEWORK

☐ Complete a Daily Diary for the week.

NOTE: These checklists are to be used as guidelines only. The number of sessions spent in change initiation and maintenance for a particular client will depend on his or her readiness for change and rate of progress.

THERAPIST CHECKLIST

Counselling Session 2: Initiation of Change

The counselling sessions in this Initiation of Change phase focus on avoiding alcohol and other drug use situations, and on seeking support from reliable friends and family members.

BEFORE THE COUNSELLING SESSION

☐ Bring the client's SCQ-8 profile.

Bring the following blank forms:

    ☐ Weekly Planning Form: Initiation of Change

    ☐ Daily Diary

    ☐ selected coping skills exercise

DURING THE COUNSELLING SESSION

☐ Review the client's assignment as outlined on the Weekly Planning Form and discuss any problems that have arisen.

☐ Review the client's SCQ-8 profile.

☐ Discuss anticipated risk situations for the coming week and possible coping alternatives.

☐ Complete a new Weekly Planning Form with the client.

☐ Discuss or assign a coping skills topic relevant to the client.

CLIENT HOMEWORK

☐ Anticipate and plan for a high-risk situation.

☐ Complete a Daily Diary for the week.

☐ Complete the assigned coping skills exercise (if any).

NOTE: These checklists are to be used as guidelines only. The number of sessions spent in change initiation and maintenance for a particular client will depend on his or her readiness for change and rate of progress.

THERAPIST CHECKLIST

Counselling Session 3: Initiation of Change

The counselling sessions in this Initiation of Change phase focus on avoiding alcohol and other drug use situations, and on seeking support from reliable friends and family members.

BEFORE THE COUNSELLING SESSION

Bring the following blank forms:

- ☐ Weekly Planning Form: Initiation of Change
- ☐ Daily Diary
- ☐ selected coping skills exercise
- ☐ Cope Alert Card

DURING THE COUNSELLING SESSION

- ☐ Review the client's assignment as outlined on the Weekly Planning Form and discuss any problems that have arisen.
- ☐ Discuss anticipated risk situations for the coming week and possible coping alternatives.
- ☐ Complete a new Weekly Planning Form with the client.
- ☐ Discuss or assign a coping skills topic relevant to the client.
- ☐ Have the client complete a Cope Alert Card.

CLIENT HOMEWORK

- ☐ Anticipate and plan for a high-risk situation.
- ☐ Complete a Daily Diary for the week.
- ☐ Complete the assigned coping skills exercise (if any).

NOTE: These checklists are to be used as guidelines only. The number of sessions spent in change initiation and maintenance for a particular client will depend on his or her readiness for change and rate of progress.

THERAPIST CHECKLIST

Counselling Session 4: Initiation of Change

The counselling sessions in this Initiation of Change phase focus on avoiding alcohol and other drug use situations, and on seeking support from reliable friends and family members.

BEFORE THE COUNSELLING SESSION

Bring the following blank forms:

- ☐ Weekly Planning Form: Initiation of Change
- ☐ Daily Diary
- ☐ selected coping skills exercise

DURING THE COUNSELLING SESSION

- ☐ Review the client's assignment as outlined in the Weekly Planning Form and discuss any problems that have arisen.
- ☐ Discuss anticipated risk situations for the coming week and possible coping alternatives.
- ☐ Complete a new Weekly Planning Form with the client.
- ☐ Discuss or assign a coping skills topic relevant to the client.

CLIENT HOMEWORK

- ☐ Anticipate and plan for a high-risk situation.
- ☐ Complete a Daily Diary for the week.
- ☐ Complete the assigned coping skills exercise (if any).

NOTE: These checklists are to be used as guidelines only. The number of sessions spent in change initiation and maintenance for a particular client will depend on his or her readiness for change and rate of progress.

Name: _____ Date: _____

WEEKLY PLANNING FORM

Initiation of Change

STRATEGIES FOR STARTING TO MAKE CHANGES TO YOUR SUBSTANCE USE

The early weeks of changing your substance use can be a hard time, but there are some things you can do to make it a little easier. Research has shown that starting to make changes is easier and more effective when you use some of the following powerful strategies:

- Avoid risky places and stay away from people who use substances.
- Call a friend, a family member or an AA or NA sponsor to ask for help and support.
- Ask yourself: "What will I lose if I use?" "What will I gain by not using?"
- If possible, consider living in a supportive place (a treatment centre or a hospital) during the first couple of weeks of changing your substance use.
- Ask your doctor about medications that can help with cravings to use substances.
- Make a commitment to yourself by setting a substance use goal.
- Figure out what situations are going to be risky for you this week.
- Do something nice for yourself. For example, eat a favourite meal or make a point of doing something you really enjoy.

Now fill out the form on the following page to help you think about what you would like to accomplish in the coming week, and how you will do so.

INITIATION OF CHANGE PLAN FOR THIS WEEK

Below is some space for you to think about what you would like to accomplish in the coming week, and how you will do so.

My goal: _____

My level of confidence that I will achieve this goal:

☐ 0% ☐ 20% ☐ 40% ☐ 60% ☐ 80% ☐ 100%

Substance Use Trigger	Plans for Coping
What is my substance use trigger for this week? (E.g., meeting a friend who uses drugs)	**How can I cope with this trigger?** ☐ Avoid the situation. ☐ Go to a self-help group. ☐ Call a friend, family member or sponsor. ☐ Remind myself of what will happen if I use. ☐ Other things I can do to cope:
Where might this happen?	
What time of the day or night?	
What will I be doing, thinking and feeling?	

Name: _____ Date: _____

Daily Diary

By monitoring the risky situations that you encounter, and any urges and temptations that you feel to drink or use other drugs, you can develop better coping strategies and alternative behaviours. Keeping track of any drinking or other drug use that does occur helps you to get an overall picture of how well you are doing. The simple exercise of daily monitoring can, in itself, help you to achieve your goals.

For each day this week:

Describe the most risky situation (urges, temptations and cravings) that you experienced during the day. Write down where you were; what time of day it was; who (if anyone) you were with; what you were doing, thinking and feeling; and what happened.	Describe what you did to cope in this situation (e.g., went for a walk, left the situation, thought of the negative consequences of using).	If you did use any alcohol or other drugs, record what and how much.
MONDAY		
TUESDAY		
WEDNESDAY		
THURSDAY		
FRIDAY		
SATURDAY		
SUNDAY		

Name: _____ Date: _____

Situational Confidence Questionnaire (SCQ-8)

Complete Part 1 with your therapist. You can complete Part 2 either during the session with your therapist or as a homework assignment. If you complete it at home, bring it with you to your next appointment.

PART 1: IDENTIFYING CAUSES

In order to change your substance use habits and patterns for good, you need to identify the reasons that lead to your use of alcohol or other drugs. Eight typical causes, or "trigger situations," are outlined below.

Which ones have tended to trigger your substance use over the past year? (Check any or all that apply.)

- ☐ unpleasant emotions
  (e.g., when angry, frustrated, bored, sad or anxious)
- ☐ physical discomfort
  (e.g., when feeling ill or in pain)
- ☐ pleasant emotions
  (e.g., when enjoying yourself or just feeling happy)
- ☐ testing personal control
  (e.g., when you started to believe you could handle alcohol or other drugs)
- ☐ urges and temptations to use
  (e.g., when walking by a pub or after seeing something that reminded you of drinking or other drug use)
- ☐ conflict with others
  (e.g., after an argument or when not getting along with someone)
- ☐ social pressure to use
  (e.g., when someone offered you alcohol or other drugs)
- ☐ pleasant times with others
  (e.g., when out with friends or at a party).

Rank the trigger situations you checked above in terms of how frequently they are linked to problem drinking or other drug use:

Rank 1 (most frequently a problem): _____

Rank 2 (next most frequent): _____

Rank 3 (next most frequent): _____

PART 2: SITUATIONAL CONFIDENCE QUESTIONNAIRE

Imagine yourself, as you are right now, faced with in each of the following trigger situations. Place an **X** along the line in the scale provided to show how confident you feel **right now** that you would be able to resist problem drinking or other drug use. In the example below, the person feels that he or she is about 48% confident— a little less than halfway—about resisting in this situation.

I feel . . .

0%	25%	**X** 50%	75%	100%	=	48%

Not at all confident   Totally Confident

Right now, I feel I would be able to resist the urge to drink or use other drugs in situations involving . . .

1. Unpleasant emotions

0%	25%	50%	75%	100%	=	%

Not at all confident   Totally Confident

2. Physical discomfort

0%	25%	50%	75%	100%	=	%

Not at all confident   Totally Confident

3. Pleasant emotions

0%	25%	50%	75%	100%	=	%

Not at all confident   Totally Confident

4. Testing personal control

0%	25%	50%	75%	100%	=	%

Not at all confident   Totally Confident

5. Urges and temptations

0%	25%	50%	75%	100%	=	%

Not at all confident   Totally Confident

6. Conflict with others

0%	25%	50%	75%	100%	=	%

Not at all confident   Totally Confident

7. Social pressures

0%	25%	50%	75%	100%	=	%

Not at all confident   Totally Confident

8. Pleasant times with others

0%	25%	50%	75%	100%	=	%

Not at all confident   Totally Confident

Adapted from: H.M. Annis and G. Martin, Inventory of Drug-Taking Situations *(4th ed.). Toronto: Addiction Research Foundation © 1985*

Cope Alert Card

The Cope Alert Card is a wallet-sized card on which a client can record a variety of coping strategies that can be put into action anywhere, anytime. The rationale behind encouraging clients to carry Cope Alert Cards is that, as much as one can plan for certain situations, unexpected events do occur.

Examples of such unexpected events might include:
• spontaneous after-work get-togethers
• running into a dealer or a friend who uses
• unexpected major life events (e.g., unemployment, the end of a relationship or the death of a friend).

When a person is faced with situations like the above, coping strategies may not readily come to mind. The Cope Alert Card is an easy retrieval method, a way to remind clients whenever and wherever they are of coping strategies that have worked in the past.

Urge clients to be as specific as possible in completing their cards. In addition, suggest that they tape to the card a quarter for a telephone call, or a public transit token (or both).

Examples of coping strategies might include:
• Recognize and acknowledge the craving.
• Use relaxation techniques or imagery.
• Use positive self-talk.
• Think about the positive and negative consequences of using.
• Leave the situation and go somewhere safe.
• Call someone who can help.
• Find an alternative way to deal with the feelings.

Point out to clients that Cope Alert Cards are also useful for times when they know that they will be in high-risk situations, such as family gatherings. Some clients may want to carry several different Cope Alert Cards to help with different types of situations; for example, one for feeling negative emotions and another for wanting to socialize with old friends.

The following is an example of a Cope Alert Card. Copies of the card can be printed from the CD that accompanies this manual.

✂ (Cut along this line)

COPE ALERT
My plan for unexpected situations
is . . . _____   _____
_____   _____
_____   _____
_____   _____   25¢
_____   _____
_____   _____

(Fold here)

Name: _____ Date: _____

ABC Analysis Chart

An ABC analysis (or "functional analysis") is a helpful tool for analyzing your alcohol or other drug use episodes. It can help you to understand the function of substance use, and therefore to develop strategies for avoiding future alcohol or other drug use.

The simple format shown in the table below can help you to identify both triggers and consequences of your substance use. You are encouraged to view your substance use as a behavioural pattern or habit that you can change. Remember to consider both the positive and negative—as well as both short-term and long-term—consequences of your substance use.

You may carry out an ABC analysis during a group or individual counselling session, or it may be assigned as homework.

A ACTIVATORS	B BEHAVIOUR	C CONSEQUENCES
Example: **Had a fight with partner, felt angry.**	Example: **Drank 8–12 beers.**	Example: **Forgot problems for a while, my partner didn't speak to me, was late for work the next day, felt bad about myself.**

Phase 5: Maintenance of Change

In the Maintenance of Change phase of SRP counselling, the performance aids used in the Initiation of Change phase are gradually withdrawn as the focus shifts to the client's own coping strategies for preventing a relapse. This phase usually features from four to eight counselling sessions.

Clients are asked to construct a hierarchy of risk situations, and to systematically plan to enter these situations (beginning with lower-risk situations and progressing toward more challenging situations).

Some of the clinical tools used earlier in the SRP process can be helpful in working with clients to identify situations of progressively greater risk. For example, a client's IDTS-8 profile (completed during the Assessment phase) and his or her responses in the exercise Identifying Problem Substance Use Situations (completed in the Individualized Treatment Planning phase) can provide an overview of the specific categories of risk that he or she faces.

Clients should plan to enter situations that are going to occur in their day-to-day lives. For example, carrying money or credit cards, a risk situation that a client may have avoided during the Initiation of Change phase of counselling, can be an important experience as part of the Maintenance of Change phase, as it is an area where good coping skills need to be developed in order to successfully maintain change.

Powerful strategies for maintaining a change in behaviour include:
- graduated real-life exposure to a hierarchy of risk situations
- multiple homework tasks within each type of risk situation
- fading of all use of external aids to performance (i.e., all Initiation of Change phase strategies)
- homework tasks designed to let clients take control and then attribute their success to their own efforts.

Homework assignments should increase clients' confidence (self-efficacy), as clients perceive that:
- the homework assignments are challenging (i.e., clients acknowledge that they were able to control alcohol or other drug use in formerly high-risk situations)

- only a moderate degree of effort was needed to successfully control alcohol or other drug use in the homework situations
- little external aid was involved in the successes
- the successes are part of an overall pattern of improvement in alcohol or other drug use
- personal control over alcohol or other drug use was responsible for the successes
- the successes were relevant to high-risk drinking or other drug use situations that the clients frequently encounter.

Description	Clinical Tools
• The client and therapist together prepare a weekly plan of anticipated risk situations and coping alternatives. The focus is on exposure to risk situations.	• Weekly Planning Form: Maintenance of Change . . . . p. 69 • Daily Diary . . . . p. 71 • SCQ-8 . . . . p. 59 • "If I Were to Relapse . . ." Exercise . . . . p. 72 • Client Satisfaction Questionnaire . . . . p. 73

THERAPIST CHECKLIST

Counselling Session 5: Maintenance of Change

Sessions 5 to 8 involve counselling clients on how to maintain the changes they have achieved in their substance use behaviour and avoid relapse. Having practised alternative ways to cope during the Initiation of Change phase, clients now learn strategies for entering pre-planned risk situations.

BEFORE THE COUNSELLING SESSION

Bring the following blank forms:

☐ Weekly Planning Form: Maintenance of Change

☐ Daily Diary

☐ selected coping skills exercise

DURING THE COUNSELLING SESSION

☐ Review the client's assignment as outlined on the Weekly Planning Form and discuss any problems that have arisen.

☐ Encourage the client to develop a weekly plan that involves exposure to situations that are challenging but which the client feels confident to handle. Complete the left column of the Weekly Planning Form with the client. Help the client prepare to try new coping skills in these high-risk situations.

☐ Discuss or assign a coping skills topic relevant to the client.

CLIENT HOMEWORK

☐ Fill in the right column (outcome report) of the Weekly Planning Form: Maintenance of Change.

☐ Complete a Daily Diary for the week.

☐ Complete the assigned coping skills exercise (if any).

NOTE: These checklists are intended as guidelines only. The number of sessions spent in change initiation and maintenance for a particular client will depend on his or her readiness for change and rate of progress.

Counselling Session 6: Maintenance of Change

Sessions 5 to 8 involve counselling clients on how to maintain the changes they have achieved in their substance use behaviour and avoid relapse. Having practised alternative ways to cope during the Initiation of Change phase, clients now learn strategies for entering pre-planned risk situations.

BEFORE THE COUNSELLING SESSION

Bring the following blank forms:

- ☐ Weekly Planning Form: Maintenance of Change
- ☐ Daily Diary
- ☐ selected coping skills exercise

DURING THE COUNSELLING SESSION

- ☐ Review the client's assignment as outlined on the Weekly Planning Form and discuss any problems that have arisen.
- ☐ Encourage the client to develop a weekly plan that involves exposure to situations that are challenging but which the client feels confident to handle. Complete the left column of the Weekly Planning Form with the client. Help the client prepare to try new coping skills in these high-risk situations.
- ☐ Discuss or assign a coping skills topic relevant to the client.

CLIENT HOMEWORK

- ☐ Fill in the right column (outcome report) of the Weekly Planning Form.
- ☐ Complete a Daily Diary for the week.
- ☐ Complete the assigned coping skills exercise (if any).

NOTE: These checklists are intended to be used as guidelines only. The number of sessions spent in change initiation and maintenance for a particular client will depend on his or her readiness for change and rate of progress.

THERAPIST CHECKLIST

Counselling Session 7: Maintenance of Change

Sessions 5 to 8 involve counselling clients on how to maintain the changes they have achieved in their substance use behaviour and avoid relapse. Having practised alternative ways to cope during the Initiation of Change phase, clients now learn strategies for entering pre-planned risk situations.

BEFORE THE COUNSELLING SESSION

Bring the following blank forms:

- ☐ Weekly Planning Form: Maintenance of Change
- ☐ Daily Diary
- ☐ SCQ-8
- ☐ "If I Were to Relapse . . ." Exercise

DURING THE COUNSELLING SESSION

- ☐ Review the client's assignment as outlined on the Weekly Planning Form and discuss any problems that have arisen.

- ☐ Encourage the client to develop a weekly plan that involves exposure to situations that are challenging but which the client feels confident to handle. Complete the left column of the Weekly Planning Form with the client. Help the client prepare to try new coping skills in these high-risk situations.

- ☐ Discuss or assign the "If I Were to Relapse . . ." Exercise.

- ☐ Have the client complete the SCQ-8.

CLIENT HOMEWORK

- ☐ Fill in the right column (outcome report) of the Weekly Planning Form.
- ☐ Complete a Daily Diary for the week.
- ☐ Complete the "If I Were to Relapse . . ." Exercise.
- ☐ Complete the assigned coping skills exercise (if any).

NOTE: These checklists are to be used as guidelines only. The number of sessions spent in change initiation and maintenance for a particular client will depend on his or her readiness for change and rate of progress.

Counselling Session 8: Maintenance of Change

Sessions 5 to 8 involve counselling clients on how to maintain the changes they have achieved in their substance use behaviour and avoid relapse. Having practised alternative ways to cope during the Initiation of Change phase, clients now learn strategies for entering pre-planned risk situations.

BEFORE THE COUNSELLING SESSION

☐ Bring a blank Client Satisfaction Questionnaire.

☐ Bring the client's completed SCQ-8 profile from Session 7, and a copy of the SCQ-8 profile he or she completed in Session 1.

DURING THE COUNSELLING SESSION

☐ Review the client's assignment as outlined on the Weekly Planning Form and discuss any problems that have arisen.

☐ Review the "If I Were to Relapse . . ." Exercise.

☐ Discuss upcoming risk situations and coping plans.

☐ Compare the client's SCQ-8 profiles from Sessions 1 and 7. Explore the strengths and vulnerabilities shown by the results.

☐ Have the client complete a Client Satisfaction Questionnaire.

NOTE: These checklists are to be used as guidelines only. The number of sessions spent in change initiation and maintenance for a particular client will depend on his or her readiness for change and rate of progress.

Name: _____ Date: _____

WEEKLY PLANNING FORM

Maintenance of Change

STRATEGIES AND TIPS FOR MAINTAINING CHANGES TO YOUR SUBSTANCE USE

Congratulations! You've successfully made some changes in your substance use. The next step is to maintain those changes and prevent relapse. Here are two of the most powerful strategies for maintaining your substance use goal:

- Think about all the high-risk situations you are likely to encounter as a part of your lifestyle.
- Gradually enter these situations, starting with lower risk and working your way up.

Why plan to enter situations where you might be tempted to use substances? Well, if these situations are likely to come up some time, it's better for you to be in control of where and when they do.

Here are a few more tips for keeping to your goal:

- Put yourself in each risk situation a few times before moving on to the next one.
- Make sure that you take the credit for your successes! For example, in the early weeks of change, we encouraged you to ask for help from other people. Now that you are learning to maintain change, it's important to know that you can do it on your own if you have to.
- Make sure that the situation you plan to enter is challenging, but not **too** challenging.
- If you find that you are having trouble with the risky situations you are in, you might be moving too fast. Take your time! You can always go back to using some of the early strategies (like avoiding people, places and things, or relying on the support of others) until you feel more confident.

Your substance use pattern didn't start overnight, so it makes sense that it will take some time to feel strong and confident in making positive changes. Setting a goal and planning to enter risky situations are two powerful strategies to help you keep to your goals. On the next page is a form where you can write down your plan for the coming week.

MAINTENANCE OF CHANGE PLAN FOR THIS WEEK

Below is some space for you to think about what you would like to accomplish in the coming week, and how you will do so.

My goal: _____

My level of confidence that I will achieve this goal:

☐ 0%   ☐ 20%   ☐ 40%   ☐ 60%   ☐ 80%   ☐ 100%

Planning Fill in this column **before** the situation.	**Outcome Report** Fill in this column **after** the situation.
Describe the risky situation: _____ _____ _____ When? _____ Where? _____ Who will be there? _____ _____ _____ What is your coping plan? (Describe exactly what you will say and do, what you will be thinking, etc.)	Did you attempt this assignment? ☐ Yes ☐ No Were you successful? ☐ Yes ☐ No Comment: _____ _____ _____ _____ _____ Did you use substances? ☐ Yes ☐ No If Yes, how much? _____ What, if anything, might you try doing differently next time?

Name: _____ Date: _____

Daily Diary

By monitoring the risky situations that you encounter, and any urges and temptations that you feel to drink or use other drugs, you can develop better coping strategies and alternative behaviours. Keeping track of any drinking or other drug use that does occur helps you to get an overall picture of how well you are doing. The simple exercise of daily monitoring can, in itself, help you to achieve your goals.

For each day this week:

Describe the most risky situation (urges, temptations and cravings) that you experienced during the day. Write down where you were; what time of day it was; who (if anyone) you were with; what you were doing, thinking and feeling; and what happened.	Describe what you did to cope in this situation (e.g., went for a walk, left the situation, thought of the negative consequences of using).	If you did use any alcohol or other drugs, record what and how much.
MONDAY		
TUESDAY		
WEDNESDAY		
THURSDAY		
FRIDAY		
SATURDAY		
SUNDAY		

Name: _____ Date: _____

"If I Were to Relapse . . ." Exercise

In what kind of situation would you be most likely to relapse?

Describe where you would be, who you might be with (if anyone), what else you would be doing, and what you would be thinking about and feeling before you used alcohol or other drugs.

_____

_____

_____

What coping strategies could you use to avoid this relapse?

1. _____

2. _____

3. _____

4. _____

5. _____

6. _____

7. _____

8. _____

9. _____

10. _____

How confident are you that you will use one or more of these coping strategies in this situation? (Place an **X** on the line below to show your answer.)

$$\longleftarrow\!\longrightarrow$$

Not at all confident   Very confident

What is the first coping strategy that you would use?

_____

_____

_____

Client Satisfaction Questionnaire

PART 1: SATISFACTION LEVELS

Please help us improve our program by answering some questions about the services you have received. We are interested in your honest opinions, whether they are positive or negative. We also welcome your comments and suggestions.

Circle your answers. Please answer all questions.

1. How would you rate the quality of service you received?

4	3	2	1
Excellent	Good	Fair	Poor

2. Did you get the kind of service you wanted?

4	3	2	1
Yes, definitely	Yes, generally	No, not really	No, definitely not

3. To what extent has our program met your needs?

4	3	2	1
Almost all of my needs have been met	Most of my needs have been met	Only a few of my needs have been met	None of my needs have been met

4. If a friend were in need of similar help, would you recommend our program to him or her?

4	3	2	1
Yes, definitely	Yes, generally	No, not likely	No, definitely not

5. Have the services you received helped you to deal more effectively with your problems?

4	3	2	1
Yes, a great deal	Yes, somewhat	No, not really	No, they seemed to make things worse

6. Overall, how satisfied are you with the service you have received?

4	3	2	1
Very satisfied	Mostly satisfied	Indifferent or mildly dissatisfied	Quite dissatisfied

7. If you were to seek help again, would you come back to our program?

4	3	2	1
Yes, definitely	Yes, generally	No, not really	No, definitely not

PART 2: COMMENTS AND SUGGESTIONS

The following questions provide an opportunity for you to comment on our services, if you wish to do so.

8. In your opinion, what was the most helpful part of the services you received?

_____

_____

_____

_____

_____

_____

9. In your opinion, what was the least helpful part of the services you received?

_____

_____

_____

_____

_____

_____

10. What improvement(s) would you like to see in our services?

_____

_____

_____

_____

_____

_____

11. What could the therapist do differently in order to improve the program?

_____

_____

_____

_____

_____

_____

PART 3: HOMEWORK ASSIGNMENTS

During the treatment program, you were given the following types of homework assignments. Please let us know how useful you found each type of assignment.

Circle your answers.

12. Identifying Problem Substance Use Situations

1	2	3	4	5
Very useful		Useful		Not at all useful

13. Weekly Planning Forms

1	2	3	4	5
Very useful		Useful		Not at all useful

14. Daily Diaries or Weekly Diaries

1	2	3	4	5
Very useful		Useful		Not at all useful

15. "If I Were to Relapse . . ." Exercise

1	2	3	4	5
Very useful		Useful		Not at all useful

16. Coping Skills Exercises (e.g., Refusing Alcohol and Other Drugs, Coping with Cravings, Increasing Social Support, Assertiveness, Relaxation, Anger Management)

1	2	3	4	5
Very useful		Useful		Not at all useful

PART 4: FEEDBACK ON USE TRIGGERS

17. Following your assessment, you were given feedback on your reported triggers to alcohol or other drug use. How useful did you find this feedback?

1	2	3	4	5
Very useful		Useful		Not at all useful

We appreciate your help! Thank you for your comments.

PART III:
Coping Skills
Exercises

Introduction

Coping responses vary in complexity and quality. They range from simple behavioural acts (such as avoiding a risky situation) to complicated cognitive strategies (such as managing negative thoughts). Some clients are able to cope as necessary to maintain their goals by relying on their existing strengths and resources, but most people will benefit from acquiring and practising a greater repertoire of coping responses.

A coping response can be defined as any response that enables a person to prevent—or minimize the severity of—a relapse. In other words, clients use coping strategies when they anticipate, and face, high-risk situations. Research has shown that people who practise a variety of coping skills tend to be at lower risk of relapse.

Clinical staff at CAMH have developed a number of coping skills exercises that can be used in a discussion format in individual or group sessions, or assigned to a client as homework. The following exercises are presented here:

The initial choice of topics should be guided by the client's perceptions of areas that present an immediate, serious risk for relapse. The IDTS-8 (page 24) and the Coping Skills Checklist (page 48) can also help you choose appropriate skills training exercises.

In our experience, these are the topics clients have found to be most useful in the early phase of treatment:
- Refusing Alcohol and Other Drugs
- Coping with Cravings
- Early Coping Strategies
- Increasing Social Support.

However, to keep clients engaged in treatment, a flexible approach and consideration of clients' preferences is recommended.

Coping with Cravings

Quitting drinking or other drug use is likely to lead to cravings, especially in high-risk situations. Learning to deal with urges and temptations is a very important part of preventing relapse. We experience urges to use at different levels of intensity, which can be viewed as being on a continuum, as illustrated below.

fleeting thoughts   very strong urges

⟵──⟶

     mild   moderate   severe

We can decrease cravings for alcohol and other drugs by using specific coping strategies. Remember that cravings do not last forever and will decrease in number and strength over time.

Try some of the following suggestions to help you cope:

Behaviour (What I Do)	Cognition (What I Think)
• Self-monitor: Write out your thoughts and feelings. • Seek support: Tell someone what you are experiencing. • Distract yourself: Do something unrelated to substance use. • Substitute another behaviour (e.g., eat something or drink a non-alcoholic beverage). • Leave the situation, or do something to change it. • Take deep breaths (in through your nose, out through your mouth) to relax yourself. • Delay the response: Put off the decision to drink or use other drugs for 15 minutes.	• Normalize the craving: "I am experiencing an urge to drink/use drugs. It is OK to feel like using." • Use imagery (e.g., visualize the craving as a wave that rises and falls, with you riding it out). • Use positive self-statements (e.g., "I can cope with it," or "I have been clean for two weeks and I don't want to spoil it now." • Use thought stopping (e.g., picture a STOP sign). • Think of the negative consequences of using alcohol or other drugs. • Think of the benefits of not using alcohol or other drugs.

PRACTICE EXERCISE

Now, come up with your own plan to deal with urges and temptations to use. Be specific.

Describe a recent high-risk situation you experienced that resulted in a craving.

_____

_____

_____

_____

Using your example above, plan ways to deal with urges and temptations to use in a similar future situation.

Whom are you going to seek support from?

_____

_____

_____

_____

What will you do to distract yourself?

_____

_____

_____

_____

What messages (positive self-talk) will you give yourself?

_____

_____

_____

_____

What else can you do in this situation?

_____

_____

_____

_____

Early Coping Strategies

The first few weeks after cutting down or stopping substance use can be a difficult time. Some people compare their substance to a best friend or a lover, and can feel sadness and grief without it.

There are, however, some important things you can do right away to help prevent a relapse back to problem using behaviour. Try out as many of the following suggestions as you can! The more action you can take, the easier it will be to keep to your substance use goal during this early time in your recovery:

- Throw out alcohol, other drugs and paraphernalia. If this is difficult for you, let a supportive, non-using friend help you.
- Break off all contact with people who drink heavily or use other drugs, and with dealers. This can be done by clearly telling these people that you don't want any further contact with them. If you are concerned about your safety, discuss your plans with a professional. Do not put yourself at risk of being harmed.
- If you live in an area where there is a lot of drug activity (using and dealing drugs), explore whether you can stay with supportive friends or family members for a while. Consider moving to a more substance-free area and do not tell drinking buddies, friends who use other drugs, or dealers where you have moved.
- Change your telephone number. Throw out telephone numbers of dealers.
- Have cheques automatically deposited into your bank account. Throw out 24-hour cash cards. Have someone hold on to your money for you.
- Try a new drug-free activity.
- Give self-help groups a try. This means trying out a number of different types and locations of meetings so that you can make an informed decision about whether there is a self-help group that is right for you.
- Talk to supportive friends, family or health professionals about situations that are difficult for you.
- Tell supportive friends (those who will not encourage you to use alcohol or other drugs) that you are no longer using substances.

PRACTICE EXERCISE

Now come up with your own plan to help you cope in early recovery.

1. What high-risk people do you need to avoid at this time?

_____

_____

_____

_____

_____

_____

2. What high-risk places do you need to avoid at this time?

_____

_____

_____

_____

_____

_____

3. What high-risk things (e.g., drug paraphernalia, bottles) do you need to throw out or avoid at this time?

_____

_____

_____

_____

_____

_____

4. What are some safe activities that you can get involved in now?

_____

_____

_____

_____

_____

_____

5. Where can you seek support, or who can give you support?

_____

_____

_____

_____

_____

_____

Increasing Social Support

It's important to have a network of people who are supportive and with whom you can discuss your feelings and experiences safely. People with such a network usually feel more capable of coping with day-to-day life, as well as with any problems that come up. Social support is particularly crucial for people who have quit or cut down on substance use. It can help them cope with stresses in relationships, at work and within the family.

WHO CAN PROVIDE SUPPORT?

Support can come from anyone you trust and feel comfortable approaching; for example:
• your partner or a family member (parent, brother, sister, adult son or daughter)
• a trusted friend
• a health professional (therapist or family physician).

DIFFERENT KINDS OF SUPPORT

Work on building your support network. While you may already have one or two people you can talk to or spend your time with, developing a network that includes a number of different people lets you give—and receive—support to meet different needs you may have. The kinds of support you might find helpful as you work to change your alcohol or other drug use include:
• emotional support: someone with whom you can discuss feelings
• moral support: someone who can give you encouragement
• instrumental support: someone who can help you with practical tasks such as child care or transportation.
• support from a mentor: someone who can give you guidance and instruction
• recreational support: someone you would like to share your free time with.

PRACTICE EXERCISE

Mapping Your Support System

Take a look at your support system. The circles below are like a map of your network. You are in the middle of the circles, surrounded by different people and organizations that can be helpful to you in your recovery.

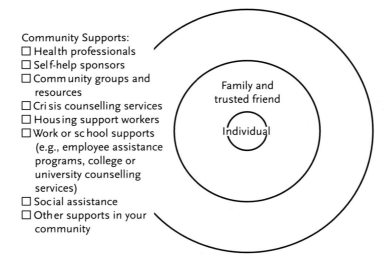

Community Supports:
☐ Health professionals
☐ Self-help sponsors
☐ Community groups and resources
☐ Crisis counselling services
☐ Housing support workers
☐ Work or school supports (e.g., employee assistance programs, college or university counselling services)
☐ Social assistance
☐ Other supports in your community

Family and trusted friend

Individual

Which individuals, groups or organizations do you have in place right now that can offer you support? Put a checkmark beside these.

Which individuals, groups or organizations could you access to get more support? Underline these.

Considering Your Support System

Ask yourself the following questions:

1. Who is currently supporting me? (Be specific.)

_____

_____

2. What needs are met in my relationships with these individuals? (See "Different Kinds of Support," on page 85.)

_____

_____

3. What needs of mine are going unmet?

_____

_____

Strengthening Your Support System
Now ask yourself the questions in the table below about making your support network stronger.

What problems do I have with getting support?	Whom could I approach to help?	How will I plan to do it? (Be specific.)
1.		
2.		
3.		

Refusing Alcohol and Other Drugs

When you quit using alcohol or other drugs, one of the highest-risk situations you might experience is when someone offers you a drink or urges you to use another drug. Saying No requires some practice. In many cases, saying No is not enough.

Read the following suggestions to help you cope in situations where you are being offered alcohol or other drugs. Which ones would work for you?

- Don't hesitate to say No.
- Look the person in the eye.
- Tell the person to stop offering.
- Suggest an alternative—something else to do or something else to drink or eat.
- Change the subject.
- Remind yourself of your goal.
- Think about the negative consequences of using and the benefits of not using.
- Leave the situation.
- Don't feel guilty about refusing.
- Feel good about yourself for not using.

PRACTICE EXERCISE

In what situations do you anticipate being offered alcohol or other drugs?

1. _____
   _____
2. _____
   _____
3. _____
   _____

Look at the strategies you checked off in the first part of this exercise. What will you do, think or say in each of the three situations you listed above?

1. _____
   _____
2. _____
   _____
3. _____
   _____

Dealing with Physical Discomfort

Substance use is often a quick way to get relief from physical discomfort or pain. Many people "self-medicate" with alcohol and other substances, and others use substances to prevent symptoms of withdrawal. The substances people use to deal with pain or withdrawal include:

- prescription medication (taken in ways other than as prescribed by a physician, or medication bought on the street)
- legal drugs, such as alcohol and over-the-counter medication (for example, cough medicine or Tylenol 1)
- illegal drugs, such as cannabis, heroin or cocaine.

Although substance use can work in the short term to reduce pain or withdrawal symptoms, there are some major risks and possible consequences to using substances in this way. For example, taking more of your medication than your doctor prescribed carries the risk of overdose or other negative health consequences. High doses of over-the-counter medication are also risky—for example, liver damage is associated with high doses of Tylenol 1. Using "street drugs" can also have legal consequences, along with other possible health and social consequences.

Another problem is that substance use can "mask" the existence or seriousness of other health and mental health issues. Remember, pain is a signal that requires a response to promote healing (e.g., rest). **If your pain is severe or does not go away, seek medical attention.**

If you find that you rely on substance use to relieve physical discomfort, here are some important strategies to consider:

- Talk with a doctor about your symptoms, and about whether there are other, less risky medications that can help you cope with physical discomfort or withdrawal symptoms.
- Be honest with your doctor about all of the substances (including over-the-counter medications) you are taking. If you don't feel comfortable discussing this issue with your physician, talk about it with your therapist, community outreach worker or nurse.
- Try out some alternative ways of coping with pain or discomfort; for example:
  - Get plenty of sleep (average eight hours a night).
  - Increase your physical activity (e.g., daily walks, stretching exercises).
  - Eat a balanced diet (check out Canada's Food Guide at www.hc-sc.gc.ca/fn-an/food-guide-aliment/fg_rainbow-arc_en_ciel_ga_e.html; you can find suggested cultural adaptations at www.opha.on.ca/resources/foodguides.html).
  - Drink plenty of fluids, including water.
  - Avoid too much caffeine (no more than three cups of coffee per day is recommended).
  - Massage tense, painful areas, or apply heat to sore, tense muscles.
  - Apply ice packs to injured areas.
  - Reduce stress and tension with "time outs" or relaxation exercises.
  - Distract yourself (e.g., read a magazine, watch television, play with your kids).
  - Use imagery (e.g., imagine yourself being healthy and whole, or imagine muscles that are loose and limp).
  - Practise positive emotions, such as humour and optimism.
  - Maintain a balance between work and play.

- Make an appointment at a pain management clinic or read pain management self-help books.
- Join a support group.

PRACTICE EXERCISE

1. What kind of physical discomfort is a trigger for you to use alcohol or other drugs (e.g., tension headaches, difficulty sleeping, withdrawal symptoms)?

_____

_____

_____

_____

_____

2. How have you coped in the past with your physical discomfort triggers?

_____

_____

_____

_____

3. What were the consequences (short-term and long-term) of using substances to cope with pain or withdrawal?

_____

_____

_____

_____

4. What other things could you do to cope?

_____

_____

_____

_____

Problem Solving

Learning how to be an effective problem solver is a skill. You can use problem-solving strategies to deal with substance use as well as with other challenging situations in your life. Problem solving can also help you set and stick to goals (both short-term and long-term).

In this exercise you will learn the steps to effective problem solving, and ways to set concrete and achievable goals.

- Three basic steps are the keys to solving problems:
  - Identify and acknowledge that there is a problem.
  - Make a plan—decide what to do about the problem.
  - Take action!

PRACTICE EXERCISE

Think of an example of a problem you want to deal with. Perhaps you would like to find a nicer place to live, or you want to find a job that interests you. The following exercise will take you through the three steps.

Step 1: Identify the Problem

State the problem using "I" statements, such as, "I can't find a job." If the problem you identify is very large, break it down into smaller parts (e.g., "I need employment counselling," "I need help writing a résumé").

Step 2: Come up with Possible Solutions

List and evaluate the solutions (think of as many solutions as possible, including a silly one just for fun). Brainstorm! Then weigh the pros (good things) and cons (not-so-good things) for each solution. What is your best option?

Here is an example:

Problem area I want to work on: **I need work experience.**

SOLUTION 1

Do some volunteer work.

Pros: **Gain experience, add structure to my day, get a reference for a job I'm really interested in.**

Cons: **Take up time I could use to look for a paying job, even if not's one that I would be happy in for long.**

SOLUTION 2

Enrol in a job-training program.

Pros: **Gain experience, add structure to my day, get a reference for I job I'm really interested in.**

Cons: **Might be a long waiting list, might not get accepted.**

SOLUTION 3

See an employment counsellor.

Pros: **Might find some opportunities I never knew or thought of, could give me some support and encouragement.**

Cons: **I'd like to do it on my own—asking for help is hard.**

Best Option: **I think an employment counsellor would be worth a try. If that doesn't work out, I can look at some places to volunteer.**

Now it's your turn! What would areas would you like to work on?

Problem area I want to work on: _____

_____

SOLUTION 1

_____

Pros: _____

Cons: _____

SOLUTION 2

_____

Pros: _____

Cons: _____

SOLUTION 3

_____

Pros: _____

Cons: _____

Based on your own evaluation of each possible solution above, what is your best option—Solution 1, 2 or 3?

_____

_____

Step 3: Take Action!

Now it is time to come up with your own realistic action plan. Think about the two following questions and then write down your own action plan.

How you will act on your best solution (where, with whom, with what and how)?

Are there any other skills or practice required?

My Action Plan:

_____.

_____.

_____.

_____.

Now work toward your goal by setting up a timeline for putting your solution into practice:

In three months I would like to: _____.

In six months I would like to: _____.

In one year I would like to: _____.

In two years I would like to: _____.

DO IT!

After you have given the approach a fair trial, is it working?

If not, try one of the other approaches.

Remember to keep your goals realistic and to break them up into small steps. Even if your progress is slow, every time you move forward, you get closer to achieving your goal!

Spirituality

Many people who are trying to quit or cut down on alcohol or other drugs consider spirituality to be a key factor in helping them to achieve their substance use goals.

Spirituality is hard to define, because it can mean different things to different people. For some, spirituality is understood as a feeling, experience or personal faith that may or may not mean being part of an organized religion. For others, spirituality is expressed through prayer, meditation or attending places of worship. Spirituality can help motivate us, give meaning to our lives and allow us to feel that we are a part of a larger community.

The following are examples of some things that may help you to enhance your spirituality:

- Be honest with yourself and others.
- Look for ways to make life a positive and satisfying experience.
- Find a place where you feel calm and peaceful (e.g., go to where nature has been relatively untouched by people).
- Volunteer in your community.
- Ask or allow a higher power to help you achieve your goals.
- Attend self-help groups, such as Alcoholics Anonymous (AA), Narcotics Anonymous (NA) or Cocaine Anonymous (CA).
- Read AA, NA or CA literature.
- Attend spiritual or religious ceremonies.
- Read religious literature and learn more about your own or another religion.
- Talk to a spiritual leader, member of the clergy or elder.
- Do yoga or meditate.
- Read about mindfulness meditation—for example, John Kabat-Zinn's *Full Catastrophe Living* (Doubleday, 1990).
- Keep a journal.
- Get in touch with the spiritual side of your heritage.

Spirituality is a very personal and individual experience. Take a moment to list some of the things that **you** can do to develop your spirituality:

_____

_____

_____

_____

_____

_____

_____

_____

_____

_____

Assertiveness

Assertiveness means being able to tell others how you feel without putting them down or becoming aggressive and angry. Assertive behaviour is also direct and honest. It allows you to feel good about yourself, and to get your needs met—but not at the expense of others.

Many people have never learned how to communicate assertively. Assertive behaviour is a skill. And like any skill, it takes practice before it comes naturally and feels comfortable. Aggressive and/or passive behaviour can trap you in a cycle that involves using substances to deal with unpleasant emotions like anger. One of the ways to break that cycle is through assertiveness.

In this exercise you will work on identifying your communication style and begin to learn some of the skills involved in giving clear and direct verbal and non-verbal messages.

CYCLE OF AGGRESSIVE/PASSIVE BEHAVIOUR

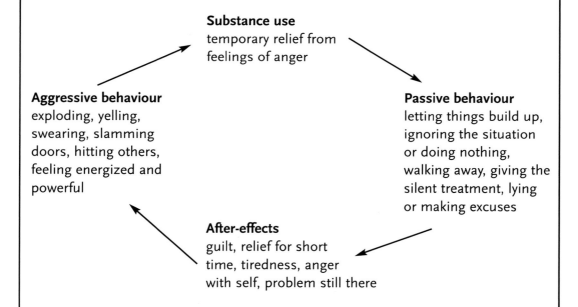

Substance use
temporary relief from
feelings of anger

Aggressive behaviour
exploding, yelling,
swearing, slamming
doors, hitting others,
feeling energized and
powerful

Passive behaviour
letting things build up,
ignoring the situation
or doing nothing,
walking away, giving the
silent treatment, lying
or making excuses

After-effects
guilt, relief for short
time, tiredness, anger
with self, problem still there

GETTING OUT OF THE CYCLE

Here are some techniques for behaving assertively:
- Practice what you want to say. You can do this by yourself or with someone you trust.
- Set a specific time for the conversation.
- Make direct eye contact with the other person.
- Watch your posture—stand or sit up straight.
- Speak in a clear, firm, controlled voice.
- Remind yourself that anger is a normal emotion.
- Use "I" statements (e.g., "I feel angry when . . ." or "I feel angry that . . .")
- Make your point and stick to it—calmly.
- Be brief! Avoid long explanations.
- Don't attack or blame the other person.

- Repeat your point, if necessary.
- Don't drag in old issues.
- Listen to the other person's response.
- Look for possible compromises.
- Leave the situation if you feel unsafe because the other person may become violent.
- Close the discussion and move on.

PRACTICE EXERCISE

In this exercise you will work on identifying your communication style and begin to learn some of the skills involved in giving clear and direct verbal and non-verbal messages.

Think about situations in the past year where you wish you had been better at standing up for yourself, or where you lost control and later regretted it.

1. Describe one of those situations:

    Where were you? _____

    _____

    Who else was there? _____

    _____

    What were you thinking? _____

    _____

    What were you feeling? _____

    _____

    What was the outcome? _____

    _____

2. List three statements you could make in a similar situation in the future that would lead to a positive (assertive) outcome:

    i. _____

    _____

    _____

    ii. _____

    _____

    _____

    iii. _____

    _____

    _____

3. Role-play or think about how you could respond to the following scenarios:

My roommate or partner is extremely messy and I am always picking up after him or her. _____

_____

_____

A member of my family is always asking to borrow money from me.

_____

_____

_____

My partner interrupts me and finishes my thought or sentence in public.

_____

_____

_____

Someone asks me for money or a cigarette. _____

_____

_____

Other: _____

_____

_____

Exercise adapted from Susan Cox, Anger Management Program, Kitchener Probation and Parole Office, Kitchener, Ont. 1995.

Anger Management

Anger is a normal human emotion. However, the ways in which we express anger can have negative consequences both for others and for ourselves. For example, anger might make it difficult to think clearly, perhaps leading to actions we later regret. Anger can also lead to verbal and physical aggression or violence. Many people identify anger as a trigger to substance use.

WHEN IS ANGER A PROBLEM?

If your anger is frequent, if it is intense, if it lasts a long time, if it leads to aggression or violence or if it disturbs your work or relationships, these are warning signs that your anger is creating problems for you.

There are different styles of expressing anger:

- Some people tend to be **passive** when they are angry. Such people would likely avoid confrontations, and perhaps allow others to take advantage of them. Passive anger means "bottling it up" inside.
- Other people express their anger **aggressively**. Such people may try to dominate others with anger and blame others for their own behaviour.
- The ideal way of expressing anger is by being **assertive**. Assertive people express their feelings in an open and honest manner, and in a way that shows respect for others. They try to solve problems by attempting to change the behaviours that create anger.

Here are some suggestions for dealing with anger:

- Be aware of your body (e.g., tight muscles, clenched fists). Try to recognize the warning signs that your anger is being expressed either passively (e.g., headache, depressed feelings) or aggressively (e.g., raising your voice).
- Take a few deep breaths to relax. Stay calm.
- Remember that anger is a signal that something needs to change.
- Look for positives; don't jump to conclusions.
- Tell yourself, "I'm not going to get pushed around, but I'm not going to lose control of myself either."
- Leave the situation if necessary (take a "time out").
- Ask yourself if you can you laugh about the situation.

PRACTICE EXERCISE

1. Describe a recent situation where you have felt angry:

_____

_____

_____

_____

_____

2. What were the physical signs of anger? (e.g., tight muscles)

_____

_____

_____

_____

_____

3. How did you react in this situation?

_____

_____

_____

_____

_____

4. What anger style did you express?

_____

_____

_____

_____

_____

5. What did you like about how you coped? What would you do differently in the future?

_____

_____

_____

_____

_____

_____

Adapted from Anger Management Program Manual, *John Howard Society of Windsor-Essex County, Ont., 1992.*

Coping with Boredom

One of the hardest things about "staying quit" or changing substance use is finding things to do that are interesting or exciting. Many people say that in order to give up drinking and other drug use, they also had to give up some old (or new) friends, and stay away from risky places, such as bars, social gatherings or even celebrations.

People who have changed their substance use often ask these kinds of questions:
- How can I have fun without going to a bar or nightclub?
- Who can I hang out with, since all my friends drink or use other drugs?
- What do I do with my time now?
- How do I deal with these feelings of loneliness or boredom?
- What can I do when I don't have money to spend?

Coping with boredom means finding new activities, interests, friends and hobbies. Like any lifestyle change, this might be hard at first. Being out and active in the community is an important part of recovery. Yet even leaving the safety of your home for short periods of time can be risky, as many people and places can make it hard to stay substance-free.

PRACTICE EXCERCISE

In this exercise, you will have a chance to think about:
- some things you can do right away in situations where you are feeling bored or lonely
- other things that might take longer to put in place, but will add meaning and interest to your life in the future.

Use this exercise to take a look at some things you can do that will add fun and interest to your life—without alcohol or other drugs.

PART 1: THINGS TO DO AND PLACES TO GO

First, think about some of the things that you used to enjoy doing (maybe it was a long time ago), or some new things that you think you might like to try. Check off any of the ideas on the lists below that might interest you, and add anything else that **you** like the idea of.

Physical Activities	
☐ Walking or hiking	☐ Fishing
☐ Jogging or running	☐ Bowling
☐ Bike riding	☐ Martial arts
☐ Swimming	☐ Tennis, badminton or other
☐ Basketball	racquet sports
☐ Working out or lifting weights	☐ Dancing
☐ Yoga	☐ Other: _____
☐ Volleyball	☐ Other: _____
☐ Soccer or football	

Hobbies

☐ Writing	☐ Painting
☐ Collecting things	☐ Pottery making
☐ Woodwork	☐ Other: _____
☐ Sewing	☐ Other: _____

Other Interests

☐ Watching movies	☐ Playing an instrument
☐ Reading	☐ Playing video games
☐ Listening to music	☐ Other: _____
☐ Surfing the Internet	☐ Other: _____
☐ Playing chess, cards or other games	

Now look over some the things that you checked off. What activities do you think you could try doing?

Activity	How Realistic Is It That I Will Do This?	How Fun or Interesting Is This Activity?
1.	◄──────────► not very realistic realistic	◄──────────► not very fun/ interesting fun/ interesting
2.	◄──────────► not very realistic realistic	◄──────────► not very fun/ interesting fun/ interesting
3.	◄──────────► not very realistic realistic	◄──────────► not very fun/ interesting fun/ interesting

PART 2: MEETING NEW PEOPLE

In addition to having activities and interests, it's also important to have people around whom you like and trust. Some people who stop using substances say that, since many of their friends used substances, they need to find a new "support network"—new friends to talk to and do things with.

The list below has some ideas for places to meet new people who can help you in your recovery. Which ideas are you willing to try?

☐ Self-help groups or meetings (such as: _____)

☐ Social clubs (such as: _____)

☐ Drop-in programs (such as: _____)

☐ Educational courses or programs (such as: _____)

☐ Counselling or therapy groups (such as: _____)

☐ Religious or spiritual groups or services (such as: _____)

☐ Volunteer work (such as: _____)

☐ Other: _____

☐ Other: _____

☐ Other: _____

Look over the things that you checked off. What places do you think you could try going to in order to meet new people?

Place	How Realistic Is It That I Will Go?	How Fun or Interesting Will It Be for Me?
1.	◄─────────────► not very realistic → realistic	◄─────────────► not very fun/ interesting → fun/ interesting
2.	◄─────────────► not very realistic → realistic	◄─────────────► not very fun/ interesting → fun/ interesting
3.	◄─────────────► not very realistic → realistic	◄─────────────► not very fun/ interesting → fun/ interesting

PART 3: TAKING ACTION

Doing new things may not be easy. But as with anything new, the more you do it, the easier it becomes. To finish this exercise, write down three things you could do right away when you're feeling bored:

1. _____

2. _____

3. _____

Can you try one of these things this week?

You might find it helpful to keep this exercise in a place where you can refer back to it easily to inspire and motivate yourself. Good luck!

Relaxation

A common reason people drink or use other drugs is to relax. Some people turn to substances to reduce tension, stress or anxiety. When you quit or cut down on your substance use, you may feel discomfort—in the form of sleep problems, headaches or tension.

Maintaining your substance use goal may mean developing other ways to deal with these feelings and issues. Relaxation techniques are a way to reduce tension in your body and quiet your emotions and thinking. The techniques listed below can help you develop skills to relax without needing to use substances.

Relaxation is marked by a state of calm, a feeling of well-being and easy breathing. To achieve a relaxed feeling, there are different paths you can take.

Try the following while sitting with your back well supported and your eyes closed.

Focus on Your Body
- Slowly scan your body and relax all your muscles, starting with your feet and moving slowly up to your face.
- Tell yourself to let go of the tension as you focus on each area of your body.
- When you have finished, think of yourself as relaxed and comfortable.

Focus on Your Breathing
- Breathe out.
- Breathe in slowly—way down into your abdomen.
- Breathe out slowly.
- Try this with your hand on your upper abdomen to be more aware of your breathing.

Focus on Images
- Picture a calm, peaceful scene (e.g., imagine yourself sitting or lying on a beach feeling the warmth of the sun).
- Think of yourself as completely relaxed. Enjoy the sensation.

Try one of the above techniques, or all of them together, to help you sleep or deal with anxiety, or to reduce a tension headache.

Other Things You Can Do to Relax
- Say the word "relax" or "calm" to yourself as you breathe out.
- Stretch.
- Tense your muscles, then let go (e.g., shrug your shoulders up, hold for a few seconds, then let go and notice the difference).
- Remember a time you felt relaxed, and recall the feeling.
- Listen to relaxation tapes.
- Talk to your therapist about where you can learn more about relaxation techniques.

PRACTICE EXERCISE

Be aware of your tension. What part of your body gets tense when you are stressed or craving substances?

_____

_____

_____

_____

Try one of the techniques suggested above. What changes do you notice in your muscle tension or breathing?

_____

_____

_____

_____

Practise the techniques daily. What works best for you?

_____

_____

_____

_____

Think of ways to help yourself remember to use these techniques (e.g., use them every time you notice tension building, or use them at the same time every day).

_____

_____

_____

_____

Coping with Unpleasant Feelings and Memories of Trauma

Substance use is often a coping strategy for dealing with unpleasant feelings. Many people who have a history of substance use have experienced trauma in their lives, such as physical, sexual or emotional abuse. When people who have a history of being traumatized stop using substances, they may feel a range of negative, overwhelming feelings. It is common to experience flashbacks and nightmares. Flashbacks are recurrent, distressing memories of the traumatic event. When you are having a flashback, you may feel as if you are reliving the event.

Here is a list of symptoms you may have experienced if you have been traumatized. Put a check beside any of the symptoms that are triggers for you—in other words, warning signs that can spark a relapse of alcohol or other drug use.

HYPERAROUSAL (being in a constant state of anxiety)

☐ Never feeling really safe
☐ Being easily startled, reacting irritably to small things
☐ Having a feeling of potential danger
☐ Sleeping poorly (especially having problems falling asleep)

INTRUSION (unwelcome or difficult thoughts and feelings)

☐ Flashbacks
☐ Suicidal thoughts
☐ Traumatic nightmares, causing you to wake up feeling very frightened
☐ Body memories (feelings in your body that were with you at the time of the traumatic event, such as smells, tastes and sounds, and which trigger memories of the event)

CONSTRICTION (shutting down for self-protection)

☐ Feelings of numbness
☐ Lack of any feelings
☐ Dissociation (observing events from outside your body)
☐ Suicidal thoughts
☐ Generalized fear (e.g., sleeping with a weapon, or checking under the bed)
☐ Sleep problems

You may also experience physical symptoms (e.g., racing heartbeat, disorientation) or emotional symptoms (e.g., feeling like you are going crazy, or feeling intense anger).

All the above symptoms are common and normal if you have experienced trauma. People often speak about feeling overwhelmed or out of control; they may say, "I feel like I am going crazy," or "I feel I don't know who I am."

Take a few moments to write down some symptoms that you experience when you feel overwhelmed. It is important to know your symptoms as a first step to managing these symptoms.

_____

_____

_____

_____

_____

You may want to talk to your therapist if these symptoms are common for you. Your therapist may be able to refer you for treatment that helps people cope with these feelings.

Developed by Eva Ingber, MSW, RSW, Centre for Addiction and Mental Health.

Coping with Flashbacks and Unpleasant Emotions

Here is a list of strategies you can practise to help you cope with flashbacks, body memories, feelings of anxiety and cravings. The goal is to help yourself get out of your unpleasant thoughts and feelings and get into the present.

You can use these strategies anywhere. Consider carrying these instructions with you as a reminder.

BREATHE

- Become aware of your breathing (holding your breath is a fear reaction).
- Tell yourself to breathe—repeat the word "breathe."
- Breathe from your diaphragm, taking slow, deep breaths. Breathe in for a count of 3, hold your breath for a count of 3, and release your breath to a count of 3. Repeat this pattern.

BRING YOURSELF BACK INTO YOUR ENVIRONMENT

Become aware of your senses:
- Sight: Try to keep your eyes open, so you can see your environment. If someone is with you, make eye contact.
- Hearing: Pay attention to the sounds around you (e.g., traffic, people's voices).
- Smell: Pay attention to smells (e.g., coffee, food).
- Touch: Hold onto the chair you are sitting on. Feel the chair underneath you, and notice your feet on the ground. Repeat to yourself, "I am here in the room" (you may want to specify your living room, your group therapy room, etc.).

ESTABLISH A COMFORTABLE AND NURTURING ENVIRONMENT

Carry things with you that bring you comfort (e.g., a journal, or a picture of yourself or someone you care about).

SAY POSITIVE THINGS TO YOURSELF

For example, remind yourself of a good thing that you have done or that has happened to you.

Developed by Eva Ingber, MSW, RSW, Centre for Addiction and Mental Health.

PRACTICE EXERCISE

Part 1: Be Prepared

List two grounding techniques you will try to use the next time you need to cope with your feelings.

1. _____

2. _____

Write something you can say to yourself to feel better.

_____

_____

_____

Part 2: Create a Safe Place

Another way of coping with negative feelings is to choose a place in your living environment where you feel safe, and to make it as safe, nurturing and comfortable as possible. You can carry out your grounding techniques in this place.

1. Where is this place?

_____

_____

_____

2. What does it look like?

_____

_____

_____

3. What will you put in this place to bring you comfort?

_____

_____

_____

4. Is there anything you need to change to make this place more comfortable?

_____

_____

_____

At times when you are physically unable to go to this safe place, you can feel comfort by carrying the image of it with you.

Coping with Anxiety

Although almost everyone feels somewhat anxious in unfamiliar situations, some people feel such high levels of anxiety, making them extremely uncomfortable, that they find it easier to avoid certain situations. Others may rely on alcohol or other drugs to reduce their anxiety to a tolerable level. Neither solution works well in the long run. Using alcohol or other drugs to cope with anxiety can become a vicious cycle, in which people come to believe that they can't function in a given situation without using substances.

What you think and what you tell yourself have a big influence on how you feel. Many people have responded to situations in the same way for so long that their thinking becomes almost automatic. These "automatic thoughts" are the negative messages people give themselves that contribute to feelings of anxiety. Becoming aware of your own automatic thoughts, then challenging them, can help you break a common cycle of substance use. This cycle is illustrated below.

anxiety-provoking ➜ automatic ➜ high level ➜ substance use to
situation   thoughts   of anxiety   decrease anxiety

The first step is to identify ways that you might engage in automatic, or faulty, thinking. Here are some examples of automatic thoughts:

- Perfectionism ("I still sometimes think about drinking—so I've really failed in treatment.")
- Mind reading ("My boss thinks I'm incompetent." "This person must think I'm boring.")
- Emotional reasoning—the idea that, if you feel it, therefore it must be true ("I feel so stupid, I must really look stupid.")
- All or nothing thinking ("I had one drink, so I'm headed back to living on the street!")
- "Should" statements ("I should always be in control." "I shouldn't show others how nervous I am.")
- Jumping to conclusions ("My parole officer/boss called me today; I must be in trouble.")
- Labelling ("I'm just an alcoholic/ex-convict/junkie.")
- Dwelling on the negatives ("I always screw things up. Why should this time be any different?")

PRACTICE EXERCISE

1. Can you think of any other examples of automatic thoughts? _____
   _____

2. Describe a situation in which you have felt stressed or anxious, and have used
   alcohol or other drugs to cope: _____
   _____

3. List the consequences of drinking or other drug use in that situation (positive
   and negative, short-term **and** long-term): _____
   _____

4. List the automatic thoughts that go along with this situation: _____
   _____

5. How do you feel as a result of these thoughts? _____
   _____

What are some things you could say to yourself in the future in order to replace the
negative thoughts outlined above? For example, you could say something neutral or
positive to yourself ("I'm trying and that is a start").

_____

_____

If you are in a group treatment setting, you may wish to role-play the above
scenario, or ask your counsellor for help in coming up with some alternatives. In
any case, it is important to practice your coping plan in anxiety-provoking situations.

Here are some strategies that have worked for others in coping with automatic thoughts:
- Relabel your negative feelings (e.g., stress, anxiety)—and the cravings that go along with
  them—as an important signal to take action.
- Practise "thought stopping." When you recognize negative automatic thoughts appearing,
  shout "STOP!" and picture a large stop sign in your imagination.
- Pay attention to the positive things that happen, and keep track of them. You may even
  want to write them down.
- Challenge the automatic thought. Ask: Does it make sense? What is the evidence for it? Is
  there a more realistic way to interpret the situation?
- Pat yourself on the back! Say something positive to yourself or reward yourself when
  you successfully cope with an anxiety-producing situation without drinking or using
  other drugs.
- Remember that some anxiety and stress is normal for everyone. Concentrate on reducing
  your anxiety to a manageable level, not on eliminating it entirely.
- It is important for you to become an observer of your thoughts. That way you can
  be aware of messages you tell yourself. Observe your positive and negative judgments
  about yourself.

Coping with Loss

Loss is a normal part of the human experience, and grief is a normal reaction to any kind of loss. People associate the word "grief" with death or dying, but grief is a natural response to any loss, such as ending a relationship, moving to a new community or even saying goodbye to substance use.

A moment of grief is like the tip of an emotional iceberg: it can trigger other emotional experiences that linger beneath the surface. Taking time to grieve the loss of a lifestyle can be very helpful to you in the early stages of changing your substance use.

PRACTICE EXERCISE

This exercise helps you identify some of your emotional reactions as you embark on changing your use of alcohol or other drugs. The objective is to encourage you to identify and then normalize the feelings that accompany the absence of old habits related to alcohol and other drug use.

In the spaces below, fill in the people, places or things you have lost as a result of quitting your old alcohol or other drug use habits. Then, on the same line, write in the feelings and the new behaviours that accompanied each of these losses in your life.

What I Have Lost	Feeling	New Behaviours
Example: **Friends who still use drugs; having fun and partying**	Example: **Sad, bored, frustrated**	Example: **Spend time at home with partner**

Using your imagination, picture yourself as an iceberg. There are some things about you that are seen, like the tip of the ice, above the water, and some things that remain unseen, like the ice that floats below the water. Both parts are very much a part of who you are as a person. On the iceberg shown on the next page, above the waterline, write some of the changes in your attitude and behaviour that are now visible to you and to others as you work on your substance use. Below the waterline, write less visible thoughts and feelings (both positive and negative) that you are experiencing in your new lifestyle.

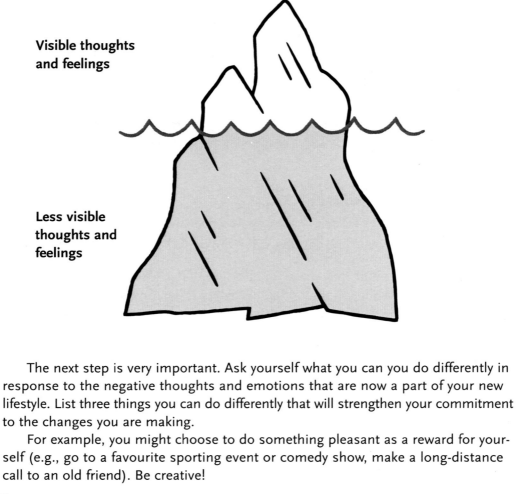

Visible thoughts and feelings

Less visible thoughts and feelings

The next step is very important. Ask yourself what you can you do differently in response to the negative thoughts and emotions that are now a part of your new lifestyle. List three things you can do differently that will strengthen your commitment to the changes you are making.

For example, you might choose to do something pleasant as a reward for yourself (e.g., go to a favourite sporting event or comedy show, make a long-distance call to an old friend). Be creative!

1. _____

_____

_____

2. _____

_____

_____

3. _____

_____

_____

Adapted from Mark Balfe, Grief & Bereavement Services, Mount Sinai Hospital, Toronto, Ont.

Healthy Relationships

When you have substance use issues, you may become isolated and disconnected from significant people in your life. But healthy relationships are especially important to your sense of self-worth and personal growth.

In all relationships, including intimate ones, it is important to maintain appropriate personal boundaries. In other words, you have a right to your own unique feelings and needs. Boundaries are like a fence with a gate. You decide when and how much to open the gate based on how you feel emotionally and physically. Pay attention to your thoughts, feelings and immediate ("gut") reactions.

In healthy relationships, your needs and feelings are heard and respected. Taking care of others, or rescuing, changing or controlling other people, can contribute to an imbalance in your relationships. Examples of how you can take care of yourself include telling yourself, "I won't allow alcohol or other drugs in my home," "I won't allow anyone to verbally abuse me" or "I won't lend money to anyone except my family members." Resources such as support groups, family services and drop-in centres are easy to access, and they can support you in making decisions and help you to improve your relationships with others.

Good, healthy relationships are a fair exchange. The costs to you should be about equal to the rewards. Keep in mind that the value of costs and rewards is personal. The value of something to one person may not be the same to another.

PRACTICE EXERCISE

Think about the current relationship(s) in your life as you answer the questions below.

1. What kinds of things do you value in a relationship?

_____

_____

_____

2. How have alcohol and other drugs affected your relationships?

_____

_____

_____

3. What do you need to change about your relationship(s) in order to help you meet your goals for changing your use of alcohol and other drugs?

_____

_____

_____

4. What steps must you take to make these changes and improve your relationship(s)?

_____

_____

_____

Sexual Relationships and Dating

INTRODUCTION

Many people who have who quit or cut down on their substance use find that meeting people to date and having sexual relationships are big challenges. For some, alcohol or other drugs were a way to feel more confident with others. Also, many people have met their sexual partners by going to bars and clubs. Dating is challenging at the best of times—when dealing with substance use recovery at the same time, it can be positively frightening!

Forming healthy relationships takes time and effort. But there are ways to connect with others that don't involve alcohol or other drugs. This exercise will help you think about and plan how you are going to go about trying some of those ways.

People who are trying to quit using substances and want to date or start a sexual relationship often ask these kinds of questions:
- What does "healthy dating" mean?
- How and where do I meet people who don't misuse substances, and are supportive of my recovery?
- How much information about my substance use issues should I tell someone I'm interested in?

Many people who have substance use issues have also had difficulties having a close relationship. It is OK to choose **not** to focus on dating.

PART 1: WHAT IS A HEALTHY RELATIONSHIP?
PRACTICE EXERCISE

In this exercise, you will learn:
- what a healthy relationship looks like
- how to ask someone for a date
- where you can meet people where drinking or using other drugs is not expected.

Below is a list of qualities that are usually part of a healthy relationship. There is room for you to add some of your own.

How many of these qualities have you had in past relationships? Which ones needed work or were missing? These are some areas to think about as you start dating or meeting potential partners.

- ☐ You are with someone who has values and interests similar to yours.
- ☐ It takes time to get to know each other and see whether the relationship is right for you.
- ☐ The needs of both partners are being met.
- ☐ Both partners feel comfortable and safe with one another.
- ☐ You can trust the other person with your feelings, ideas, wishes and desires.
- ☐ The two partners respect one another's boundaries (e.g., how often to see each other, whether to have sex, what each other's sexual preferences are).

☐ If you make a commitment not to date other people, you both trust each other's loyalty to the relationship.

☐ Your partner accepts you for who are (and you accept him or her)—both the good and the bad things.

☐ If one or both partners aren't looking (or ready) for a serious relationship, this is talked about, understood and accepted.

☐ One or both partners don't need to use substances in order to feel intimate or have sex.

☐ Other: _____

☐ Other: _____

☐ Other: _____

PART 2: HOW DO I ASK FOR A DATE?

It can take some courage to ask someone you like for a date, especially if you are not using alcohol or other drugs. Here are some simple steps and suggestions that may help:

• It doesn't have to be a big deal! Try thinking about asking someone for a date in these terms: "I'm asking someone to join me in a fun activity—if they say Yes, that's great; if they say No, there's always someone else out there."

• Make eye contact and smile at the person.

• Use a pleasant greeting in an upbeat tone.

• Tell the person about the activity and when it takes place.

• Ask if he or she would like to join you—be direct.

• If the person says he or she is busy, suggest another activity at another time.

• If the person still says No, thank the person and move on. Sometimes people just don't feel a connection.

• If the person says Yes, say that you are pleased, and set a meeting place and time.

PART 3: WHEN AND HOW DO I TALK ABOUT MY SUBSTANCE USE HISTORY?

You may want to wait until you've had a couple of dates with someone before you disclose information about your substance use history and recovery. However, once you have begun to get to know the person, it is important to be honest about what you are going through. Of course, there is always the possibility that the person will decide that he or she does not want to continue the relationship. But if so, it's better to know this sooner rather than later. Your willingness to be honest shows respect for the other person, as well as commitment to yourself and your recovery.

Pick a time when you are both feeling relaxed, and make sure the conversation happens in a private place where you aren't likely to be interrupted.

You might want to start the conversation with a statement such as this: "There's something on my mind that I've been concerned about telling you. I really like you, and I'm hoping that it doesn't get in the way of our spending time together. Is this a good time to talk a bit about this?"

Reread the suggested opening sentence on the previous page, and try putting the same ideas into your own words:

_____

_____

_____

PART 4: PLACES TO GO AND PEOPLE TO MEET
PRACTICE EXERCISE

Now explore some possible places to meet people and things you can do together.

Where to Go*

What other places can you think of to meet people? Brainstorm a list (e.g., special-interest clubs, sporting events, walkathons, health clubs, neighbourhood and community gatherings, volunteer opportunities, continuing education workshops, courses).

_____

_____

What other places can you think of to go with someone? Brainstorm a list (e.g., coffee shops, bookstores, movies, film festivals, shopping malls and food courts, museums, libraries, craft fairs, church and community centres, bowling, restaurants).

_____

_____

Tips for Success

- Tell your friends that you are interested in meeting someone. They might know someone who is single who might be right for you.
- Pick places that are easy to get to by public transportation and don't cost too much money (e.g., museums, parks, free community concerts or other events).
- Stay out of bars and clubs and the old "playgrounds" where you may be tempted to use substances.
- Pay attention to your personal hygiene.
- Keep your interactions light and friendly.
- Ask open-ended questions instead of questions that would get a Yes or No answer (e.g., "What made you decide to join this art class?" rather than, "Do you like this class?").
- Do not disclose everything about yourself on the first date. People need time to get to know each other.

    Trying out new ways of meeting people may not be easy, but as with anything new, the more you do it, the easier and more natural it becomes.

*List of places to go adapted from Mary Faulkner (2004), Easy Does It Dating Guide for People in Recovery. Center City, MN: Hazelden Publishing (p. 93).

PART 5: WHAT DO YOU VALUE IN A RELATIONSHIP?
PRACTICE EXERCISE

For the last part of this exercise, write down what you value in a relationship and what kind of person you are looking for. Take some time to think about it. Knowing what you want in a partner will help you to reach your goal of developing healthy relationships.

What do you value in a relationship?

1. _____

2. _____

3. _____

What kind of person are you looking for?

1. _____

2. _____

3. _____

AN IMPORTANT NOTE ON SEXUAL HEALTH

If you have any physical issues that make having sex uncomfortable or difficult (e.g., vaginal dryness or difficulty getting or maintaining an erection), talk to your doctor. Problems such as these may be related to substance use, and may disappear as you quit or cut down on your use of alcohol or other drugs. If they are still an issue, they may be treatable with medication, depending on the type of problem, the length of time it has been an issue for you, your age and your medical history.

You might find it helpful to keep this exercise in a place where you can refer back to it easily to inspire and motivate yourself. Good luck!

Money Issues

Money is important for many reasons. With money we can pay for food, rent and clothes. We also use money to pay for things that aren't absolutely necessary, such as eating out in restaurants, or special things we want but may not need. We also count on money for security for the future. Generally speaking, when people have enough money, they have more choices in our society.

For people with substance use issues, having or not having money can be a trigger to drink or use other drugs. It is important to think about how money and substance use are connected.

Consider the role that money plays in your life around substance use:
• In what ways is money a trigger for you?
• How have you managed your money in the past to avoid buying alcohol and other drugs?
• Is it safe for you to carry money around right now?

HAVING MONEY

If money is a trigger for you to use substances, here are some ideas you can try:
• Don't carry a bank card or credit card.
• Only carry enough money for transportation and the day's expenses.
• Have someone you trust manage your money for a period of time, until your confidence and coping strategies are stronger.
• Have any money coming to you (such as paycheques or government cheques) deposited directly into your bank account.
• Avoid borrowing or lending money.
• Stay away from "easy money" from drug deals or other crime.
• Have a plan for the times when you know you are going to receive money—stay busy, and attend self-help or support groups.

PRACTICE EXERCISE

Which of the above suggestions might you try in order to feel less at risk for relapsing as a result of having money?

_____

_____

_____

_____

What other strategies can you think of that might be helpful?

_____

_____

_____

_____

NOT HAVING MONEY

Having no money can be very stressful. You may feel very vulnerable and afraid that you won't be able to take care of yourself or others. As a result of not having money, some people might turn to risky behaviours. These might include legal behaviours such as gambling (e.g., buying lottery tickets), or illegal behaviours (e.g., theft, dealing drugs). These are behaviours that can trigger substance use.

In what ways does not having money put you at risk for returning to substance use?

_____

_____

_____

_____

How have you coped in the past with not having enough money?

_____

_____

_____

_____

Here is a list of suggestions for dealing with money problems:
- Seek help at an agency that counsels people around money management (such as a credit counselling bureau). Many are free.
- Talk to a professional from a social assistance (welfare) agency.
- Explore with a counsellor whether you are eligible for disability benefits.
- Get on a waiting list for subsidized housing.
- Find out about resources and programs in your community, such as food banks, drop-in centres and support groups.
- Use self-care strategies that are low-cost or free to help you stick to your substance use goals.
- Join (or start) a group that lobbies government around social justice and anti-poverty issues.
- Set long-term goals around returning to school or getting job training, to help you to find a better-paying job in the future.

Which of the above suggestions might you try in order to feel less at risk for relapsing as a result of not having money?

_____

_____

_____

_____

What other strategies can you think of that might help you to feel less at risk for relapsing as a result of not having money?

_____

_____

_____

_____

There are no easy answers for dealing with the challenges of having or not having money. It might be helpful to talk with other people about how they cope.

PART IV:
SRP for Clients with Concurrent Disorders

Adapting the SRP Approach

MARILYN HERIE, ANDREA TSANOS AND LYN WATKIN MEREK

Introduction

Client Profile: Steve

Steve is 32. He has a diagnosis of schizophrenia and is connected to the outpatient mental health program. He has a psychiatrist and a case manager, and medication is part of his treatment plan. Steve uses crack cocaine, typically in binges, particularly when his monthly disability cheque arrives. He also smokes marijuana and drinks alcohol. His substance use has had negative consequences for his mental health (it has produced psychotic symptoms), and also may jeopardize his housing situation (since substance use is not tolerated in the supportive housing where he lives). Steve calls crack "the Devil's drug," but feels he is hooked, and still values the escape and social enjoyment he gets from it. He says it is difficult for him to resist when drugs are offered to him, and he finds it hard to be assertive in refusing drugs if he is approached by dealers in his neighbourhood and has money in his pocket. He is open to receiving help to explore his use of crack, but does not see his marijuana and alcohol use as problematic.

This chapter addresses the issue of how we can work effectively with clients like Steve, who present with concurrent substance use and mental health issues. In what follows, we outline an adapted version of SRP for clients with concurrent disorders (CD). The first section of the chapter discusses the prevalence of concurrent disorders and summarizes some of the key research findings related to working with clients with concurrent disorders. It also includes some tips for running SRP groups with this population. The following sections provide session outlines and clinical tools that have been adapted for use with clients with concurrent disorders.

Over the past decade, there has been an increasing appreciation of the needs of people with concurrent mental health and substance use issues. A variety of studies seeking to establish the prevalence rate of concurrent disorders have shown that *roughly half* of individuals with either a mental health or substance use disorder had concurrent disorders at some point in their life (Health Canada, 2002; Kessler et al., 1996; Regier et al., 1990). In an Ontario study of clients seeking treatment for substance use problems, 68 per cent had a concurrent mental health disorder (Ross et al., 1995). As expected, the study indicates that the prevalence rates are higher in agency and hospital populations than in the general population. However, the rates in clinical populations varies considerably, depending on the setting and the method of diagnosis.

What is clear is that this traditionally underserved (even, often, ignored) population comprises a high proportion of clients presenting for service in either specialized substance use or mental health settings, as well as other contexts (such as hostels and shelters, criminal justice and corrections systems, child protection and family services, employee assistance programs and primary care settings). The increasing recognition of the high co-prevalence rates has led clinicians to screen routinely for the presence of concurrent disorders. Ignoring or not properly recognizing concurrent disorders can affect clients' ability to recover successfully from both disorders, and negative effects can include:
• premature dropout from treatment
• higher risk of relapse
• risk of harmful interactions between drugs of abuse and psychiatric medications
• misinterpretation of symptoms (e.g., are they signs of a mental health problem, the effects of substance use or signs of withdrawal from substances?)
• likelihood of the client needing more expensive services in future.

However, a variety of factors, have made it difficult for agencies and health care organizations to respond adequately to the needs of people with concurrent disorders: lack of specialist knowledge and skills in substance use, mental health or both; limited access to specialist diagnostic and other treatment services and providers; agency exclusion criteria; problem complexity; and fragmented treatment systems. Nonetheless, people with concurrent disorders are often best served where they present; at the very least, they are best served within the context of an integrated treatment program or system (Health Canada, 2002).

Because research is still lacking in this area, our current understanding of best practices in screening, assessment and treatment of people with concurrent disorders must be seen as still in development. What we do have, though, is an emerging consensus regarding how best to design programs and systems to provide more seamless and integrated care, and how to respond clinically to clients with concurrent disorders. Integrated treatment for concurrent disorders started in the early 1980s as a solution to the difficulties and poor outcomes associated with "sequential" and "parallel" treatment systems that were not co-ordinated. Integrated treatment occurs when "mental health treatments and substance abuse treatments are brought together by the same clinicians/support workers, or team of clinicians/support workers, in the same program, to ensure that the individual receives a consistent explanation of illness/problems and a coherent prescription for treatment rather than a contradictory set of messages from different providers" (Health Canada, 2002, p. 15).

Minkoff (2001) has articulated the following key principles of integrated treatment for concurrent disorders:

- comprehensive programs and services designed to respond to the substance use, mental health and other issues with which clients present
- continuity of treatment over time, as many clients with concurrent disorders require long-term follow-up, aftercare and community support
- accessibility in the location of services; flexibility in hours and service delivery
- acceptance by practitioners of both mental health issues and substance use issues
- a sense of optimism about the possibility of recovery, even for clients with very severe or complex problems
- treatment that is tailored to individual needs
- culturally competent treatment.

The end result of a fully integrated approach is essentially a "no wrong door" response for individuals with concurrent disorders. Within this approach, new clients presenting to either a mental health or a substance use facility receive screening, assessment and treatment services both for substance use and for mental health problems.

Screening and Assessment

While there is no consensus about the best screening and assessment tools for people with concurrent disorders, the components of an integrated treatment process are addressed by Health Canada's (2002) *Best Practices* document:

- identifying potential substance use and/or mental health problems by properly screening clients
- for those who screen positive, conducting a comprehensive assessment to investigate the nature and severity of the substance use and mental health problems, and exploring their interrelations
- for those who have been diagnosed as having concurrent substance use and mental health problems, providing treatment and support.

With respect to screening to identify people with potential concurrent disorders, the principles of best practice suggest "level 1 screening procedures," where all people presenting in mental health services are screened for concurrent substance use problems (Health Canada, 2002). Level 1 screening procedures include asking a few key questions regarding substance use, being alert to social and clinical indicators that raise the clinician's index of suspicion, and drawing on the judgment and experience of a case manager. These procedures are summarized below.

ASKING A FEW KEY QUESTIONS

By asking a few key questions regarding, for example, a client's perception that others are concerned about his or her substance use, you can make better decisions about whether or not the client requires more intensive assessment of a potential concurrent substance use disorder. A Yes response to any one of the three following questions suggests that further investigation into the possibility of concurrent disorders is warranted:

- Have you ever had any problems related to your use of alcohol or other drugs?
- Has a relative, friend, doctor or other health worker been concerned about your drinking or other drug use, or suggested you cut down?
- Have you ever said to another person, "No, I don't have an alcohol (or other drug) problem," when, around the same time, you questioned yourself and felt, "Maybe I do have a problem"?

Do not rely only on client self-disclosure, because clients may minimize their problems. For this reason, additional screening procedures may be helpful.

INDEX OF SUSPICION AND CLINICAL CORRELATES

If it is not possible to ask questions, or if the quality of a self-report is in question, a number of behavioural, clinical and social indicators and consequences (the "index of suspicion"), can be considered; the presence of a number of items from this index may give cause for suspecting possible concurrent substance use difficulties. The index includes:

- new or unexplained mental health symptom relapses
- history of substance use
- unstable housing
- budgeting difficulties
- treatment compliance issues
- sexual acting out
- social isolation or difficulties
- violence or threats
- suicidal thoughts or attempts
- self-harm
- hygiene or health concerns
- legal problems
- cognitive impairments
- avoidance of disclosing mental health or substance use issues.

Along with the items above, be alert to what Mueser et al. (1992), in their work with clients with severe mental illness, have identified as various "clinical correlates" of substance use disorders:

- cigarette smoking (people who smoke are three to four times more likely to misuse substances)
- male
- younger
- lower education
- single or never married
- good premorbid social functioning
- family history of substance use problems
- history of childhood conduct disorder
- antisocial personality disorder
- higher affective symptoms (e.g., depression or suicidality)
- relationship problems

- job problems
- disrupted housing or other instability
- disruptive behaviour or violence
- non-compliance with treatment (e.g., medication not taken, missed appointments)
- legal problems
- physical symptoms (e.g., dilated pupils, sweats, shakes, smell)
- physical diagnoses (e.g., liver problems).

Given the high prevalence of comorbidity, you should make screening efforts routine, and "view concurrent disorders as the *norm*, NOT the *exception*" (Mueser et al., 1992). Accordingly, the use of an index of suspicion, and bringing this lens to interactions with clients, represents good clinical practice in both substance use and mental health settings.

CASE MANAGER JUDGEMENT

Also useful is a case manager's opinion and concern about the possibility of a substance use problem, since the case manager often has the benefit of a long-standing relationship with the client. Seeking this opinion can be as simple as asking the case manager, "Do you think the client has ever had a drinking or other drug problem? Would you say definitely, probably or not at all?"

MOVING FROM SCREENING TO ASSESSMENT

If the result of the screening procedures outlined above suggests concurrent disorders, you may find it helpful to complete a brief screening tool. The Dartmouth Assessment of Lifestyle Instrument (DALI) (Rosenberg et al., 1998) is the only tool that was explicitly developed as a screen for substance use disorders among people with severe mental illness (see www.dartmouth.edu/~psychrc/pdf_files/DALI.pdf).

With respect to diagnostic assessment, the most comprehensive option for such clients is a complete assessment for psychiatric and substance use disorders, per the *Diagnostic and Statistical Manual of Mental Disorders* (DSM-IV) (American Psychiatric Association, 1994). However, several barriers may preclude a complete psychiatric and substance use assessment, including limited resources, long waiting lists for treatment and limited CD-specialized programs and services. For a more complete review of CD screening and assessment considerations, issues and instruments, see Juan Negrete's chapter, "Screening and Assessing for Concurrent Disorders" in Skinner (2005).

Treatment

Harm reduction (see Skinner & Carver, 2004) is seen as the most desirable treatment philosophy in working with a population that may not be willing or able to accept abstinence-based goals. Despite the recognition among health care professionals that abstinence is an ideal goal for people with concurrent substance use and psychiatric disorders, most experts in the field acknowledge that returns to substance use (i.e., relapses), are a reality of working with this client population. A harm reduction approach brings with it an understanding of the need to continue to work with these clients even (and especially) when they are not abstinent.

Further clinical challenges include compliance issues with taking prescribed psychiatric medication and ambivalence about changing or stopping substance use. The recommended response is to set small, incremental goals. Keeping clients engaged in treatment is preferable to mandating abstinence, as treatment engagement increases opportunities to continue to facilitate and support positive change. Finally, treatment outcomes can be measured by more than just adherence to substance use goals or medication compliance. It is important to also assess a client's overall level of functioning, use of coping strategies and support systems, community integration, vocational rehabilitation, social and interpersonal functioning, and other target areas as evidence of good treatment outcomes.

MODIFICATIONS TO COUNSELLING PROCEDURES AND CLINICAL TOOLS

Research in Motivational Interviewing approaches suggests that clinical tools and techniques developed for people with substance use problems need some adaptation when they are used with clients who have concurrent disorders (Martino et. al., 2002; Graeber et. al., 2003; Steinberg et al., 2004). Given the motivational orientation of SRP, it is not surprising that the SRP treatment sessions and clinical tools require some modification for use with this population.

This section outlines such an adapted version of SRP for use with clients with concurrent disorders. While not as rigorously evaluated as the "generic" version of SRP, the CD-adapted protocols and tools were developed in collaboration with a group of inpatient-based and community-based clients with concurrent disorders, and reviewed and revised in light of responses by a cross-disciplinary mix of clinicians working in both substance use and mental health specialties.

Although further research is needed to establish the efficacy and effectiveness of SRP with clients who have concurrent disorders, the goal of sharing our understanding and experience is to allow others to take advantage of the gains that we have made, and to join us in pursuing further knowledge in this area. Therefore, we suggest that you let your clients be your guide in implementing these tools: they are the most expert in the treatment structure, format and content that will best fit their needs.

The revisions needed for running an SRP group for clients with concurrent disorders include:

- shortening group duration (90 minutes, as opposed to two hours in the "substance-use-only" SRP group)
- using fewer clinical tools per treatment session (we found that even one or two paper-and-pencil tools could be overwhelming for some clients with concurrent disorders)
- modifying clinical tools to incorporate CD-specific treatment goals (such as taking prescribed medications, or coping with the symptoms of mental illness and/or the side-effects of prescribed medications)
- spending more time in the group processing discussion around access to services, and navigating the mental health and substance use treatment system
- making the clinical tools easier to complete.
- including a follow-up SRP group three to four months after the last weekly session, in order to review ongoing or emergent treatment needs, to help clients progress toward their goals and to identify next steps.

This section includes CD-adapted Therapist Checklists for each session, as well as revised versions of the relevant clinical tools from parts II and III of the manual.

NOTE: We have indicated the tools that have been altered for clients with concurrent disorders by appending the notation "CD Adapted." Any tools listed that are not identified as "CD Adapted" are identical to the non-adapted versions, which can be found earlier in this book.

Other Issues with CD-Adapted SRP

CO-FACILITATION

There is no research examining whether or not CD-adapted SRP groups should be co-facilitated. In fact, the overall composition of CD-adapted SRP groups is an area we hope will be the focus of further research (e.g., should groups be composed of people with similar or with differing psychiatric diagnoses?). In our clinical practice, co-facilitation has been the model for several reasons, as discussed below.

Safety

It is not uncommon when working with people who have concurrent disorders for a group member to arrive acutely psychotic, acutely suicidal, intoxicated or acting out. When a situation like this occurs, one therapist is typically required, for safety reasons, to intervene directly with the person outside of the group. It is therefore helpful to have a second therapist who can be free to stay with the group and carry on with the session.

Avoidance of Burnout

One therapist "going it alone" in running a CD group can find the work to be emotionally draining. In a co-facilitation situation, the two therapists can support each other, plan for the group together and work together to manage challenging clinical group issues that inevitably arise. Within this model, therapists are less likely to feel isolated in this challenging clinical work, and to potentially burn out.

Professional Development

Co-facilitation allows the therapists to brief for the group before the group session, and to de-brief together after the session is over. This kind of clinical exchange stimulates analysis of the CD-adapted SRP approach and related group developments, and provides a forum for peer support. Also, exposure to a co-therapist's insights can enhance professional development and skills.

Opportunities for Training and Supervision

We also believe there is value in having one seasoned, experienced therapist co-facilitating a CD-adapted SRP group along with a less experienced clinician or a student. This combination can provide a valuable real-life learning process and an ideal opportunity for close supervision.

Opportunity for Mutual CD Capacity-Building

A co-facilitation model comprised of one clinician with a substance use background and another with solid mental health preparation allows for mutual professional development, with a view toward building capacity in the area of concurrent disorders.

DETERMINING THE SUITABILITY OF SRP FOR A GIVEN CLIENT

Once the presence of concurrent substance use and mental health problems has been established, several factors contribute to determining whether SRP, among the range of other treatment options, would best fit a client's needs.

Although SRP employs written feedback, exercises and forms, the ability to complete written exercises is not essential. Where written exercises are not appropriate, we have substituted discussion and role-playing exercises (or individual therapy).

If SRP is being delivered as part of an inpatient, hospital-based program, the major criteria for SRP treatment is the client's ability to attend and participate in the group or individual sessions.

However, before considering SRP on an outpatient basis, consider the factors listed in the table below. If any of the following are present, we suggest a more intensive treatment program (such as day or residential treatment), as SRP may not be the most appropriate treatment at that juncture.

Presentation	Suggestion
Poor outcome of previous brief treatment episodes	Suggest a "stepped care" approach, where the least intrusive treatment options are attempted and, if they are unsuccessful, "stepping up" to a more intensive level of care.
Multiple concurrent problems (e.g., substance use *and* mental illness *and* housing instability *and* medication non-compliance; active symptoms *and* cognitive impairment; etc.) Severe substance use problems (i.e., DSM-IV criteria are met for substance dependence)	Suggest day treatment or residential options, which, research suggests, are better suited to these clients.
Acute or recurrent suicidality	Suggest hospitalization for stabilization.
Acute psychosis	Suggest hospitalization for stabilization.
Acute intoxication or withdrawal	Suggest withdrawal management.
Cognitive impairment (e.g., poor concentration, memory, inability to focus)	Suggest a review of medications and an inquiry into whether a cognitive impairment exists in addition to mental health and substance use issues. Use SRP tools on an ad hoc basis.
Long-term history of relapse following multiple unsuccessful treatment episodes	Suggest more intensive treatment.
Serious consequences to relapse	Suggest more intensive treatment.

If SRP is the best treatment option, it is important to give clients with concurrent disorders a thorough orientation to the format and content of the treatment sessions. In addition, for clients involved in the forensic system, there should be a discussion about how disclosures of substance use episodes, cravings and triggers, and exposure to risk situations, will be documented, as there may be legal implications for clients. The CD-adapted Therapist Checklist for the Assessment phase (page 136) notes some of these group process issues, as well as listing relevant clinical tools.

HANDLING RELAPSES

Relapse is often a part of recovery from mental health and substance use problems. Clients should be encouraged to view lapses and relapse as temporary setbacks.

Relapse to Substance Use

When clients relapse to substance use, we are careful to correct the interpretation that relapse means failure in recovery. On an emotional level, for some people, the perception that relapse equals failure often creates a significant experience of shame, pessimism about the ability to change and even self-loathing because they have continued to repeat old patterns. In settings where relapse is not normalized, clients have reported dropping out prematurely because they could not imagine returning to and facing the group. Within a CD-adapted SRP approach, we reframe experiences of relapse as an opportunity for learning and for problem solving. Relapse is also seen as an opportunity for clients to reaffirm their substance use goals and shore up their levels of motivation and commitment.

The hope is that within a harm reduction approach, clients will feel comfortable disclosing relapses—should they occur—without fearing they will be asked to withdraw from the program. Permission to be honest about a relapse in the treatment process, especially if the relapse is already over, helps to normalize it as an occurrence, and helps to prevent the client feeling he or she cannot be genuine in therapy. It is also helpful for clients to explore the trigger(s) that led to the slip, and to discuss more adaptive coping responses that could prove useful for any similar situations in the future.

Relapse of Mental Health Problems

When working with a population that has concurrent disorders, it is also important to note clinically that relapse is a common occurrence with mental health problems such as depression and psychosis. However, in our experience, clients tend not to feel the same guilt and shame with a mental health relapse as they do with a relapse to substance use. The underlying belief for many clients seems to be that the use of substances is essentially their fault, but that a relapse to psychiatric symptoms is largely beyond their control. Nevertheless, relapsing mental health symptoms are associated with a feeling of disappointment and learned helplessness, and a profoundly demoralizing sense that the psychiatric condition will be a continuing struggle, possibly for a lifetime. This is a common reaction in clients with chronic depression or bipolar disorder.

To foster a better, more helpful mindset for managing relapse, we normalize the idea that relapses occur in both domains, and then attempt to help clients identify personalized early warning signs that their mental health is deteriorating. Such signs in depression, for example, might include sensing a tendency to withdraw socially, beginning to lose interest in activities previously enjoyed and experiencing an increase in negative or pessimistic thinking.

Once the client becomes aware of these early warning signs or "red flags," he or she can develop strategies for coping and intervening early in the cycle. Such interventions might include relaying symptoms to a caregiver, implementing personal coping strategies such as good self-care and seeking social support, with the overall goal of circumventing a full relapse.

The SRP approach helps a client to anticipate substance use triggers for the coming week and identify and commit to a plan of action. Within the CD-adapted SRP approach, relapse prevention goals include, but are not limited to:

- working on a substance use goal of abstinence or reduction
- within an abstinence-based goal, having fewer and shorter-lasting slips
- using less (if any) of the problem substance, and having fewer negative consequences associated with substance use
- recognizing the impact of substance use on mental health
- learning and recognizing early warning signs for mental health relapse
- developing an action recovery plan and putting it into practice in the "real world," in between SRP sessions, which aim to support the maintenance of change.

THE SUPERSENSITIVITY HYPOTHESIS

Mueser and colleagues argue that people with severe mental illness are more sensitive to the effects of alcohol and other drugs, due to an increased biological vulnerability (Mueser et al., 1998). As a result, people with concurrent disorders may experience increased negative consequences from relatively small amounts of substance use. Thus, in someone with schizophrenia, relatively moderate use (e.g., two beers three times per week, or $20 worth of crack cocaine used once every few weeks) may result in negative consequences (such as increased psychotic symptoms), or may dramatically increase the risk of more severe substance use. A key message with respect to the supersensitivity hypothesis is that, when working with people with serious and persistent mental illness, the *quantity* of the substance use is less important than the *consequences*.

REFERENCES

We hope you find the following CD-adapted SRP tools and guidelines helpful. Even in the absence of rigorous, empirical support, deciding to run a CD-adapted SRP group is an important step in providing more accessible and integrated treatment for clients.

American Psychiatric Association. (1994). *Diagnostic and Statistical Manual of Mental Disorders* (4th ed.). Washington, DC: Author.

Graeber, D.A., Moyers, T.B., Griffith, G., Guajardo, A. & Tonigan, S. (2003). A pilot study comparing Motivational Interviewing and an educational intervention in patients with schizophrenia and alcohol use disorders. *Community Mental Health Journal, 39*(3), 189–202.

Health Canada. (2002). *Best Practices: Concurrent Mental Health and Substance Use Disorders*. Ottawa: Health Canada. Available: www.hc-sc.gc.ca/ahc-asc/pubs/drugs-drogues/bp_disorder-mp_concomitants/index_e.html. Accessed February 27, 2006.

Kessler, R.C., Nelson, C.B., McGonagle, K.A., Edlund, M.J., Frank, R.G. & Leaf, P.J. (1996). The epidemiology of co-occurring addictive and mental disorders: Implications for prevention and service utilization. *American Journal of Orthopsychiatry, 66*, 17–31.

Martino, S., Carroll, K., Kostas, D., Perkins, J. & Rounsaville, B. (2002). Dual diagnosis Motivational Interviewing: A modification of Motivational Interviewing for substance-abusing patients with psychotic disorders. *Journal of Substance Abuse Treatment. 23*, 297–308.

Minkoff, K. (2001). *Dual Diagnosis: An Integrated Model for the Treatment of People with Co-Occurring Psychiatric and Substance Disorders: A Lecture by Kenneth Minkoff* [Video]. The Mental Illness Education Project Lecture Series. Brookline Village, MA: The Mental Illness Education Project.

Mueser, K.T., Drake, R.E. & Wallach, M.A. (1998). Dual diagnosis: A review of etiological theories. *Addictive Behaviours, 23*(6), 717–734.

Mueser, K.T., Yarnold, P.R. & Bellack, A.S. (1992). Diagnostic and demographic correlates of substance abuse in schizophrenia and major affective disorder. *Acta Psychiatrica Scandinavica, 85*, 48–55.

Regier, D.A., Farmer, M.E. & Rae, D.S. (1990). Co-morbidity of mental disorders with alcohol and other drug abuse: Results from the Epidemiological Catchment Area (ECA) study. *Journal of American Medical Association, 264*, 2511–2518.

Rosenberg, S.D., Drake, R.E., Wolford, G.L., Mueser, K.T., Oxman, T.E., Vidaver, R.M. et al. (1998). Dartmouth Assessment of Lifestyle Instrument (DALI): A substance use disorder screen for people with severe mental illness. *American Journal of Psychiatry, 155*(2), 232–238.

Ross, H.E., Swinson, R., Doumani, S. & Larkin, E.J. (1995). Diagnosing comorbidity in substance abusers: A comparison of the test-retest reliability of two interviews. *American Journal of Drug and Alcohol Abuse, 21*, 167–185.

Skinner, W. (2005). *Treating Concurrent Disorders: A Guide for Counsellors*. Toronto: Centre for Additction and Mental Health.

Skinner, W. J. & Carver, V. (2004). Working in a harm reduction framework. In Susan Harrison & Virginia Carver (Eds.), *Alcohol and Drug Problems: A Practical Guide for Counsellors* (3rd ed.) (pp. 229–243). Toronto: Centre for Addiction and Mental Health.

Steinberg, M.L., Ziedonis, D.M., Krejci, J.A. & Brandan, T.H. (2004). Motivational Interviewing with personalized feedback: A brief intervention for motivating smokers with schizophrenia to seek treatment for tobacco dependence. *Journal of Consulting and Clinical Psychology, 72*(4), 723–728.

Phase 1: Assessment

Screening and assessment for clients with concurrent disorders involves special issues and challenges due to the potential complexity of clients' presenting problems. We encourage you to review the introductory material on screening and assessment of concurrent disorders in "Adapting the SRP Approach" (page 123) before using the CD-adapted clinical tools with your clients.

Description	Clinical Tools
Assessment includes a standardized set of procedures designed to: • provide an overview of the client's substance use and mental health issues • establish baseline information on alcohol and/or other drug dependence • assess the client's high-risk situations for alcohol and/or other drug use.	• Assessment Summary Form— CD Adapted . . . . p. 137 • Inventory of Drug-Taking Situations (IDTS-8) . . . . p. 24 • Personalized Alcohol Use Feedback Online Tool (*optional*) . . . . p. 20

NOTE: Tools that have been altered for clients with concurrent disorders are labelled "CD Adapted." Tools that do not have adapted versions can be found in Part II of this manual; page numbers are given above.

Assessment—CD Adapted

THERAPIST COMPLETES WITH CLIENT

☐ Assessment Summary Form—CD Adapted

CLIENT COMPLETES

☐ Inventory of Drug-Taking Situations (IDTS-8)

☐ Personalized Alcohol Use Feedback Online Tool (*optional*)

(Available at http://notes.camh.net/efeed.nsf/feedback. If the client cannot access this tool online, the therapist can print out the questions, complete them with the client in a paper and pencil format, then enter the data online and bring back the personalized feedback for discussion at the next session.)

Assessment Summary Form—CD Adapted

BACKGROUND

Name: _____

Referring program (if applicable): _____

Home phone: (_____) _____ Bus. phone: (_____) _____

Postal address: _____

_____

Age: _____ Sex: _____ Marital status: _____

Highest level of education reached: _____

Occupation: _____

Current employment status: _____

Current legal status: _____

Primary drug for which client is seeking treatment: _____

Secondary drug(s), if any: _____

Other notable presenting characteristics: _____

1. REASON FOR SEEKING TREATMENT

_____

☐ Client has been oriented to purpose of assessment and SRP treatment process.

2. SUBSTANCE USE

NOTE: Explore states of intoxication or withdrawal that may confound assessment.

Substance(s) Used	Quantity	Frequency (# days used per week)	Last Use
Primary:			
Secondary:			
Other:			

Do you have a history of quit attempts? ☐ Yes ☐ No

If Yes, how long was the longest period you did not use at all?

_____

When was this? _____

What helped you achieve this? _____

Do you have a history of cutting down? ☐ Yes ☐ No

If Yes, for how long? _____

When? _____

What helped you achieve this? _____

What problems do you expect if you continue to use? _____

3A. PSYCHIATRIC DIAGNOSES OR ISSUES

☐ Check if unknown

1. _____

2. _____

3. _____

4. _____

3B. PSYCHIATRIC DIAGNOSES OR ISSUES THAT CLIENT IDENTIFIES AS PROBLEMATIC

1. _____

2. _____

3. _____

4. _____

4. FUNCTIONAL RELATIONSHIP

Check the description that best describes the functional relationship between the client's substance use and his or her mental health symptoms:

☐ *Substance-induced symptoms*: Mental health symptoms are the result of chronic or excessive substance use or withdrawal. Mental health symptoms emerge after increased or prolonged substance use or withdrawal.

☐ *Symptom regulation (self-medication)*: Substance use is a coping response to mental health symptoms. Substance use starts or increases after the onset of mental health symptoms.

☐ *Substance-related symptoms*: Mental health symptoms develop due to the psychosocial consequences of substance use. There are no mental health symptoms until the consequences of substance use emerge.

☐ *Common risk factor*: Mental health symptoms and substance use are related to a common factor that is genetic, familial, socio-cultural or environmental.

☐ *Independent*: Mental health symptoms and substance use problems are unrelated. They don't affect each other, and change in one area does not affect the other.

☐ *Unknown*

5. PHYSICAL HEALTH ISSUES

_____

_____

_____

_____

6. CURRENT MEDICATION

☐ None

Medication	Dose	Condition Being Treated	Prescribing Clinician

7. PSYCHOSOCIAL SITUATION

Accommodation	
Relationship(s) and Family	
Employment or School	
Finances	
Legal Issues	
Child Welfare Involvement	
Other	

8. PREVIOUS TREATMENT

Addiction Treatment

☐ Residential (where? when?): _____

_____

☐ Outpatient (where? when?): _____

_____

☐ Self-help (what type? when?): _____

_____

Psychiatric or Other Mental Health Treatment

☐ Outpatient treatment (where? when? what for? group or individual?): _____

_____

☐ Hospitalization(s) (where? when? what for?): _____

_____

9. CLIENT'S EXPRESSED GOALS FOR TREATMENT

Primary Substance Use Goal

☐ Abstinence   ☐ Reduction   ☐ Continued use   ☐ Undecided

STAGE OF CHANGE

☐ Precontemplation ("It's not a problem for me.")

☐ Contemplation ("I'm ambivalent about change.")

☐ Preparation ("I'm on the verge of making change.")

☐ Action ("I'm taking steps toward change.")

☐ Maintenance ("I'm in relapse prevention mode," or "I'm trying to sustain my reduction changes.")

Secondary Substance Use Goal

☐ Abstinence   ☐ Reduction   ☐ Continued use   ☐ Undecided

STAGE OF CHANGE

☐ Precontemplation ("It's not a problem for me.")

☐ Contemplation ("I'm ambivalent about change.")

☐ Preparation ("I'm on the verge of making change.")

☐ Action ("I'm taking steps toward change.")

☐ Maintenance ("I'm in relapse prevention mode," or "I'm trying to sustain my reduction changes.")

Mental Health Goal(s)

_____

_____

_____

Other Goals

_____

_____

_____

10. CLIENT'S PERCEPTION OF PROBLEM

Prompt: People usually have several things they would like to change in their lives. Your substance use may be only one of those things. So, your feeling about the **importance** of change, as well as your **confidence** and your **readiness to change** your substance use, can vary depending on other things that are happening. On each line below, circle the number (from 0 to 10) that best fits with how you are feeling right now.

How **important** is it to you to change this behaviour?

| 0 | 1 | 2 | 3 | 4 | 5 | 6 | 7 | 8 | 9 | 10 |

Comments (What else is more important at this time? What has made this change this important to you so far—why are you not at zero? What would it take to make this change even more important to you?):

_____

_____

How **confident** are you that you could make this change?

| 0 | 1 | 2 | 3 | 4 | 5 | 6 | 7 | 8 | 9 | 10 |

Comments (Why are you at your current score and not zero? What would it take for you to move you to a higher score?):

_____

_____

3. How **ready** are you to make this change?

| 0 | 1 | 2 | 3 | 4 | 5 | 6 | 7 | 8 | 9 | 10 |

Comments (Why are you at your current score and not zero? What would it take for you to move to a higher score? What would you need to support you in making a change, if you choose to do so?):

_____

_____

11. DIVERSITY CONSIDERATIONS

Describe any barriers, strengths or resources related to diversity issues:

_____

_____

_____

_____

_____

_____

_____

12. GENERAL IMPRESSION AND SUMMARY

_____

_____

_____

_____

_____

_____

_____

Signature of Clinician

_____

Name and Credentials (print)

_____

Date (dd/mm/yyyy)

Original in client chart

Copy to referral source (if applicable)

Phase 2: Motivational Interviewing

Recent research has examined the application of Motivational Interviewing tools and techniques to people with concurrent disorders (Martino et al., 2002; Graeber et al., 2003; Steinberg et al., 2004). (See pages 132 to 133 for a list of references.) Particularly noteworthy are the adaptations to Motivational Interviewing for people with severe mental illness suggested by Martino and his colleagues (2002). Referred to as Dual Diagnosis Motivational Interviewing, or DDMI, this modified approach is designed to respond to cognitive impairments and disordered thinking. ("Dual diagnosis" is a term commonly used in the United States for concurrent disorders.) The table below presents an overview of the standard practices of Motivational Interviewing alongside the recommended DDMI modifications.

With clients who have concurrent disorders, therapists should expect to work at a slower pace, focusing on engagement and encouragement. Clients may be at the precontemplative stage for a long time (e.g., two years). With this client population, the quality of the relationship between the client and the therapist is crucial, as it can help to motivate change.

Standard Motivational Interviewing Practices and Dual Diagnosis Adaptations

Standard MI Practices	DDMI Modifications
Targets substance use.	Targets concurrent substance use and mental health issues (e.g., substance use, medication compliance, barriers to treatment).
Presumes clients are cognitively intact and logically organized.	Uses repetition, simple and direct verbal and visual materials and breaks within sessions.
	Therapist guides conversation to promote logical organization and improved reality testing.
	Group sessions meet for only 60 to 90 minutes.
Uses open-ended questions.	Avoids compound open-ended questions; poses queries in clear and concise terms.

Standard MI Practices	DDMI Modifications
Uses reflective listening.	Reflects in clear and concise terms; reduces use of reflections on disturbing life experiences; uses metaphors to anchor concepts in reality; provides plenty of time for clients to respond to reflective statements.
Uses statements of affirmation (strengths, change efforts and accomplishments).	Places heightened emphasis on affirmations.
Provides personalized feedback from objective substance use–related assessment results.	Contrasts client and therapist ratings of severity (developing discrepancy). Uses images, simple rating scales, analogies and metaphors.
Uses 2 x 2 decisional balance matrix to weigh the costs and benefits of changing substance use, and the costs and benefits of staying the same.	Uses simple decisional balance to explore client ambivalence about getting CD treatment, taking psychiatric medication and changing substance use. Focuses only on the costs and benefits of behaviour change.

Adapted from Martino et al. (2002), p. 301.

Because SRP incorporates a Motivational Interviewing style throughout all treatment phases, the guidelines in the right-hand column above should be kept in mind throughout the CD-adapted SRP treatment.

NOTE: For a more detailed discussion of the application of Motivational Interviewing techniques and principles with c+lients with concurrent disorders, see the article "Dual Diagnosis Motivational Interviewing," by Martino et al. (2002), in Appendix B.

Description	Clinical Tools
The client receives feedback on assessment findings, with a focus on exploring the client's: • reasons for change in alcohol or other drug use • pros and cons of change • strength of commitment to change • coping strengths • triggers for use (exploration of IDTS-8 profile, if undifferentiated. Clients must reach an explicit decision. In other words, they must state their definite intent to try to work toward change in alcohol and/or other drug use before proceeding to SRP counselling.	• Client's completed Assessment Summary Form—CD Adapted • Client's completed IDTS-8 • Feedback about Goal Setting and Commitment to Change—CD Adapted . . . p. 146 • Personalized Alcohol Use Feedback Online Tool (*optional*) . . . . .p. 20 • Decisional Balance Assignment—CD Adapted . . . . p. 149

NOTE: Tools that have been altered for clients with concurrent disorders are labelled "CD Adapted." Tools that do not have adapted versions can be found in Part II of this manual; page numbers are given above.

THERAPIST CHECKLIST

Motivational Interviewing—CD Adapted

BEFORE THE COUNSELLING SESSION

☐ Review the client's completed Assessment Summary Form—CD Adapted.

☐ Review the client's completed IDTS-8, and note whether it is undifferentiated.

DURING THE COUNSELLING SESSION

☐ Discuss assessment findings with the client.

☐ Complete and review with the client the form Feedback about Goal Setting and Commitment to Change—CD Adapted, and follow up with discussion. (Note that clients should take the completed form away with them.)

☐ Engage the client in a discussion of his or her reasons for wanting to change alcohol or other drug use.

☐ Have the client weigh the pros and cons of change, using the Decisional Balance Assignment. Remember to look at the benefits of use along with the losses; this exploration will help inform you why the client is continuing to use substances.

☐ Discuss coping strengths and weaknesses with the client.

☐ Review the client's problematic triggers to alcohol or other drug use, and have the client suggest some interim coping alternatives.

☐ If the client's IDTS-8 profile is undifferentiated, explore possible reasons for this (see Therapist Checklist: Troubleshooting for Undifferentiated IDTS-8 Profiles [page 27]).

NOTE: Motivational interviewing may require only one session or it may need several sessions. This checklist is intended only as a guide to areas of discussion that may help clients strengthen their commitment to change.

Name: _____ Date: _____

Feedback about Goal Setting and Commitment to Change—CD Adapted

Thank you for coming to this appointment to talk about some of the things that have been going on in your life. The purpose of this treatment process is to work with you to come up with helpful solutions that fit your personal goals and priorities.

You are asked to fill out this form because some people find that written feedback and information can help them make decisions about behaviour change, look at different treatment options, or just think about how substance use and mental health issues affect their lives.

Mental Health Issue(s)

_____
_____
_____
_____

Substance Use Issue(s)

_____
_____
_____
_____

Other Issues

_____
_____
_____
_____

What is your goal for the substance you most often use?

Substance: _____

☐ Not using at all ☐ Cutting down ☐ Continuing to use ☐ Undecided

What is your goal for any other substance(s) you use sometimes?

Substance(s): _____

☐ Not using at all ☐ Cutting down ☐ Continuing to use ☐ Undecided

A Note about Risk

How or whether you use substances is your own personal decision. However, if you continue to use alcohol or other drugs, you will expose yourself to increased risks, especially if you:

- *are pregnant*
- *have mental health issues*
- *use prescription drugs (medication)*
- *have diabetes*
- *have a seizure disorder*
- *have an active peptic ulcer or gastritis*
- *have active hepatitis*
- *are under a legal order to abstain*
- *have advanced coronary heart disease*
- *have cancer*
- *have cirrhosis of the liver*
- *are at risk of negative social consequences (such as fighting with a partner).*

TO CHANGE OR NOT TO CHANGE?

What would you like to change in your life?

Change can be hard—even making a decision to change may take a long time for some people. Change is also a process. It generally doesn't happen all at once, but in stages.

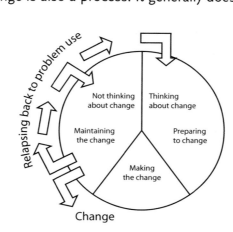

Where are you in the change process?

The questions on the next page may help you to get a better picture of:

- how important changing is to you
- how confident you feel
- how ready are you to quit or cut down your use of substances.

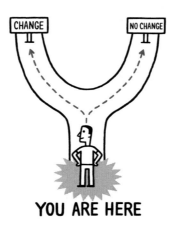

THE READINESS RULER

People usually have several things they would like to change in their lives. Your substance use may be only one of the things you hope to change. Your **motivation** to change your substance use can vary, depending on other things that are happening.

On each of the rulers below, circle the number (from 0 to 10) that best fits with how you are feeling right now.

1. How **important** is it to you to reduce or quit using alcohol or other drugs?

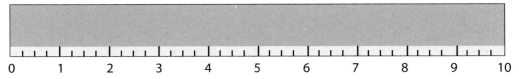

2. How **confident** are you that you will not use alcohol or other drugs?

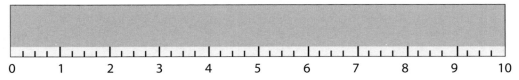

3. How **realistic** is it that you will stay away from alcohol or other drugs in the long term?

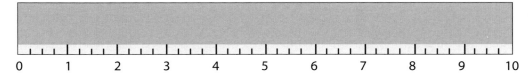

SOME QUESTIONS TO THINK ABOUT

- Why are you at your current score and not at zero?
- What would it take for you to move to a higher score?
- What has made this change important to you so far—why are you not at zero?)
- What would it take to make this change even more important to you?
- What support would you need to make a change, if you chose to do so?

This exercise can also be used to explore readiness to change other behaviours, such as taking prescribed medication, looking for a job or finding stable housing.

_____

Signature of Clinician

_____

Name and Credentials (print)

_____

Contact Information

Decisional Balance Assignment—CD Adapted

Change isn't easy. Often people feel "stuck" in their old habits and behaviours. Imagine a set of scales, with the good things about your substance use on one side, and the less good things on the other side. What's good about using substances? What about the other side—what is not so good about using substances?

Check off the boxes below that fit for you. Add any other good things and less good things that you think of about using substances.

YOUR DRINKING OR OTHER DRUG USE

What's Good about It?	**What's Not So Good about It?**
☐ I feel better right away.	☐ It makes my symptoms get worse, or makes me get sick again.
☐ It gets rid of symptoms or side-effects of my medication.	☐ I end up back in hospital.
☐ I forget about problems.	☐ It causes money problems.
☐ It makes me feel more relaxed.	☐ It gets me in trouble with the law.
☐ I have fun.	☐ I feel bad about myself.
☐ I connect with other people.	☐ I get into dangerous situations.
☐ Other good things:	☐ Other less good things:

Now let's weigh these good and less good things. Are the scales:
- evenly balanced? That might be why you are feeling stuck right now.
- tipping toward the good things? If there doesn't seem to be much that is harmful about using substances, you may not feel very motivated to change.
- tipping toward the less good things? If you feel that your substance use is costing you, then you probably want to make some changes.

Even if you aren't sure you want to make any changes, this exercise will help you understand the costs and benefits of using alcohol or other drugs. Just thinking about the good things and less good things is important.

Phase 3: Individualized Treatment Planning

Depending on the time available for treatment planning, as well as on whether SRP will be delivered in a group or an individual format, this component can be delivered separately or as part of the Initiation of Change phase (outlined in the next section).

Our experience in running SRP groups with clients who have concurrent disorders is that more time is needed for group process issues and discussion of the clinical tools—"less paper, more discussion" is a helpful guideline. You may find that in the Individualized Treatment Planning session (and in subsequent sessions), you use only a few of the tools during the actual session, and either address the content of the others in subsequent sessions or simply discuss the major ideas with clients without having them read and complete the entire assignment.

We have also made a few other adaptations in the delivery of this component for clients with concurrent disorders:

- When clients return with "homework," they are offered a choice of keeping it or handing it in to the therapist at the end of the session. All of the print material handed in is filed in a personal folder for each client, and the complete folder is returned to the client at the end of the SRP program. This approach was developed because many clients found the cumulative amount of written material overwhelming and difficult to keep track of. Clients appreciated leaving the program with all of their work filed and organized for them.
- Many clients had difficulty completing the open-ended questions on the SRP exercises. Therefore, you will notice that the CD-adapted tools have more checkboxes and other closed-ended items. These are followed by some additional space for clients to add their own ideas and comments.
- Having students or volunteers sit in on SRP group sessions is helpful for clients who require individual help to understand and complete the SRP exercises.
- Some clients in our groups with concurrent disorders were still in hospital, while others had been discharged to the community. Inpatient clients were more likely to report little or no use during the past year, and required more help to complete assignments.

Not all clients find the SRP approach helpful. The session outlines, therapist checklists and exercises are meant as guidelines only. You may want to adapt them or simply use selected tools as needed. In our own groups, we often used tools on an ad hoc basis. However, each week we made sure to cover:

- current motivation for change (group discussion)
- upcoming risk situations (Weekly Planning Form—CD Adapted) (see page 163 [Initiation] or page 173 [Maintenance])
- client self-monitoring (Weekly Diary). Note that this version of the self-monitoring form is designed to be completed weekly rather than daily. This change was based on client feedback that the open-ended, daily recording of cravings and triggers was laborious and overwhelming. Clients unanimously preferred the weekly "checkbox" format of the adapted self-monitoring form.

The most important question we asked ourselves and our clients at the beginning of each group was: "What would be most helpful for this group at this particular time?" In other words, we encourage you to use the structure of these sessions as a starting point, and let the clients guide the content and format of the sessions.

Description	Clinical Tools
The following steps are used to engage the client in developing an individually tailored treatment plan, using the following steps: • orientation to SRP counselling and signing of treatment contract • review of IDTS-8 results; exploration of specific recent alcohol or other drug use triggers; development of a personal hierarchy of risk areas that the client wishes to work on through weekly assignments • client goal setting and self-monitoring.	• Treatment Contract: Individual Counselling . . . . p. 41 • Treatment Contract: Group Counselling . . . p. 43 • Identifying Problem Substance Use Situations—CD Adapted . . . . p. 154 • Weekly Diary (replaces Daily Diary) . . . . . . p. 158

NOTE: A CD-adapted version of the Coping Skills Checklist is included in phase 4 (Initiation of Change). However, you may also find the coping skills exercises helpful at this phase of treatment.

NOTE: Tools that have been altered for clients with concurrent disorders are labelled "CD Adapted." Tools that do not have adapted versions can be found in Part II of this manual; page numbers are given above.

THERAPIST CHECKLIST

Individualized Treatment Planning—CD Adapted

BEFORE THE COUNSELLING SESSION

☐ Photocopy the client's IDTS-8.

Bring the following blank forms:

☐ Treatment Contract: Individual Counselling

or

☐ Treatment Contract: Group Counselling

☐ Identifying Problem Substance Use Situations

☐ Weekly Diary.

DURING THE COUNSELLING SESSION

☐ Provide an orientation to SRP counselling.

☐ Have the client sign a Treatment Contract.

☐ Provide the client with a copy of his or her IDTS-8 form (if this has not already been done), and engage the client in a discussion of common triggers to use.

☐ Have the client complete Part 1 of Identifying Problem Substance Use Situations—CD Adapted.

☐ Explain the rationale of self-monitoring.

☐ Have the client set a goal for the coming week.

CLIENT HOMEWORK

☐ Fill out the remainder of Identify Problem Substance Use Situations—CD Adapted.

☐ Complete a Weekly Diary.

Name: _____ Date:_____

Identifying Problem Substance Use Situations—CD Adapted

Complete Part 1 with your therapist after reviewing your assessment results on the Inventory of Drug-Taking Situations (IDTS-8).

You can complete Part 2 either during the session with your therapist or as a homework assignment. If you complete it at home, bring it with you to your next appointment.

PART 1

What situations have tended to trigger your substance use over the past year? (Check any that apply.)

☐ unpleasant emotions
   (e.g., when angry, frustrated, bored, sad or anxious)

☐ physical discomfort
   (e.g., when feeling ill or in pain)

☐ pleasant emotions
   (e.g., when enjoying yourself or just feeling happy)

☐ testing personal control
   (e.g., when you started to believe you could handle alcohol or other drugs)

☐ urges and temptations to use
   (e.g., when walking by a pub or after seeing something that reminded you of drinking or other drug use)

☐ conflict with others
   (e.g., after an argument or when not getting along well with someone)

☐ social pressure to use
   (e.g., when someone offered you alcohol or other drugs)

☐ pleasant times with others
   (e.g., when out with friends or at a party)

Now rank the situations you checked above that are most often linked to problem drinking or other drug use (put the one that was **most often** a problem for you as rank 1, then the one that was a problem second most often as rank 2, then the third as rank 3):

Rank 1 (most frequently a problem): _____

Rank 2 (next most frequent): _____

Rank 3 (next most frequent): _____

PART 2

Your therapist has helped you identify general types of situations that have tended to trigger your problem drinking or other drug use over the past year. Now, think about the situations you ranked 1, 2 and 3. Write down examples of specific incidents of problem drinking or other drug use.

Rank 1 Situation

Think carefully about the particular drinking or other drug use experience you wish to describe, and then answer the questions below in as much detail as possible.

BEFORE USING

Where were you?

☐ Where you live (e.g., house, apartment, hostel or shelter, hospital)

☐ At someone else's place (whose?): _____

☐ In a public place (where?): _____

☐ Other: _____

Was anyone else there?

☐ Yes ☐ No

Were others drinking or using other drugs?

☐ Yes ☐ No

How were you feeling (e.g., happy, sad, angry, hurt, confused)?

_____

_____

_____

_____

What were you thinking just before you drank or used other drugs?

_____

_____

_____

_____

How do you think you might handle this situation without using?

_____

_____

_____

_____

Rank 2 Situation

Think carefully about the particular drinking or drug use experience you want to describe, and then answer the questions below in as much detail as possible.

BEFORE USING

Where were you?

☐ Where you live (e.g., house, apartment, hostel or shelter, hospital)

☐ At someone else's place (whose?): _____

☐ In a public place (where?): _____

☐ Other: _____

Was anyone else there?

☐ Yes ☐ No

Were others drinking or using other drugs?

☐ Yes ☐ No

How were you feeling (e.g., happy, sad, angry, hurt, confused)?

_____

_____

_____

_____

What were you thinking just before you drank or used other drugs?

_____

_____

_____

_____

How do you think you might handle this situation without using?

_____

_____

_____

_____

Rank 3 Situation

Think carefully about the particular drinking or drug use experience you want to describe, and then answer the questions below in as much detail as possible.

BEFORE USING

Where were you?

☐ Where you live (e.g., house, apartment, hostel or shelter, hospital)

☐ At someone else's place (whose?): _____

☐ In a public place (where?): _____

☐ Other: _____

Was anyone else there?

☐ Yes ☐ No

Were others drinking or using other drugs?

☐ Yes ☐ No

How were you feeling (e.g., happy, sad, angry, hurt, confused)?

_____

_____

_____

_____

What were you thinking just before you drank or used other drugs?

_____

_____

_____

_____

How do you think you might handle this situation without using?

_____

_____

_____

_____

Adapted from: H.M. Annis and G. Martin, Inventory of Drug-Taking Situations *(4th ed.). Toronto: Addiction Research Foundation © 1985*

Weekly Diary

By keeping track of the risky situations that you encounter, and of any urges or temptations that you feel to drink or use other drugs, you can develop better coping strategies. The Weekly Diary can also help you to see the "big picture" of how well you're doing. Just writing things down every week can help you to achieve your goals.

ABOUT MY WEEK

Overall, my week was (write an **X** on the line below to show how your week went):

$\longleftarrow$ $\longrightarrow$

Terrible   Pretty good   Fantastic

I thought about using substances on:

☐ Monday ☐ Tuesday ☐ Wednesday ☐ Thursday ☐ Friday ☐ Saturday ☐ Sunday

I used substances on:

☐ Monday ☐ Tuesday ☐ Wednesday ☐ Thursday ☐ Friday ☐ Saturday ☐ Sunday

I took my prescribed medication on:

☐ Monday ☐ Tuesday ☐ Wednesday ☐ Thursday ☐ Friday ☐ Saturday ☐ Sunday

THINGS THAT MADE ME THINK OF USING SUBSTANCES

☐ Unpleasant emotions (e.g., feeling bored, angry or sad)

☐ Physical discomfort (e.g., using substances to get rid of pain in my body)

☐ Pleasant emotions (e.g., being in a good mood and wanting to make it even better)

☐ Telling myself, "I can drink/use other drugs just a bit this one time"

☐ Urges or temptations to use

☐ Conflict with others (e.g., a fight with a friend or partner)

☐ Social pressure to use (being around others who want me to drink or use other drugs)

☐ Pleasant times with others (e.g., being with friends who were using)

THINGS I DID TO COPE

☐ Avoided situations where I would be tempted to drink or use other drugs

☐ Thought about the consequences of drinking or using other drugs

☐ Talked to someone I trust

☐ Other:

☐ Avoided people who drink or use other drugs

☐ Distracted myself by doing something else

☐ Left the situation

Phase 4: Initiation of Change

This phase of the CD-adapted SRP approach, like the corresponding "non-adapted" phase, focuses on counselling strategies that help initiate a change in behaviour. (The subsequent phase, Maintenance of Change, concentrates on strategies for maintaining change over the long term.) This phase usually involves four sessions but, depending on the needs of the client or group, it may require more.

Adaptations made to accommodate the needs of those with concurrent disorders include changes to the self-monitoring forms and the coping skills exercises. In order to minimize the number of exercises to accomplish and forms to complete, which many in this population find potentially overwhelming, we have included fewer optional exercises (see Coping Skills Checklist—CD Adapted on p. 167).

Because CD-adapted SRP sessions tend to vary a lot from one group to another, rather than provide a checklist for each session, we have included just two lists: one for the first counselling session and a second, "generic" checklist of things to cover in subsequent sessions of the Initiation of Change phase.

At the end of the section on CD-Adapted Phase 5 (Maintenance of Change), you will find all of the adapted clinical tools.

We have found the use of videos to be very helpful in our CD groups. One video that clients have found particularly useful is *Coping with Emotional and Physical Risk Factors* (developed by Jan Swanson and Allan Cooper, Hazelden Educational Materials, 1994). Clients indicated that this video helped them to normalize their experiences of cravings, guilt, feeling at risk and social isolation. A copy of the video can be obtained from Hazelden for US $89.95, plus shipping (the order number is 5760); call 1 800 328-9000 or write to Hazelden Education Materials, 15251 Pleasant Valley Road, Center City, MN 55012-0176.

Description	Clinical Tools
The client and therapist together prepare a weekly plan of anticipated risk situations and planned coping alternatives. The focus is on avoidance and seeking support from others. • The therapist helps the client conduct a functional analysis of a recent episode of drinking or other drug use.	• Weekly Planning Form: Initiation of Change—CD Adapted . . . . p. 163 • Weekly Diary (replaces the Daily Diary) . . p. 165 • ABC Analysis Chart—CD Adapted . . . . . . p. 166 • Coping Skills Checklist—CD Adapted . . . p. 167 • Situational Confidence Questionnaire (SCQ-8) . . . . p. 59 • Cope Alert Card . . . . p. 61 • Coping Skills Exercises—CD Adapted (optional) . . . . p. 177

NOTE: Tools that have been altered for clients with concurrent disorders are labelled "CD Adapted." Tools that do not have adapted versions can be found in Part II of this manual; page numbers are given above.

THERAPIST CHECKLIST

Counselling Session 1: Initiation of Change—CD Adapted

The counselling sessions in this Initiation of Change phase focus on avoiding drinking and other drug use situations, and on seeking support from reliable friends and family members.

BEFORE THE COUNSELLING SESSION

Bring the following blank forms:

☐ Weekly Planning Form: Initiation of Change—CD Adapted

☐ Weekly Diary

☐ Coping Skills Checklist—CD Adapted

DURING THE COUNSELLING SESSION

☐ Review the SRP program goals and structure.

☐ Discuss possible barriers to participation in the program (e.g., side-effects of medication, motivation to attend treatment) and look for possible solutions.

☐ Ask, "What will make it difficult to talk about substance use (in this group)?" "What would make it possible to talk about substance use?" Acknowledge the stigma of having both a mental illness and a substance use issue. Clients may also have difficulties with concentration or other issues relating to mental health symptoms. Forensic clients may have an incentive to minimize use, cravings or risk situations.

☐ Review the client's completed homework (Identifying Problem Substance Use Situations—CD Adapted and Weekly Diary) and discuss any problems that have arisen.

☐ Discuss the client's anticipated risk situations for the coming week and possible coping alternatives.

☐ Have the client complete the Coping Skills Checklist—CD Adapted. (In a group setting, review these after the first session to identify common areas of interest.)

☐ Work with the client to complete a Weekly Planning Form: Initiation of Change—CD Adapted.

☐ Ask, "What stood out for you about this session?"

CLIENT HOMEWORK

☐ Complete a Weekly Diary.

NOTE: These checklists are to be used as guidelines only. The number of sessions spent in change initiation and maintenance for a particular client will depend on his or her readiness for change and rate of progress.

THERAPIST CHECKLIST

Counselling Sessions 2 to 4 (or Beyond): Initiation of Change—CD Adapted

The counselling sessions in this Initiation of Change phase focus on avoiding drinking and other drug use situations, and on seeking support from reliable friends and family members.

This checklist includes topics for discussion and tools to complete (or review) each week. It also lists additional topics and tools that can be incorporated into Initiation of Change sessions as time and logistics permit. We have noted the additional items in a suggested sequence. However, feel free to use them in whatever order makes the most sense for your particular client or group.

BEFORE EVERY COUNSELLING SESSION

Bring the following blank forms:

☐ Weekly Planning Form: Initiation of Change—CD Adapted

☐ Weekly Diary

DURING EVERY COUNSELLING SESSION

☐ Check in regarding possible barriers to participation.

☐ Review completed homework forms and discuss any problems that have arisen.

☐ Discuss anticipated risk situations for the coming week and possible coping alternatives.

☐ Work with the client to complete a Weekly Planning Form: Initiation of Change—CD Adapted.

☐ Ask, "What stood out for you about this session?"

CLIENT HOMEWORK FOR EACH WEEK

☐ Complete a Weekly Diary.

ADDITIONAL DISCUSSION TOPICS AND TOOLS

☐ Discuss and complete an ABC Analysis Chart—CD Adapted.

☐ Discuss and complete an SCQ-8.

☐ Show the video Coping with Emotional and Physical Risk Factors.

☐ Discuss and complete a Cope Alert Card.

☐ Assign CD-adapted coping skills exercises as appropriate.

NOTE: These checklists are to be used as guidelines only. The number of sessions spent in change initiation and maintenance for a particular client will depend on his or her readiness for change and rate of progress.

Name: _____ Date: _____

WEEKLY PLANNING FORM

Initiation of Change—CD Adapted

STRATEGIES FOR STARTING TO MAKE CHANGES TO YOUR SUBSTANCE USE

The early weeks of changing your substance use can be a hard time, but there are some things you can do to make it a little easier. Research has shown that starting to make changes is easier and more effective when you use some of the following powerful strategies:

- Avoid risky places and stay away from people who use substances.
- Take your prescribed medication.
- Call a friend, a family member or an AA, NA or Double Trouble sponsor to ask for help and support. (Double Trouble is a support group especially geared to people with both substance use and mental health issues.)
- Ask yourself: "What will I lose if I use?" "What will I gain by not using?"
- If possible, consider living in a supportive place (a treatment centre or a hospital) during the first couple of weeks of changing your substance use.
- Ask your doctor about medications that can help with cravings to use substances.
- Make a commitment to yourself by setting a substance use goal.
- Figure out what situations are going to be risky for you this week.
- Do something nice for yourself. For example, eat a favourite meal or make a point of doing something you really enjoy.

Now fill out the form on the following page to help you think about what you would like to accomplish in the coming week, and how you will do so.

INITIATION OF CHANGE PLAN FOR THIS WEEK

Below is some space for you to think about what you would like to accomplish in the coming week, and how you will do so.

My goal: _____

My level of confidence that I will achieve this goal:

☐ 0% ☐ 20% ☐ 40% ☐ 60% ☐ 80% ☐ 100%

Substance Use Trigger	Plans for Coping
What is my substance use trigger for this week?	**How can I cope with this trigger?**
(E.g., meeting a friend who uses drugs)	☐ Avoid the situation.
	☐ Go to a self-help group.
	☐ Call a friend, family member or sponsor.
	☐ Remind myself of what will happen if I use.
	☐ Take my medication.
	☐ Other things I can do to cope:
Where might this happen?	
What time of the day or night?	
What will I be doing, thinking and feeling?	

Weekly Diary

By keeping track of the risky situations that you encounter, and of any urges or temptations that you feel to drink or use other drugs, you can develop better coping strategies. The Weekly Diary can also help you to see the "big picture" of how well you're doing. Just writing things down every week can help you to achieve your goals.

ABOUT MY WEEK

Overall, my week was (Write an **X** on the line below to show how your week went):

⟵————————————————————————————————⟶

Terrible   Pretty good   Fantastic

I thought about using substances on:

☐ Monday ☐ Tuesday ☐ Wednesday ☐ Thursday ☐ Friday ☐ Saturday ☐ Sunday

I used substances on:

☐ Monday ☐ Tuesday ☐ Wednesday ☐ Thursday ☐ Friday ☐ Saturday ☐ Sunday

I took my prescribed medication on:

☐ Monday ☐ Tuesday ☐ Wednesday ☐ Thursday ☐ Friday ☐ Saturday ☐ Sunday

THINGS THAT MADE ME THINK OF USING SUBSTANCES

☐ Unpleasant emotions (e.g., feeling bored, angry or sad)

☐ Physical discomfort (e.g., using substances to get rid of pain in my body)

☐ Pleasant emotions (e.g., being in a good mood and wanting to make it even better)

☐ Telling myself, "I can drink/use other drugs just a bit this one time"

☐ Urges or temptations to use

☐ Conflict with others (e.g., a fight with a friend or partner)

☐ Social pressure to use (being around others who want me to drink or use other drugs)

☐ Pleasant times with others (e.g., being with friends who were using)

THINGS I DID TO COPE

☐ Avoided situations where I would be tempted to drink or use other drugs

☐ Thought about the consequences of drinking or using other drugs

☐ Talked to someone I trust

☐ Avoided people who drink or use other drugs

☐ Distracted myself by doing something else

☐ Left the situation

☐ Other: _____

Name: _____ Date: _____

ABC Analysis Chart—CD Adapted

An ABC analysis helps you to better understand how your substance use is "triggered" by thoughts, feelings or things that happen. We call these triggers "activators." This exercise also shows some of the consequences of substance use, both good and not so good.

Look at the table below. Under A, write down an example of an **activator**—the thing that triggers you to use substances. Under B, write down your **behaviour**— what substances you might typically use, and how much. Under C, write down the **consequences** of your substance use. These consequences include the good things and the not-so-good things that happen. They include both things that happen right away and things that happen later.

Your substance use is something you can change!

A ACTIVATORS	B BEHAVIOUR	C CONSEQUENCES
Example: **Someone in my neighbourhood offers me a joint.**	**Smoke the joint.**	RIGHT AWAY: **Feel good and forget problems for a while.** LATER ON: **Get in trouble with the law, have to go back to the hospital because of how it affects my mind.**
Now write your example of an "activator" or substance use trigger:	Write down the substance(s) and amount you would usually use:	Describe the consequences: RIGHT AWAY: LATER ON:

Think about how you could take care of yourself when you are faced with a trigger to use. Are there ways to cope without using? _____
_____
_____

Name: _____ Date: _____

Coping Skills Checklist—CD Adapted

During your treatment sessions, you will work with your therapist to come up with some ways you can cope with situations where you could feel at risk of drinking or using other drugs.

Here is a list of some areas you might want to work on while you are attending this treatment program. Look at the different topics and check off the **three** topics that you think are the **most important** for you.

Your therapist will provide you with exercises that address the specific areas you choose.

☐ Coping with cravings (strong urges to drink or use other drugs)

☐ Coping with boredom (this topic includes having nothing interesting to do, feeling lonely, and wanting to meet people who don't have a substance use problem)

☐ Refusing alcohol and other drugs

☐ Sexual relationships and dating

☐ Coping with symptoms and side-effects.

Phase 5: Maintenance of Change

In the Maintenance of Change phase of SRP counselling, performance aids that were used in the Initiation of Change phase are gradually withdrawn as the focus shifts to the client's own coping strategies for preventing a relapse. However, for clients with concurrent disorders, we encourage continuing with some key strategies from the Initiation of Change phase. These include taking medications, developing social support networks and avoiding extremely high-risk situations.

The Maintenance of Change phase usually features four to eight counselling sessions, but may continue longer depending on the needs of the client or group.

Because of the variable format and length of CD-adapted SRP counselling sessions, the checklists in this section have been consolidated into a single checklist of tools for all but the final session. A specific checklist for the last SRP session is included, since certain tools are particularly recommended for use at a final session: the SCQ-8, which highlights treatment gains, and the "If I Were to Relapse . . ." Exercise, which can facilitate a discussion of areas for continued monitoring and attention.

Description	Clinical Tools
• The client and therapist together prepare a weekly plan of anticipated risk situations and coping alternatives. The focus is on exposure to risk situations.	• Weekly Planning Form: Maintenance of Change—CD Adapted . . . . p. 173 • Weekly Diary (replaces Daily Diary) . . . . . . p. 175 • Decisional Balance Assignment—CD Adapted . . . . p. 149 • Readiness Ruler Exercise . . . . p. 176 • SCQ-8 . . . . p. 59 • "If I Were to Relapse . . ." Exercise . . . . . . p. 72 • Client Satisfaction Questionnaire . . . . p. 73

NOTE: Tools that have been altered for clients with concurrent disorders are labelled "CD Adapted." Tools that do not have adapted versions can be found in Part II of this manual; page numbers are given above.

THERAPIST CHECKLIST

Counselling Sessions 5 to 7 (or Beyond): Maintenance of Change—CD Adapted

Sessions 5 to 7 (or beyond, depending on the needs of the client or group) involve Maintenance of Change counselling procedures. Having practised alternative ways to cope during the Initiation of Change phase, clients now learn strategies for entering pre-planned risk situations—although for clients with concurrent disorders, we encourage also keeping up with some initiation strategies.

The checklist below includes topics for discussion and tools to complete or review each week. It also lists additional topics and tools that can be incorporated into counselling sessions during this phase, as time and logistics permit. We have noted these additional items in a suggested sequence. However, feel free to use them in whatever order makes the most sense for your particular client or group.

BEFORE EVERY COUNSELLING SESSION

Bring the following blank forms:

- [ ] Weekly Planning Form: Maintenance of Change—CD Adapted
- [ ] Weekly Diary

DURING EVERY COUNSELLING SESSION

- [ ] Check in regarding possible barriers to participation.
- [ ] Review completed homework forms and discuss any problems that have arisen.
- [ ] Discuss the client's planned risk situations for the coming week and possible coping alternatives.
- [ ] Encourage the client to develop a weekly plan that involves exposure to situations that are challenging but that the client feels confident to handle. With the client, complete the left column of the Weekly Planning Form: Maintenance of Change—CD Adapted. Help the client prepare to try new coping skills in these high-risk situations.
- [ ] Ask the client, "What stood out for you about this session?"

WEEKLY CLIENT HOMEWORK

- [ ] Complete a Weekly Diary.
- [ ] Complete the right column (outcome report) of the Weekly Planning Form.

ADDITIONAL TOPIC AND TOOLS

☐ Decisional Balance Assignment: for review, and for comparison with the previous Decisional Balance Assignment clients completed during the Motivational Interviewing phase.

☐ Readiness Ruler Exercise: to facilitate a discussion of confidence, importance of goal and readiness, and for comparison with the Readiness Ruler completed as part of the form Feedback about Goal Setting and Commitment to Change, in the Motivational Interviewing phase. For convenience, it has been reproduced as a discrete form at the end of this section.

☐ CD-adapted coping skills exercises

☐ "If I Were to Relapse . . ." Exercise: we suggest completing this in the second-last SRP session.

NOTE: These checklists are to be used as guidelines only. The number of sessions spent in change initiation and maintenance for a particular client will depend on his or her readiness for change and rate of progress.

THERAPIST CHECKLIST

Counselling Session 8 or Final Session: Maintenance of Change—CD Adapted

The final SRP session is an opportunity to review the key strategies for maintaining changes to their substance use that have been helpful to clients, for identifying areas still requiring support and for discussing next steps.

BEFORE THE COUNSELLING SESSION

Bring the following blank forms:

☐ SCQ-8

☐ Client Satisfaction Questionnaire

☐ Weekly Planning Form: Maintenance of Change—CD Adapted (*multiple copies*)

☐ Weekly Diary (*multiple copies*)

DURING THE COUNSELLING SESSION

☐ Review the client's assignment as outlined on the Weekly Planning Form: Maintenance of Change—CD Adapted. Discuss any problems that have arisen.

☐ Discuss the "If I Were to Relapse . . ." Exercise.

☐ Discuss upcoming risk situations and coping plans.

☐ Have the client complete an SCQ-8, and compare the results with the SCQ-8 completed early in the Initiation of Change phase. Explore the strengths and vulnerabilities shown by the results, and discuss areas that have changed over the treatment process.

☐ Discuss the client's next steps. Review the coping skills plans made using the coping skills exercise Coping with Boredom—CD Adapted (page 181).

☐ Ask, "What has stood out for you about this group? What are the most important ideas or tools that you will take away?"

☐ Return the client's homework folder.

☐ Have the client complete a Client Satisfaction Questionnaire.

CLIENT HOMEWORK

☐ Provide clients with multiple blank copies of the Weekly Planning Form: Maintenance of Change—CD Adapted and the Weekly Diary.

NOTE: These checklists are to be used as guidelines only. The number of sessions spent in change initiation and maintenance will depend on the client's readiness for change and rate of progress.

Name: _____ Date: _____

WEEKLY PLANNING FORM

Maintenance of Change—CD Adapted

STRATEGIES AND TIPS FOR MAINTAINING CHANGES TO YOUR SUBSTANCE USE

Congratulations! You've successfully made some changes in your substance use. The next step is to maintain those changes and prevent relapse. Here are two of the most powerful strategies for maintaining your substance use goal:

- Think about all of the high-risk situations you are likely to encounter as a part of your lifestyle.
- Gradually enter these situations, starting with lower risk and working your way up.

Why plan to enter situations where you might be tempted to use substances? Well, if these situations are likely to come up some time, it's better for you to be in control of where and when they do.

Here are a few more tips for keeping to your goal:

- Put yourself in each risk situation a few times before moving on to the next one.
- Make sure that you take the credit for your successes! For example, in the early weeks of change, we encouraged you to ask for help from other people. Now that you are learning to maintain change, it's important to know that you can do it on your own if you have to.
- Make sure that the situation you plan to enter is challenging, but not **too** challenging.
- If you find that you are having trouble with the risky situations you are in, you might be moving too fast. Take your time! You can always go back to using some of the early strategies (like avoiding people, places and things, or relying on the support of others) until you feel more confident.

Your substance use pattern didn't start overnight, so it makes sense that it will take some time to feel strong and confident in making positive changes. Setting a goal and planning to enter risky situations are two powerful strategies to help you keep to your goal. On the next page is a form where you can write down your plan for the coming week.

MAINTENANCE OF CHANGE PLAN FOR THIS WEEK

Below is some space for you to think about what you would like to accomplish in the coming week, and how you will do so.

My goal: _____

My level of confidence that I will achieve this goal:

☐ 0% ☐ 20% ☐ 40% ☐ 60% ☐ 80% ☐ 100%

Plan to Enter a Risky Situation Fill in this column **before** the situation.	**What Happened?** Fill in this column **after** the situation.
Describe the risky situation: _____ _____ _____	Did you attempt this assignment? ☐ Yes ☐ No
When? _____ _____ _____	Were you successful? ☐ Yes ☐ No
	Comment: _____ _____ _____
Where? _____ _____ _____	_____
Who will be there? _____ _____ _____	Did you use substances? ☐ Yes ☐ No
Describe exactly what you will say and do. Describe what you will be thinking. (This is your coping plan.) _____ _____ _____ _____ _____ _____ _____ _____ _____ _____ _____	What, if anything, will you do differently next time? _____ _____ _____ _____ _____ _____ _____ _____ _____ _____ _____ _____ _____

Weekly Diary

By keeping track of the risky situations that you encounter, and of any urges or temptations that you feel to drink or use other drugs, you can develop better coping strategies. The Weekly Diary can also help you to see the "big picture" of how well you're doing. Just writing things down every week can help you to achieve your goals.

ABOUT MY WEEK

Overall, my week was (Write an **X** on the line below that tells how your week went.)

←—————————————————————————————————————→

Terrible   Pretty good   Fantastic

I thought about using substances on:

☐ Monday ☐ Tuesday ☐ Wednesday ☐ Thursday ☐ Friday ☐ Saturday ☐ Sunday

I used substances on:

☐ Monday ☐ Tuesday ☐ Wednesday ☐ Thursday ☐ Friday ☐ Saturday ☐ Sunday

I took my prescribed medication on:

☐ Monday ☐ Tuesday ☐ Wednesday ☐ Thursday ☐ Friday ☐ Saturday ☐ Sunday

THINGS THAT MADE ME THINK OF USING SUBSTANCES

☐ Unpleasant emotions (e.g., feeling bored, angry or sad)

☐ Physical discomfort (using substances to get rid of pain in my body)

☐ Pleasant emotions (e.g., being in a good mood and wanting to make it even better)

☐ Telling myself, "I can drink/use other drugs just a bit this one time"

☐ Urges or temptations to use

☐ Conflict with others (e.g., a fight with a friend or partner)

☐ Social pressure to use (being around others who want me to drink or use other drugs)

☐ Pleasant times with others (e.g., being with friends who were using)

THINGS I DID TO COPE

☐ Avoided situations where I would be tempted to drink or use other drugs

☐ Thought about the consequences of drinking or using other drugs

☐ Talked to someone I trust

☐ Avoided people who drink or use drugs

☐ Distracted myself by doing something else

☐ Left the situation

☐ Other: _____

Readiness Ruler Exercise

People usually have several things they would like to change in their lives. Your substance use may be only one of the things you hope to change. Your **motivation** to change your substance use can vary, depending on other things that are happening.

On each of the rulers below, circle the number (from 0 to 10) that best fits with how you are feeling right now.

1. How **important** is it to you to reduce or quit using alcohol or other drugs?

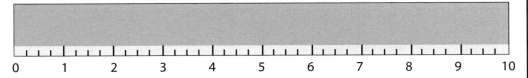

2. How **confident** are you that you will not use alcohol or other drugs?

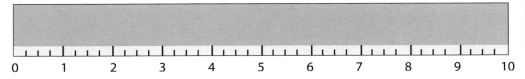

3. How **realistic** is it that you will stay away from alcohol and other drugs in the long term?

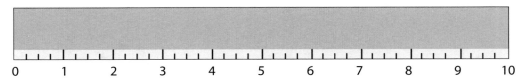

SOME QUESTIONS TO THINK ABOUT

• Why are you at your current score and not at zero?
• What would it take for you to move to a higher score?
• What has made this change important to you so far—why are you not at zero?
• What would it take to make this change even more important to you?
• What support would you need to make a change, if you chose to do so?

This exercise can also be used to explore readiness to change other behaviours, such as taking prescribed medication, looking for a job or finding stable housing.

_____

Signature of Clinician

_____

Name and Credentials (print)

_____

Contact Information

CD-Adapted Coping Skills Exercises

Introduction

People with concurrent substance use and mental health problems face the difficult task of coping with triggers and risk situations for substance use while also dealing with issues related to their mental illness. Added to this dual challenge is the reality that such clients are doubly stigmatized for having concurrent disorders. Therefore, we have developed CD-adapted versions of a few key coping skills exercises.

These exercises can be used in a discussion format in individual or group sessions, or assigned to clients as homework. In our groups, we found that a discussion format worked best, with clients then being assigned to reinforce and further practice the coping skill being targeted. In some groups, we did not hand out the assignment at all, but simply used the exercise as a framework for discussion and practice within the session through the use of role playing, group brainstorming, etc.

The following adapted exercises are presented here:

The choice of topics should be guided by the client's perceptions of areas that present an immediate, serious risk for relapse. The IDTS-8 and the Coping Skills Checklist—CD Adapted can also help you choose appropriate skills training exercises. Flexibility and consideration of client preferences will help keep clients engaged in treatment.

Coping with Cravings—CD Adapted

One of the hardest things about "staying quit" from substance use is coping with the urge to drink or use other drugs. An urge to use can be anything from a passing thought to feeling a very strong "need" to use substances. Learning to deal with these urges is a very important part of preventing relapse

People who have quit using substances often ask these kinds of questions:
• Will the cravings ever go away?
• How do I cope with thinking about substances all the time?
• How can I not give in, when the need is so strong?
• How can I ever enjoy life without alcohol or other drugs?

Remember that these feelings are normal. Have you ever tried to make some other change in your life (e.g., exercising more or eating healthier food)? Chances are, it took more than one try to make the change. Maybe you are still trying to make some of these other changes. It's the same with stopping substance use—it can take a while before the cravings and urges become a distant memory. But change is possible. You can do things to lessen your cravings for substances.

PRACTICE EXERCISE

In this exercise, you will learn that:
• cravings do not last forever—in fact, they become weaker and happen less often as time goes by
• there are some things you can do right away in situations when you are thinking about using substances
• there are other things that might take longer to put in place, but which will be powerful in stopping the strong cravings you might be feeling right now.

PART 1: SOME STRATEGIES TO HELP YOU COPE

Here are some suggested strategies that have helped many people to deal with urges to use alcohol or other drugs. Check off the ones that you think might be useful for you. There are spaces left to add your own ideas.

Things You Can Do Right Now

☐ Throw out all reminders of your substance use (e.g., crack pipes, rolling papers, liquor bottles, telephone numbers of dealers).

☐ Keep a diary—write down your thoughts and feelings.

☐ Break off contact with people who continue to use heavily.

☐ Take deep breaths (in through your nose and out through your mouth) to relax yourself.

☐ Meditate, do yoga or use prayer to help you deal with urges to use.

☐ Take your prescribed medication regularly and talk to your doctor or psychiatrist. Ask about any symptoms you might be having—there are medications that can help with strong cravings, and one of them might be right for you.

☐ Put off using for 15 minutes. By then the craving often goes away or is much less than before.

☐ Call someone who can help (a friend, your therapist or an AA or NA sponsor).

☐ Get busy and distract your self—try a new drug-free activity (e.g., see a movie, go to a self-help group, take a walk in the park, get some exercise).

☐ Leave the situation, or do something to change it.

☐ Wait out the feeling—it will pass.

☐ Other: _____

☐ Other: _____

☐ Other: _____

Things You Can Think about besides Using

☐ Remember that it is normal to have cravings. It is OK.

☐ Try holding a picture in your mind of the craving being a wave that you are surfing. Visualize the wave getting smaller as you reach shore.

☐ Use positive self-statements, such as, "I can cope with it" or "I have been clean for weeks, and I don't want to spoil it now."

☐ Use thought stopping (picture a stop sign or a dead-end street)

☐ Think of your therapist, friends or family members. What would they be saying to you?

☐ Think of the problems or bad things that would happen if you continued using (e.g., becoming ill, getting arrested, going back to the hospital).

☐ Think of the good things about not using (e.g., feeling proud of yourself, staying healthy).

☐ Other: _____

☐ Other: _____

☐ Other: _____

PART 2: TAKING ACTION

Taking action and doing new things may not be easy but, like anything new, the more you do it, the easier it becomes. Write down three things you could do right away when you are having a craving:

1. _____

2. _____

3. _____

Now write down three things that you will practise to try to deal with cravings in the next week:

1. _____

2. _____

3. _____

You might find it helpful to keep this exercise in a place where you can refer back to it easily to inspire and motivate yourself. Good luck!

Coping with Boredom—CD Adapted

One of the hardest things about "staying quit" or changing your substance use is finding things to do that are fun, interesting or exciting. Many people say that in order to give up drinking and other drug use, they also had to give up some old (or new) friends, and stay away from risky places, such as bars, social gatherings or even celebrations.

People who have changed their substance use often ask these kinds of questions:
- How can I have fun without going to a bar or nightclub?
- Who can I hang out with, since all my friends drink or use other drugs?
- What do I do with my time now?
- How do I deal with these feelings of loneliness or boredom?
- What can I do when I don't have money to spend?

Coping with boredom means finding new activities, interests, friends and hobbies. Like any lifestyle change, this might be hard at first.

PRACTICE EXERCISE

In this exercise, you will have a chance to think about:
- some things you can do right away in situations where you are feeling bored or lonely
- other things that might take longer to put in place, but which will add meaning and interest to your life in the future.

PART 1: THINGS TO DO AND PLACES TO GO

First, what are some of the things that you used to enjoy doing (maybe it was a long time ago), or new things that you think you might like to try?

Physical Activities	
☐ Walking or hiking	☐ Fishing
☐ Jogging or running	☐ Bowling
☐ Bike riding	☐ Martial arts
☐ Swimming	☐ Tennis, badminton or other
☐ Basketball	racquet sports
☐ Working out or lifting weights	☐ Dancing
☐ Yoga	☐ Other: _____
☐ Volleyball	☐ Other: _____
☐ Soccer or football	

Hobbies	
☐ Writing	☐ Painting
☐ Collecting things	☐ Pottery making
☐ Woodwork	☐ Other: _____
☐ Sewing	☐ Other: _____

Other Interests

- ☐ Watching movies
- ☐ Reading
- ☐ Listening to music
- ☐ Surfing the Internet
- ☐ Playing chess, cards or other games

- ☐ Playing an instrument
- ☐ Playing video games
- ☐ Other: _____
- ☐ Other: _____

Now look over some of the things that you checked off. What activities do you think you could try doing?

Activity	How Realistic Is It That I Will Do This?	How Fun or Interesting Is This Activity?
1.	←————————→ not very realistic realistic	←————————→ not very fun/ interesting fun/ interesting
2.	←————————→ not very realistic realistic	←————————→ not very fun/ interesting fun/ interesting
3.	←————————→ not very realistic realistic	←————————→ not very fun/ interesting fun/ interesting
4.	←————————→ not very realistic realistic	←————————→ not very fun/ interesting fun/ interesting
5.	←————————→ not very realistic realistic	←————————→ not very fun/ interesting fun/ interesting

PART 2: MEETING NEW PEOPLE

In addition to having activities and interests, it's also important to have people around whom you like and trust. Some people who stop using substances say that, since many of their friends used substances, they need to find a new "support network"—new friends to talk to and do things with.

The list below has some ideas for places to meet new people who can help you in your recovery. Which ideas are you willing to try?

☐ Self-help groups or meetings: (such as: _____)

☐ Social clubs (such as: _____)

☐ Drop-in programs (such as: _____)

☐ Educational courses or programs (such as: _____)

☐ Counselling or therapy groups (such as: _____)

☐ Religious or spiritual groups or services (such as: _____)

☐ Volunteer work (such as: _____)

☐ Other: _____

☐ Other: _____

☐ Other: _____

Look over some of the things that you checked off. What places do you think you could try go to in order to meet new people?

Place	How Realistic Is It That I Will Go?	How Fun or Interesting Will It Be for Me?
1.	←————————→ not very · · · · · · realistic realistic	←————————→ not very fun/ · · · · fun/ interesting · · · · interesting
2.	←————————→ not very · · · · · · realistic realistic	←————————→ not very fun/ · · · · fun/ interesting · · · · interesting
3.	←————————→ not very · · · · · · realistic realistic	←————————→ not very fun/ · · · · fun/ interesting · · · · interesting

PART 3: TAKING ACTION

Doing new things may not be easy. But as with anything new, the more you do it, the easier it becomes. Write down three things you could do right away when you're feeling bored:

1. _____

2. _____

3. _____

Can you try one of these things this week?

You might find it helpful to keep this exercise in a place where you can refer back to it easily to inspire and motivate yourself. Good luck!

Refusing Alcohol and Other Drugs—CD Adapted

When you quit using alcohol or other drugs, one of the highest-risk situations you might experience is when someone offers you a drink or another drug. Saying No requires some practice. In some cases, saying No is not enough.

Learning to deal with friends or relatives who offer substances, or dealers that "push" them on you, is a very important part of preventing relapse. One difference between a drug dealer and the friends or relatives who offer substances is that you may want to keep the relationship with your friends and family. It can be really hard to say No to people you care about. Also, some drug dealers are really good salespeople. They may not give up easily. Sometimes, you may consider your dealer a friend—or someone you are afraid to say No to.

Part of you might not be totally sure you want to give up substances completely. This makes it even harder to resist. Whatever the reason, you can get better at dealing with the very high-risk situation of being offered alcohol or other drugs.

People who are trying to quit using substances often ask these kinds of questions:
• How do I say no to my family or friends?
• How do I say no to my drug dealer ?
• How do I keep a good relationships with the people I care about?
• Other people drink and use other drugs—why can't I?

PRACTICE EXERCISE

In this exercise, you will learn:
• how to successfully refuse alcohol or other drugs
• how to keep a good relationship with the people you care about—and who really care about what's best for you
• how to get a friend or relative to stop offering you substances
• how to leave a situation without using.

PART 1: HOW TO SAY NO TO A DEALER

What You Can Do

☐ Look the other way and don't make eye contact.

☐ Leave the situation—walk away quickly.

☐ Say, "I don't want any, thanks." Use a firm tone. Repeat it as many times as necessary, with meaning!

☐ Stand tall and gesture with your hands as if you are pushing away the person who is offering you the substance.

☐ Keep your hands close to your body so nothing can be put into them.

☐ Break off contact with people who continue to push drugs on you.

☐ Talk to supportive friends, family members or health care professionals about what you are going through.

- ☐ Have a supportive person with you when you say No, especially if you are concerned a dealer may be violent.
- ☐ Put off the decision to use for 15 minutes.
- ☐ Other: _____
- ☐ Other: _____
- ☐ Other: _____

What You Can Think About

- ☐ Remind yourself of your goal.
- ☐ Use positive self-statements, such as, "I have been clean for weeks, and I don't want to spoil it now."
- ☐ Ask yourself, "Who are my real friends? Who really wants what's best for me?"
- ☐ Remind yourself that you are the one in control—only you can decide to use substances or not.
- ☐ Think of what will happen if you use (e.g., becoming ill, getting arrested, going back to the hospital).
- ☐ Think of the good things about not using (e.g., respecting yourself, staying healthy).
- ☐ Other: _____
- ☐ Other: _____
- ☐ Other: _____

PART 2: HOW TO SAY NO TO FRIENDS AND FAMILY

What You Can Do

- ☐ Look the person in the eyes.
- ☐ Be direct. Tell the person you are not interested, or that it's really important for you to not use substances.
- ☐ Keep repeating the message that you want to stay healthy and not use substances.
- ☐ Be honest with the person about your goal (e.g., "I have quit using drugs because it interferes with my medication.").
- ☐ Tell the other person how you feel when they offer you alcohol or other drugs (e.g., "It bothers me that you pour me a drink every time you have one," or "I'm worried that if I don't use drugs with you, it will affect our friendship—and I really care about you.")
- ☐ Break off contact with people who continue to pressure you to use and who don't respect your decision.
- ☐ Talk to your sponsor, your therapist, or another health care professional about what you are feeling.

☐ Take your prescribed medication regularly and talk to your doctor or psychiatrist about any symptoms you might be having.

☐ Suggest something else to do instead of using substances.

☐ If the person continues to pressure you, leave the situation.

☐ Other: _____

☐ Other: _____

☐ Other: _____

PART 3: TAKING ACTION

Doing new things may not be easy. But as with anything new, the more you do it, the easier it becomes. Write down three things you could do if you are being pressured to use substances by a dealer:

1. _____

2. _____

3. _____

Now write down three things you plan to do when your friends or family offer you substances:

1. _____

2. _____

3. _____

You might find it helpful to keep this exercise in a place where you can refer back to it easily to inspire and motivate yourself. Good luck!

Sexual Relationships and Dating—CD Adapted

INTRODUCTION

Many people who have who quit or cut down on their substance use find that meeting people to date and having sexual relationships are big challenges. For some, alcohol or other drugs were a way to feel more confident with others. Also, many people have met their sexual partners by going to bars and clubs. Dating is challenging at the best of times—when dealing with a mental illness and substance use recovery at the same time, it can be positively frightening!

Forming healthy relationships takes time and effort. But there are ways to connect with others that don't involve alcohol or other drugs. This exercise will help you think about and plan how you are going to go about trying some of those ways.

People who are trying to quit using substances and want to date or start a sexual relationship often ask these kinds of questions:
• What does "healthy dating" mean?
• How and where do I meet people who don't misuse substances and support my recovery?
• How much information about my mental illness or substance use issues should I tell someone I'm interested in?

Many people who have mental health and substance use issues have also had difficulties having a close relationship. It is OK to choose **not** to focus on dating.

PART 1: WHAT IS A HEALTHY RELATIONSHIP?
PRACTICE EXERCISE

In this exercise, you will learn:
• what a healthy relationship looks like
• how to ask someone for a date
• where you can meet people where drinking or using other drugs is not expected.

Below is a list of qualities that are usually part of a healthy relationship. There is room for you to add some of your own.

How many of these qualities have you had in past relationships? Which ones needed work or were missing? These are some areas to think about as you start dating or meeting potential partners.

☐ You are with someone who has values and interests similar to yours.

☐ It takes time to get to know each other and see if the relationship is right for you.

☐ The needs of both partners are being met.

☐ Both partners feel comfortable and safe with one another.

☐ You can trust the other person with your feelings, ideas, wishes and desires.

☐ The two partners respect one another's boundaries (e.g., how often to see each other, whether to have sex, what each other's sexual preferences are).

☐ If you make a commitment not to date other people, you both trust each other's loyalty to the relationship.

☐ Your partner accepts you for who are (and you accept him or her)—both the good and the bad things.

☐ If one or both partners aren't looking (or ready) for a serious relationship, this is talked about, understood and accepted.

☐ One or both partners don't need to use substances in order to feel intimate or have sex.

☐ Other: _____

☐ Other: _____

☐ Other: _____

PART 2: HOW DO I ASK FOR A DATE?

It can take some courage to ask someone you like for a date, especially if you are not using alcohol or other drugs. Here are some simple steps and suggestions that may help:

• It doesn't have to be a big deal! Try thinking about asking someone for a date in these terms: "I'm asking someone to join me in a fun activity—if they say Yes, that's great; if they say No, there's always someone else out there."
• Make eye contact and smile at the person.
• Use a pleasant greeting in an upbeat tone.
• Tell the person about the activity and when it takes place.
• Ask if he or she would like to join you—be direct.
• If the person says he or she is busy, suggest another activity at another time.
• If the person still says No, thank the person and move on. Sometimes people just don't feel a connection.
• If the person says Yes, say that you are pleased, and set a meeting place and time.

PART 3: WHEN AND HOW DO I TALK ABOUT MY MENTAL HEALTH AND SUBSTANCE USE HISTORY?

You may want to wait until you've had a couple of dates with someone before you disclose information about your mental illness and your substance use history and recovery. However, once you have begun to get to know the person, it is important to be honest about what you are going through. Of course, there is always the possibility that the person will decide that he or she does not want to continue the relationship. But if so, it's better to know this sooner rather than later. Your willingness to be honest shows respect for the other person, as well as commitment to yourself and your recovery.

Pick a time when you are both feeling relaxed, and make sure the conversation happens in a private place where you aren't likely to be interrupted.

You might want to start the conversation with a statement such as this: "There's something on my mind that I've been concerned about telling you. I really like you, and I'm hoping that it doesn't get in the way of our spending time together. Is this a good time to talk a bit about this?"

Reread this suggested opening sentence, and try putting the same ideas into your own words:

_____

_____

_____

_____

PART 4: PLACES TO GO AND PEOPLE TO MEET

Now explore some possible places to meet people and things you can do together.

Where to Go*

What other places can you think of to meet people? Brainstorm a list (e.g., special-interest clubs, sporting events, walkathons, health clubs, neighbourhood and community gatherings, volunteer opportunities, continuing education workshops, courses).

_____

_____

What other places can you think of to go with someone? Brainstorm a list (e.g., coffee shops, bookstores, movies, film festivals, shopping malls and food courts, museums, libraries, craft fairs, church and community centres, bowling, restaurants).

_____

_____

Tips for Success

- Tell your friends that you are interested in meeting someone. They might know someone who is single who might be right for you.
- Pick places that are easy to get to by public transportation and don't cost too much money (e.g., museums, parks, free community concerts or other events).
- Stay out of bars and clubs and the old "playgrounds" where you may be tempted to use substances.
- Pay attention to your personal hygiene.
- Keep your interactions light and friendly.
- Ask open-ended questions instead of questions that would get a Yes or No answer (e.g., "What made you decide to join this art class?" rather than, "Do you like this class?").
- Do not disclose everything about yourself on the first date. People need time to get to know each other.

    Trying out new ways of meeting people may not be easy, but as with anything new, the more you do it, the easier and more natural it becomes.

*List of places to go adapted from Mary Faulkner (2004), Easy Does It Dating Guide for People in Recovery. Center City, MN: Hazelden Publishing (p. 93).

PART 5: WHAT DO YOU VALUE IN A RELATIONSHIP?

For the last part of this exercise, write down what you value in a relationship and what kind of person you are looking for. Take some time to think about it. Knowing what you want in a partner will help you to reach your goal of developing healthy relationships.

What do you value in a relationship?

1. _____
2. _____
3. _____

What kind of person are you looking for?

1. _____
2. _____
3. _____

AN IMPORTANT NOTE ON SEXUAL HEALTH

Talk to your doctor or your psychiatrist about how to deal with any potential sexual side-effects of your mental illness or your medication. These symptoms or side-effects may be treatable, depending on the type of mental illness you have, the type of problem (e.g., vaginal dryness or difficulty getting or maintaining an erection), the length of time it has been an issue for you, your age and your medical history.

You might find it helpful to keep this exercise in a place where you can refer back to it easily to inspire and motivate yourself. Good luck!

Coping with Symptoms and Side-Effects

When you quit, or cut down on, using alcohol or other drugs, some of the highest-risk situations you might end up in are when you experience symptoms of your mental illness, or the side-effects of some of the medications you might be taking. Substance use can be a quick way of dealing with symptoms or side-effects in the short term, but often the substance use just makes things worse in the long term. Using alcohol or other drugs can keep your prescribed medication from working as well as it should, or it can make your mental illness symptoms even more intense. Substance use can also affect your overall health—both physical and mental—and make it hard to reach other goals, such as living independently, finding or keeping a job, or forming and keeping relationships.

People who are trying to quit using substances often ask these kinds of questions:
• How do substances affect my mental illness?
• What will it be like living with mental illness, without using alcohol or other drugs?
• What are the common side-effects of my medications, and how can I deal with them?
• How can I deal with my symptoms and medication side-effects in a healthier way?

PRACTICE EXERCISE

In this exercise, you will learn about:
• common symptoms of mental illness
• common side-effects of medications
• ways of dealing with your symptoms and side-effects without substance use
• how to be more aware (watch for your "warning signs") and to take action when you're at risk for using substances.

COMMON SYMPTOMS AND SIDE-EFFECTS

Here are some of the symptoms of mental illness and side-effects of medication that many people experience. Check off any that apply to you. There is room for you to add any others that you might have had.

Bring this list to your next appointment with your therapist or other health care professional, for help and advice.

Mental Illness Symptoms	Medication Side-Effects
☐ Hearing voices or seeing visions	☐ Drowsiness
☐ Paranoia or fear	☐ Blurry vision
☐ Depression and/or anxiety	☐ Dry mouth
☐ Lack of interest or energy	☐ Constipation or diarrhea
☐ Poor concentration	☐ Restlessness
☐ Sleep and/or eating disturbance	☐ Shakes or tremors
☐ Avoiding other people	☐ Muscle stiffness
☐ Other: _____	☐ Weight gain
☐ Other: _____	☐ Other: _____
☐ Other: _____	☐ Other: _____

HOW SUBSTANCES AFFECT THE SYMPTOMS OF MENTAL ILLNESS

Alcohol and other drugs can:

- make your prescribed medications less effective
- make your mental illness symptoms worse (e.g., make you feel paranoid)
- hide the symptoms of your mental illness, making it harder to get good treatment
- increase the risk of violence or other illegal behaviour (e.g., stealing things to get money for drugs)
- cause symptoms that are the same as those of some mental illnesses, so that you may be wrongly diagnosed.

WHAT CAN YOU DO TO STAY HEALTHY?

Now look at some of the things you can do to deal with some of the common side-effects of psychiatric medications. In the table below, on the left is a list of typical side-effects, and on the right is a list of some things that you can do to help, instead of using substances.

Medication Side-Effects	Things That Can Help
Drowsiness	See your doctor or psychiatrist about adjusting your medication.
	Take a short rest during the day.
Blurry vision	See your doctor or psychiatrist about adjusting your medication.
Dry mouth	Drink fluids, but not too much—six to eight glasses of water, juice, etc. each day).
	Use lip balm and sugarless gum.
Constipation or diarrhea	Make sure that you are eating regular, healthy meals and snacks.
	Eat high-fibre foods (e.g., bran flakes, whole wheat bread, fresh fruits and vegetables) to help with constipation.
	Eat foods that are lower in fibre (e.g., rice, bananas, applesauce) to help with diarrhea.
Restlessness Shakes or tremors	Cut down on drinks with caffeine (such as coffee and cola).
	If you smoke cigarettes, try to cut down or quit. There are some excellent medications to help you with this.
	See your doctor or psychiatrist about adjusting your medication.
Muscle stiffness	See your doctor or psychiatrist about adjusting your medication.
Weight gain	Go for walks and other exercise.
	Eat healthier food.

OTHER THINGS THAT CAN HELP

- Talk to your nurse, case worker, social worker, or psychiatrist about what you are feeling and the symptoms you are experiencing.
- Be honest with the health professionals involved in your treatment about any use of substances. Your health professionals can be more helpful if they know about your substance use. They can refer you to specialized treatment if they think it is appropriate.
- Take your medications regularly, as directed.
- Remember that you have the right to good health care! Many communities have consumer/survivor groups that advocate for patient rights. Some hospitals have patient councils that are there to help if you feel you are not getting the care you need.

TAKING ACTION

Doing new things may not be easy—but as with anything new, the more you do it, the easier it becomes. Write down three "warning signs"—symptoms or side-effects that make you really want to use substances.

1. _____

2. _____

3. _____

Now look back over this exercise and decide what things you can do—other than using substances—to deal with these warning signs. Write them down:

1. _____

2. _____

3. _____

How confident are you that you will actually try doing the things you wrote on the lines above? Circle the number on the ruler below that shows how confident you feel:

```
0   1   2   3   4   5   6   7   8   9   10
```

Now write down one thing you could do to increase your confidence by one point on the ruler. _____

_____

_____

_____

You might find it helpful to keep this exercise in a place where you can refer back to it easily to inspire and motivate yourself. Good luck!

Results from a Pilot Program

The adaptations to SRP for clients with concurrent disorders were based on client and clinician feedback from a number of sources, including:

- practice wisdom gleaned from our SRP groups over the years, in which we always had three or more clients with mental health diagnoses in addition to their substance use issues
- the invaluable feedback of clinicians at CAMH, whose knowledge and experience with concurrent disorders helped further shape the content in this section.

Finally, we pilot-tested the CD-adapted version of SRP with a group of 11 clients who had concurrent disorders. These clients were part of the CAMH Law and Mental Health Program, which works with people in the forensic system whose index offences were found by the courts to be related to their mental illness (i.e., a judgement of "not criminally responsible"). We chose to pilot the SRP materials with these clients for the following reasons:

- risk of reoffending—clients with concurrent disorders in the forensic system are at increased risk of reoffending, particularly when the substance use and mental health symptoms were related to the index offence; thus, there was some pragmatic urgency in implementing SRP within the Law and Mental Health Program
- client diversity—clients in the program are diverse with respect to problem substance, metal health diagnosis, age, cultural and socio-economic background, and motivation for change; therefore, we felt that we would be able to get a better representation of diverse clients in the pilot group
- inpatient versus outpatient status—the group comprised a combination of inpatients (hospitalized) and outpatients (living in the community); this allowed us to tailor the material to clients in both treatment contexts.

We delivered the SRP program to this group in eight 90-minute sessions, and included an additional follow-up session three months after the final session. The follow-up session allowed us to reconnect with the group and to review whether clients were continuing to apply the coping skills and anticipation of risk situations learned during SRP treatment. Although this pilot group was not a representative sample (e.g., no women were included in the group—an important shortcoming of the pilot test), and further research is needed to determine the efficacy of this revised version of SRP, the lack of CD-adapted tools and treatment programs justifies, in our opinion, its inclusion in this revised volume.

The following is a summary of the client satisfaction data from our pilot CD-adapted SRP group.

NOTE: The evaluation instrument differs from the one included in Appendix A. This is because the Law and Mental Health Program uses its own standardized evaluation tool for all groups.

Group Evaluation Form: SRP, Law and Mental Health Program, CAMH

Evaluation Summary prepared by Shannon Costigan, PhD candidate

Date Survey Completed:	July 21, 2005
Group:	Structured Relapse Prevention (SRP)
Facilitators:	Lyn Watkin-Merek, RN & Marilyn Herie, PhD
Average Age:	32 years (SD=8.01)
Gender:	11 males

Subjects were asked to respond to the question, "Do you agree or disagree with the following statements?"

	Strongly Disagree	Disagree	Agree	Strongly Agree	Undecided
1. The topics in the group were interesting and informative.	9% (N=1)		55% (N=6)	27% (N=3)	9% (N=1)
2. The facilitators clearly discussed the topics so I could understand.			55% (N=6)	45% (N=5)	
3. The topics covered in the group were relevant to my personal situation.			64% (N=7)	36% (N=4)	
4. The facilitators clearly responded to issues that came up in discussion.			45% (N=5)	45% (N=5)	9% (N=1)
5. The group helped me prepare for community living.	9% (N=1)		55% (N=6)	36% (N=4)	
6. I was satisfied with the group.			64% (N=7)	36% (N=4)	

SAMPLE CLIENT COMMENTS

What aspects of this group did you find most helpful?

- Coping skills
- Learning that one drink is too many and a thousand not enough
- The discussions we would have in the group were very helpful and informative
- Discussing strategies to avoid and deal with substances
- How to prevent a relapse
- The discussion that we had about how not to relapse.

What aspects of this group did you find least helpful?

- Processing how you stay sober
- The relapse prevention group was good, but I think the group was too lengthy
- Trying to find what will help you stay quit.

Feedback Summary

Overall, the participants were satisfied with the group. Clients were satisfied with the facilitators and topics, and felt the group was relevant to their lives and discharge planning. Coping with relapse and high-risk situations were described as the most helpful aspects of the group. Discussions on how to remain sober were described as the least helpful aspect of the group.

Selected Resources on Concurrent Disorders

PRINT RESOURCES

Carroll, K.M. (2004). Behavioural therapies for co-occurring substance use and mood disorders. *Biological Psychiatry, 56*(10), 778–784.

Graham, H.L., Copello, A., Birchwood, M.J. & Mueser, K.T. (Eds.). (2003). *Substance Misuse in Psychosis: Approaches to Treatment and Service Delivery*. West Sussex, UK: John Wiley & Sons.

Health Canada. (2002). *Best Practices: Concurrent Mental Health and Substance Use Disorders*. Minister of Public Works and Government Services Canada, Cat. #H39-599/2001-2E. Available: www.hc.-sc.gc.ca/ahc-asc/pubs/drugs-drogues/bp_disorder-mp_concomitants/index_e.html. Accessed April 5, 2006.

Minkoff, K. (2001). *AACP Position Statement on Program Competencies in a Comprehensive Continuous Integrated System of Care for Individuals with Co-occurring Psychiatric and Substance Disorders*. Dallas, TX: American Association of Community Psychiatrists.

Minkoff, K. (2001). *Behavioural Health Recovery Management Service Planning Guidelines: Co-Occurring Psychiatric and Substance Disorders*. Bloomington, IL: University of Chicago.

Minkoff, K. & Rossi, A. (1998). *Co-occurring Psychiatric and Substance Disorders in Managed Care Systems: Standards of Care, Practice Guidelines, Workforce Competencies, and Training Curricula*. Washington, DC: Center for Mental Health Services.

Mueser, K.T., Noordsy, D.L., Drake, R.E., Fox, L. & Barlow, D.H. (Eds). (2003). *Integrated Treatment for Dual Disorders: A Guide to Effective Practice. Treatment Manuals for Practitioners*. New York, NY: Guilford Press.

Najavits, L. (2002). *Seeking Safety: A Treatment Manual for PTSD and Substance Abuse*. New York: Guilford Press.

Najavits, L.M., Weiss, R.D. & Liese, B.S. (1996). Group cognitive behavioural therapy for women with PTSD and substance use disorder. *Journal of Substance Use Treatment, 13,* 13–22.

National Association of State Mental Health Program Directors (NASMHPD)/National Association of State Alcohol and Drug Abuse Directors (NASADAD). (1998). *National Dialogue on Co-occurring Mental Health and Substance Abuse Disorders.* Alexandria, VA and Washington, DC: Authors.

National Drug Strategy and National Mental Health Strategy. (2003). *Comorbidity of Mental Health Disorders and Substance Abuse: A Brief Guide for the Primary Care Clinician.* Canberra, Australia: Commonwealth Department of Health and Ageing.

National Drug Strategy and National Mental Health Strategy. (2003). *Current Practice in the Management of Clients with Comorbid Mental Health and Substance Use Disorders in Tertiary Care Settings.* Canberra, Australia: Commonwealth Department of Health and Ageing.

New Mexico Department of Health. (2002). *A Strengths-Based Systems Approach to Creating Integrated Services for Individuals with Co-occurring Psychiatric and Substance Use Disorders.* Santa Fe, NM: Author.

Puddicombe, J., Rush, B. & Bois, C. (2004). *Concurrent Disorders Treatment Models for Treating Varied Populations.* Program Models Project 2003–2004. Toronto: Centre for Addiction and Mental Health.

Roberts, L.J., Shaner A. & Eckman, T.A. (1999). *Overcoming Addictions: Skills Training for People with Schizophrenia.* New York: Norton.

Skinner, W. J. (Ed.). (2005). *Treating Concurrent Disorders: A Guide for Counsellors.* Toronto: Centre for Addiction and Mental Health.

Skinner, W. J. & Carver, V. (2004). Working in a harm reduction framework. In *Alcohol and Drug Problems: A Practical Guide for Counsellors (3rd ed.)* (pp. 229–243). Toronto: Centre for Addiction and Mental Health.

Substance Abuse and Mental Health Services Administration (SAMHSA). (2003). *Strategies for Developing Treatment Programs for People with Co-occurring Substance Abuse and Mental Disorders.* Washington, DC: Author.

Weiss, R.D. (2004). Treating patients with bipolar disorder and substance dependence: Lessons learned. *Journal of Substance Abuse Treatment, 27*(4), 307–312.

Weiss, R.D., Najavits, L.M. & Greenfield, S.F. (1999). A relapse prevention group for patients with bipolar and substance use disorders. *Journal of Substance Abuse Treatment 16,* 47–54.

Ziedonis, D., Smelson, D., Rosenthal, R., Batki, S., Green, A., Henry, R. et al. (2005). Improving the care of individuals with schizophrenia and substance use disorders: Consensus recommendations. *Journal of Psychiatric Practice, 11*(5), 315–339.

APPENDIX A:
Additional Sample Forms

Introduction

This manual includes samples of forms for use when working with clients in the Structured Relapse Prevention program. The next few pages feature samples of two additional forms that you may decide to use in SRP counselling. Your organization may already have similar forms that will suit your needs.

The Progress Note helps therapists keep a record of each client's treatment progress, and the Professional Chart Audit Checklist provides guidelines for keeping and organizing client records.

Progress Note

Name: _____ File No.: _____

Date: _____ Session No.: _____

Target substance: _____

ATTENDANCE

☐ Client attended

☐ Client cancelled

☐ No-show

☐ Therapist cancelled

OVERALL TREATMENT GOAL

☐ Abstinence

☐ Reduction

☐ No change

ASSESSMENT SESSION ONLY

☐ Inventory of Drug-Taking Situations (IDTS-8)

☐ Commitment to Change Algorithm (alcohol or drugs)

☐ Alcohol Dependence Scale (ADS)

☐ Drug Abuse Screening Test (DAST)

MOTIVATIONAL COUNSELLING SESSION ONLY

☐ Discussed Decisional Balance Assignment

☐ Reviewed client's reasons for change and strength of commitment to change

☐ Explored possible reasons for an undifferentiated IDTS-8 profile

Client reached an explicit decision to work toward change Yes ☐ No ☐

INDIVIDUALIZED TREATMENT PLANNING SESSION ONLY

☐ Reviewed terms of agreement

☐ Gave client copy of IDTS-8 profile results and discussed

☐ Discussed structure and rationale of treatment model

SUBSTANCE USE MONITORING

Substance used: _____

Indicate on calendar number of standard drinks or number of uses

Date	Sun	Mon	Tues	Wed	Thurs	Fri	Sat
Amount							

Date	Sun	Mon	Tues	Wed	Thurs	Fri	Sat
Amount							

STRUCTURE OF TREATMENT MODEL

The treatment program generally consists of eight treatment sessions, with the possibility of negotiating additional sessions. Based on the client's Inventory of Drug-Taking Situations (IDTS-8), risk situations (including thoughts and feelings) that are associated with substance use are identified and discussed. The treatment further focuses on learning and practising alternative coping strategies during planned and gradual exposure to identified risk situations in the client's daily environment. For a more detailed outline of the treatment program, refer to the Structured Relapse Prevention manual.

	Completed	Not Completed	Assigned
Weekly Activity			
_____	☐	☐	☐
_____	☐	☐	☐
Coping Skills Assignment (optional)			
_____	☐	☐	☐
_____	☐	☐	☐

Session Content

(including homework assignments not completed, changes in overall treatment goal, high-risk situations and triggers encountered and anticipated, coping strategies planned and employed)

_____

_____

_____

_____

Signature and credentials   Date

Name: _____ File no.: _____

SRP COUNSELLING (INDIVIDUAL OR GROUP)

Professional Chart Audit Checklist

Audit Criteria	Counselling Sessions 1 2 3 4 5 6 7 8 (additional)	Audit Scores
1. Indication is given that homework assignments were completed OR if not completed, discussion of steps taken.	N/A ☐☐☐☐☐☐☐☐☐☐☐☐	/ = ☐ 1
2. Overall treatment goal is set weekly, with any change in substance use goal discussed in note.	☐☐☐☐☐☐☐☐☐☐☐☐☐	/ = ☐ 2
3. Abstinence or non-abstinence is documented.	N/A ☐☐☐☐☐☐☐☐☐☐☐☐	/ = ☐ 3
4. Client's experiences of high-risk situations are documented.	☐☐☐☐☐☐☐☐☐☐☐☐☐	/ = ☐ 4
5. Client's coping strategies are documented.	☐☐☐☐☐☐☐☐☐☐☐☐☐	/ = ☐ 5
6. Discharge note or summary includes:		
• referral source and circumstances surrounding referral	☐	
• number of sessions attended (indicating completion of program or early discharge)	☐	
• identification of risk situations and coping strategies	☐	
• overall progress (abstinence/nonabstinence) andsubstance use goal at discharge	☐	
• documentation of future treatment plans aftercare arrangements.	☐	/ 5 = ☐ 6

```
┌─────────────────────────────────────────────────────────────────────────┐
│                        OVERALL AUDIT SCORE                                │
│                                                                           │
│  Total number of items present                                            │
│  ─────────────────────────────  = ─────────────────  x 100 =             │
│  Total number of items applicable                    ───────────── %      │
│                                                                           │
└─────────────────────────────────────────────────────────────────────────┘
```

- N/A should be entered if the client did not attend the session or the criteria item was not relevant.

- Additional sessions are optional and apply only to individual Structured Relapse Prevention counselling.

Scoring

- **X** indicates a deficiency; ✓ indicates criterion is met.

- N/A neither adds to nor subtracts from the score.

- The individual audit score for each of the six criteria items is calculated by dividing the total number of points accumulated for that criterion (numerator) by the total number of sessions attended for which that criterion was relevant (denominator). The number is rounded off to two decimal points.

$$\begin{array}{cccccccc} 1 & 2 & 3 & 4 & 5 & 6 & 7 & 8 \end{array}$$

(e.g., | N/A | ✔ | ✔ | X | ✔ | ✔ | ✔ | ✔ | = 6/7 = .86)

- The same applies to criteria item 6, Discharge Note, except that the denominator is always 5.

- The overall audit score is derived by dividing the total number of items present by the total number of applicable (relevant) items, and multiplying by 100.

APPENDIX B: Clinical Background Articles

Motivational Interviewing

ELSBETH TUPKER AND LORNA SAGORSKY

Introduction

Motivational interviewing (MI) is one of the most significant innovations of the past 30 years in the way counsellors approach their clients who use substances (Health Canada, 1999; Project MATCH Research Group, 1997; Miller et al., 1998). Instead of struggling with people's resistance and lack of motivation to change their alcohol or other drug use, the MI counsellor expects to encounter ambivalence, sees it as a natural aspect of behaviour change and makes it the focus of counselling. In this approach the counsellor understands that change is a process that goes through stages. The counsellor starts "where the client is at," and explores and builds motivation. The relationship between the counsellor and the client is based on equality: rather than the counsellor telling or teaching the client how to deal with problems, the client is seen as the expert on his or her own situation. In the end, it is the client who talks about changing, not the counsellor.

MI is best defined as "a client centered, directive method for enhancing intrinsic motivation to change by exploring and resolving ambivalence" (Miller & Rollnick, 2002, p. 25). MI is unique in being simultaneously client centred and directive. The interview focuses on the concerns and perspectives of the client, but the counsellor directs the interview by responding selectively and strategically to resolve ambivalence, facilitate talk about change and diminish resistance.

Counsellors intending to use motivational interviewing in their work must not only learn the strategies and techniques, but must also embrace the underlying spirit and principles of MI. This chapter will discuss these issues, as well as the stages of change, how to deal with resistance, the use of MI at assessment, and the adaptation of MI for clients with concurrent addiction and mental health disorders.

Reprinted from S. Harrison and V. Carver (Eds.). (2004). *Alcohol and Drug Problems: A Practical Guide for Counsellors* (3rd ed.). Toronto: Centre for Addiction and Mental Health.

The Spirit of Motivational Interviewing

Motivational interviewing is an interpersonal style, or a "way of being" with the client. It is client centred in that the focus is on the client's concerns, and directive in that the therapist plays an active role in moving the client toward change. Thetherapeutic relationship is a partnership in which the counsellor takes a supporting rather than an authoritarian role. He or she creates a positive, collaborative interpersonal environment. The counsellor's focus is not on giving information or instilling insight, but rather on eliciting these things from the client. The counsellor respects the client's autonomy and freedom to choose his or her own course of action (Miller & Rollnick, 2002).

Motivation to change is a process that emerges from client-counsellor interactions. In the early stages, the counsellor's central task is to structure the sessions so the client talks about his or her concerns and ambivalence about changing. The counsellor encourages the client to explore the pros and cons of changing and of not changing. By asking evocative questions, the counsellor helps the client talk about how drug use fits with his or her life goals and values. This process lets the client see the discrepancy between a life of drug use and what he or she truly values, and leads the client to realize that something needs to change. When the client starts totalk about changing, the counsellor helps increase the client's confideence and commitment to change.

The counselling style of MI is gentle elicitation, rather than teaching or persuasion. Persuasion tends to put clients in a defensive position, and entrenches resistance as the client tries to convince the counsellor that his or her perspective is right. Resistance by the client is a sign that the counsellor is moving too fast, and needs to change his or her motivational strategy. The stages of change model, described below, helps the counsellor choose strategies appropriate to the client's readiness to change (Miller & Rollnick, 2002).

The Stages of Change Model

An important theoretical contribution to motivational interviewing is Prochaska and DiClemente's "transtheoretical" or "stages of change" model (DiClemente & Velasquez, 2002). The theory initially explained how people who smoke go about changing their behaviour (Prochaska & DiClemente, 1983). The model has since been generalized to other addictive behaviours. It is usually depicted as a wheel or spiral of different change stages. In each stage, the client needs to focus on specific tasks that will enable movement to the next stage. The stages of change model asserts that a "slip" or relapse is part of the cyclical nature of changing substance use. This model of change has also been successfully applied to various other behaviours, including weight control, high-fat diets, adolescent delinquency, condom use, sunscreen use and mammography screening (Prochaska et al., 1994; Soden & Murray, 1997).

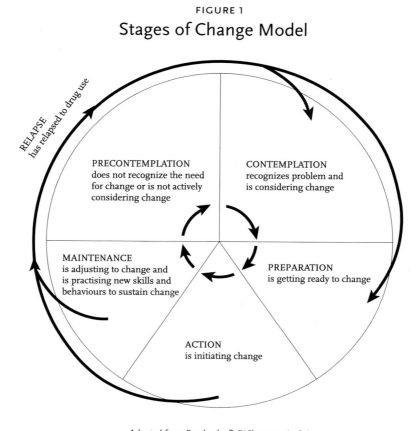

FIGURE 1

Stages of Change Model

Adapted from Prochaska & DiClemente (1982).

PRECONTEMPLATION STAGE

Clients at the precontemplation stage do not recognize that they have a problem and are not thinking about change. They usually resist treatment; they feel others are pushing them and they do not intend to change. The therapeutic tasks at this stage are to build the client-counsellor relationship, and to let the client know the consequences of his or her behaviour. Strategies include providing clinical feedback that is relevant to clients and that may elicit concern, or asking clients to weigh the good things and less good things about their substance use.

CONTEMPLATION STAGE

Clients in this stage recognize some of the negative consequences of their substance use, but are ambivalent about changing. They see a need to change but are not ready to do it. This stage may last a long time, so it is important to keep the client engaged. The counsellor's task at this stage is to resolve the client's ambivalence. Strategies include exploring the pros and cons of changing and of not changing, and helping clients to see discrepancies between their drug use and their values.

PREPARATION STAGE

In this stage, clients are thinking about changing in the near future. They may still be ambivalent, so the therapeutic task is to build commitment to change. The counsellor should set goals and make plans for change at a pace that is comfortable for the client. Clinical strategies at this stage focus on eliciting the client's ideas for change, and providing options, advice and direction.

ACTION STAGE

Clients in the action stage are changing; they are giving up old behaviour patterns and replacing them with new ones. There is a lot of activity and energy to try new things. The therapeutic task is to build self-belief and continue with goal setting and implementation. Counsellors can do this by exploring the importance of change and the client's level of confidence about making a change.

MAINTENANCE STAGE

In the maintenance stage, clients are making more profound and long-term changes that support the new behaviours of the action stage. The counsellor's task is to generalize new behaviours, focus on preventing relapse, and prepare clients to cope with high-risk situations and to deal constructively with relapse, should this occur.

RELAPSE

In this model, relapse is considered not as a failure, but as a common and useful aspect of lasting change. Clients in relapse may revert back to an earlier stage, such as precontemplation or contemplation. The therapeutic task in this case is to encourage clients to learn from the relapse and to re-evaluate their goals and strategies.

Practitioners following the stages of change model tailor their counselling to the stage that the client is in. Moving through the stages is not necessarily a fluid process, and most people revert back to an earlier stage in the change process at some point. Therefore counsellors need to identify at assessment which stage the client is in, and to continue to monitor the client's stage of change throughout counselling. Failure to focus on the tasks of the appropriate stage can lead the client to resist treatment, or even to drop out. Motivational interviewing can be employed in all stages of change; the MI strategies appropriate to each stage are discussed further throughout this chapter (DiClemente & Velasquez, 2002).

Principles behind Motivational Interviewing

Miller and Rollnick (2002) have identified four broad clinical principles to help counsellors motivate clients:

- Express empathy.
- Support self-efficacy.
- Roll with resistance.
- Develop discrepancy.

EXPRESS EMPATHY

Empathy and its expression were identified in the work of Rogers (1965). He maintained that counsellors who show an understanding of the client's situation from the client's own perspective, without judging, criticizing or blaming, will be the most successful in treating people. The counsellor accepts the client, and listens respectfully with a desire to understand the client's perspective. Paradoxically, this acceptance of people as they are seems to give them freedom to change, whereas insistent non-acceptance ("You're not OK: you have to change") can have the effect of keeping people as they are. This attitude of acceptance and respect also builds a therapeutic alliance and supports the client's self-esteem—an important condition for change (Miller & Rollnick, 2002; Soden & Murray, 1997).

SUPPORT SELF-EFFICACY

Self-efficacy refers to a client's belief that he or she can do something (Bandura, 1977). It is an important motivator for people who are changing their use of alcohol or other drugs. To instill confidence, the counsellor can explore the client's past successes or relate examples of others who have succeeded in the same circumstances. It is also important to maintain the client's hope for change, even when progress is slow. Counsellors should let the client know there is no single way to achieve success, and that it is often a process of trial and error.

ROLL WITH RESISTANCE

Rather than challenge resistance through persuasion or argument, the counsellor uses the energy of the resistance to further explore the client's views. This approach tends to lower resistance, because the client is not forced to argue for his or her point of view. Specific strategies for dealing with resistance will be discussed later in the chapter.

DEVELOP DISCREPANCY

"Developing discrepancy," or creating cognitive dissonance, allows the counsellor "to create and amplify, in the client's mind, a discrepancy between present behavior and broader goals" (Miller & Rollnick, 1991, p. 56). Through this process, the client becomes aware of the gap between where he or she is and where he or she would like to be. This occurs when a client realizes that his or her substance use conflicts with personal goals such as good health, vocational or financial success or healthy relationships. Such awareness creates a motivating force that tips the balance of ambivalence in the direction of changing the problem. When successfully done, this process enables the client, not the counsellor, to articulate the reasons for change (Soden & Murray, 1997).

Traps to Avoid

Learning to do motivational interviewing requires not doing certain counterproductive things, as well as applying the principles and techniques of MI. To build the client's motivation to change, the counsellor must avoid certain traps, discussed below (Miller & Rollnick, 2002).

QUESTION AND ANSWER TRAP

A question and answer interview tends to make clients relatively passive, and does not encourage them to explore the deeper levels of their experience and perceptions. It also creates a hierarchy, in which the counsellor alone determines the course and content of the interview. Counsellors should avoid asking more than three questions in a row—rather, the counsellor should be listening and following along with the client.

CONFRONTATION-DENIAL TRAP

The confrontation-denial trap is only one of a number of problematic dynamics that may arise from a counsellor's need to preserve his or her own self-esteem. This situation may arise if, for example, the clinician is so task oriented that he or she gives little consideration to important process issues, such as the client's need to own the therapeutic process. The result is that the counsellor becomes more directive and prescriptive, while the client becomes more entrenched and resistant (Miller & Sovereign, 1989; Soden & Murray, 1997).

EXPERT TRAP

In the expert trap, the clinician solves the client's problems and imposes "corrective" measures to rectify dysfunctional situations. As with the confrontation-denial trap, the client's self-belief and self-esteem are not increased and may even be harmed (Miller & Rollnick, 1991; Soden & Murray, 1997).

PREMATURE FOCUS TRAP

This trap occurs when the counsellor raises the issue of the client's substance use problem before the client is prepared to discuss it. The client may then become defensive, and deny or minimize the issue. To avoid this trap, the counsellor must focus on the client's issues and concerns, rather than his or her own agenda (Miller & Rollnick, 2002; Soden & Murray, 1997).

LABELLING TRAP

This trap relates to the popular idea that in order to change, a client must first accept that he or she is an "alcoholic" or a "drug addict." Given the stigma usually attached to these labels, it is understandable that people will resist adopting them. People do not need to accept a label or diagnosis in order to change, and so MI avoids the use of labels (Miller & Rollnick, 1991).

BLAMING TRAP

Clients who blame others for their problems, and counsellors who point out that clients' difficulties are their own fault, are pursuing a course that does not help the client change. It is best to maintain a "no-fault" policy, and focus instead on what is troubling the client and what he or she can do about it (Miller & Rollnick, 1991).

Interactional Techniques

Motivational interviewing relies on four basic techniques that are captured by the acronym OARS (Miller & Rollnick, 2002):

- open-ended questions
- affirmations
- reflective listening
- summaries.

To do MI successfully, a clinician needs to become skilled in these techniques. This involves learning what to say, as well as knowing when to use each technique. A training workshop may help the counsellor learn and practise these ways of working. In addition, demonstration tapes made by Miller and Rollnick (1998) show how many of the techniques are used.

OPEN-ENDED QUESTIONS

Open-ended questions are questions that cannot be answered by a simple yes or no or by just a few words. Instead these questions invite the client to talk about his or her life and concerns. Typical opening questions are "What brings you here today?" or "Could you tell me what has happened since we met last week?" Open-ended questions are intended to create momentum, and to help the client explore his or her situation and the possibility of change (Miller & Rollnick, 2002).

AFFIRMATIONS

These are statements by the counsellor that acknowledge clients' strengths. People with substance use problems often have failures, and may doubt their ability to make things better. Pointing out strengths in a sincere way can instil much-needed hope and confidence (Miller & Rollnick, 2002).

REFLECTIVE LISTENING

Reflective listening is the most central and most challenging skill used in MI. It involves listening attentively and then responding to what the client has said. Reflective responses are a counsellor's best guess at what the client means. The reflection is not intended to question the client's meaning, but to demonstrate understanding and acceptance. Therefore the reflective listener gives this meaning back in the form of a statement, not a question; the intonation of a reflective listening statement goes down at the end, not up as it would in a question (Miller & Rollnick, 2002).

The purpose of reflections is to elicit more exploratory talk from the client, and to move the client toward thinking and talking about change. Merely echoing what the client has said would slow the momentum. Instead the counsellor reflects a part of what was said to explore it more deeply; or the counsellor can touch on what he or she wants the client to talk about next, in order to move the interview forward.

Simple reflections may focus on feelings or on the content of the client's statements, or they may link feelings, thoughts and content. Deeper reflections are about the meaning of the client's experience, or about universal, spiritual or existential issues. Simple reflections are used in the early stages of treatment, while deeper reflections become more appropriate as the relationship develops and the client presents more complex material. Typically the flow of the interview involves an open-ended question followed by two to three reflections (Miller & Rollnick, 2002). Consider the client statement below:

> I came to see you today because my mother passed away this week. You know that she was ill for a long time, and although it's a relief for her, it's very hard for me. I always wanted her to be proud of me, but I know I was always a big disappointment to her, being an alcoholic and never doing what she wanted me to do. I always felt that I never pleased her, and now it's too late to make any changes. And I loved her so much. How can you help me?

Various counsellor reflections are possible. *Echoing* is an exact repetition of the client's words.

> You loved your mother very much and now she has died.

Paraphrasing is repetition with some added content.

> You feel you were always a disappointment to your mother, and now that she has died you can't make it right.

Getting the gist involves repetition and showing understanding by using the client's words.

> Things are very hard for you now. You are mourning your mother's death and on top of that you're very saddened by the fact that you never lived up to her expectations.

Reflecting feelings is talking about the client's affect.

> There are many feelings you're experiencing now. You're very sad that your mother has died, and you're also guilty that you never did what she would have wanted for you. And now there's also a feeling of frustration because whatever you do now, you can't change the past.

Reflecting feelings and content involves linking thought, feelings and events.

> Your mother, whom you loved a great deal, has just died and has left you feeling very upset since you always wanted to do right by her, and because of your drinking you were unable to do this. Now you're in a position where nothing can be changed.

Reflecting meaning involves reflecting the experience as a whole, including personal, human, spiritual, universal or existential elements.

Living up to your mother's dreams for you was something you always felt you needed to do as a son who loved his mother. But because of your heavy drinking you never felt you achieved this, and you're very sad that now your mother has passed away those ambitions will never be fulfilled.

SUMMARIES

Summaries are a special form of reflective listening in which the counsellor reflects back what the client has been saying over a longer period of the interaction. Summaries communicate the counsellor's interest and build rapport. Summaries can focus on important aspects of the interview, make linkages, as well as change the direction of the interaction. This technique is particularly useful when the counsellor wants to move on from an interaction that is not productive.

Another important approach is eliciting change talk. This is a technique that helps the client resolve ambivalence. Change talk, or self-motivational statements, refers to statements the client makes about the need for change, the benefits of change, his or her hopes for change, or the intention to change. A central goal of motivational interviewing is for clients to make self-motivational statements that articulate concern, recognize that a problem exists, express an intention to change or show optimism about the possibility of change (Miller & Rollnick, 2002). The counsellor may elicit change talk by, for example, asking clients evocative questions, such as an open-ended question about how the client sees things or what his or her concerns are, or asking clients how important something is to them. Once clients begin to talk about change, help them elaborate. The more they hear themselves talking about change, the stronger their commitment to change will become (Miller & Rollnick, 2002).

Practical Strategies in Motivational Interviewing

Following are some simple practical strategies to create a motivating and collaborative way of working with a client, while getting the information you need in a short time.

REVIEW OF A TYPICAL DAY

The client relates what happens in a typical day, including his or her use of substances. This is a good way to build rapport without focusing on the problem. It not only helps the counsellor to know and understand the client better, but also gives a realistic picture of how substance use fits into the client's life. Reflective listening is used to further explore what the client tells you (Mid-Atlantic Addiction Technology Transfer Center, 2003).

LOOKING BACK

This involves the client discussing how things were before his or her substance use began. It gives a good picture of the client's lifestyle, and allows the client to reflect on the changes (usually losses) that have come about since the substance use started. The use of OARS techniques during this process helps the counsellor explore and elaborate on useful material, such as the impact of substance use (Miller & Rollnick, 2002).

LOOKING FORWARD

Another technique is to have the client reflect on the impact of continuing his or her current behaviours. The counsellor asks the client what things will be like in the future, given the current state of affairs and assuming things won't change. The client typically considers the impact of substance use over a long period and then examines the anticipated cumulative effects on his or her quality of life. It can also be useful for the client to contemplate the future without the problem behaviour. This helps pinpoint the effect of the problem behaviour on the client's lifestyle. Looking back and looking forward may both be used to elicit self-motivational statements, one of the principal goals of motivational interviewing (Miller & Rollnick, 2002).

LOOKING AT THE GOOD THINGS AND THE NOT-SO-GOOD THINGS

In this technique, the client is asked to look at both sides of substance use. In MI it is understood that clients use substances because there is a "payoff." The counsellor's acknowledgment of this truth is very powerful for the client. It builds rapport and allows the client to feel understood because, from this point of view, his or her substance use makes sense.

Clients are much more ready to explore the not-so-good things after they have articulated the advantages of their substance use. The phrase "not so good" has been chosen carefully to avoid the implication of a problem (e.g., the "bad things"), which can be a barrier to moving forward.

The counsellor then summarizes the two types of consequences of substance use, and gives the client time to think about this material and reflect back his or her thoughts. This helps the client contrast the positive and negative consequences, which often results in a better understanding of the full impact of the not-so-good things (Mid-Atlantic Addiction Technology Transfer Center, 2003).

DECISIONAL BALANCE

Once the client has acknowledged that the substance use has both positive and negative consequences, the counsellor can do a cost-benefit analysis. The client looks first at the pros and cons of staying the same and then at the pros and cons of change. This technique gives a good overall view of what change will mean to the client, in both positive and negative terms. It helps the client understand which payoffs of substance use will need to be compensated for, and what benefits can be anticipated. Looking at the entire picture can help the client to see how to create a different lifestyle, and to determine whom he or she can become in the future through the choices made now (Mid-Atlantic Addiction Technology Transfer Center, 2003).

EXPLORING VALUES

Focusing on a client's values can stimulate motivation for change and self-motivational statements. Often people have a vision of their "ideal self," which they feel defines them and the things that are important to them. Spending time exploring a client's values, and then examining the effect of substance use on this vision of self, can sometimes move clients quickly and powerfully toward change. As inconsistencies emerge between the person's behaviour and his or her deeper sense of self and values, the person may become increasingly aware that while substance use meets short-term needs, it does not fulfil higher values or lead to long-term satisfaction (Mid-Atlantic Addiction Technology Transfer Center, 2003).

DISCUSSING THE STAGES OF CHANGE MODEL

It can be useful to explain the stages of change model and to talk with clients about where they are in the change process. This can help them understand some of the stumbling blocks they will encounter, and help them realize that change may take more time and effort than they (and interested others) may expect. In addition, ask clients to look back at previous changes they have made, and to remember how the change process occurred at that time. A new understanding of what moved the client into action in the past may help him or her change now.

EXPLORING THE IMPORTANCE OF CHANGE

In order for clients to make changes, they need to feel that change is important. Ask clients how important a particular change is to them, on a scale of one to 10. If it does not rate very highly, change is less likely. Identifying the person's most important goal may motivate change, by helping the person realize that if the substance use does not change, the person won't reach his or her ultimate goal (Mid-Atlantic Addiction Technology Transfer Center, 2003).

EXPLORING CONFIDENCE

The more confidence a person has in his or her ability to change, the more likely it will happen. Have the client rate his or her confidence on a scale of one to 10, and then help the person find ways to become more confident (Mid-Atlantic Addiction Technology Transfer Center, 2003).

PLANNING CHANGE

Once it is established that the client wants to change, planning for change needs to be done sensitively and with the client taking the lead. As many options and choices as possible should be presented and considered. The pace of change needs to match what the client can handle. Moving too quickly can set a client back in the stages of change. Initially, work on short-term and simple plans, so it is easier for the client to succeed. Planning for change is a collaborative effort: the client is the expert on himself or herself, and on what he or she wants and can do, while the therapist gives information on possible ways to make changes (Mid-Atlantic Addiction Technology Transfer Center, 2003).

Resistance

In the substance use field it is common to encounter people who are considered resistant. In motivational interviewing, resistance is seen not as a character trait but as a specific behaviour pattern in the interaction between the client and the counsellor. The extent to which clients "resist" is strongly influenced by the therapist's style (Patterson & Forgatch, 1985). MI techniques have been developed to help decrease clients' resistance. Some signs of resistance are arguing, interrupting, negating and ignoring. These behaviours usually signal that the counsellor needs to change the interaction.

If you understand what causes resistance, you can prevent it. Often it occurs when the client and counsellor have different agendas or goals, or when the respective roles are unclear. You can prevent this by agreeing on an agenda before the session and exploring the client's hopes and goals before making any assumptions. To avoid a misunderstanding about the respective roles of the client and therapist, it is best to talk about role expectations early on.

Resistance can also arise when the counsellor uses strategies that are not appropriate for the client's stage of change. Check in regularly with the client to learn where he or she is in the change process, since the client's stage of change may fluctuate over the course of treatment.

Some counsellor behaviours can lead the client to become resistant or to increase resistance. Generally this occurs if the counsellor "takes charge" of the session, and the client-counsellor partnership is broken. It may happen if the counsellor falls into one of the traps discussed earlier, such as confrontation, blaming, labelling or acting as the expert. When a counsellor argues for change or takes up the side of the client's ambivalence that is in favour of change, the client's natural response is to provide counter-arguments. This kind of interaction, in which the therapist does all the work and provides all the change talk while the client argues against it, is unproductive and usually entrenches resistance.

There are certain times when resistance is more common. Resistance is usually a sign of ambivalence. If we think of resistance as a client's attempt to stop hidden, often painful information from becoming visible both to others and to himself or herself, then it is understandable that the client will resist at certain points. For example, a client may resist when considering whether a problem really exists (contemplation stage), when facing the loss of behaviours and lifestyle (action stage), or when facing the risks of new behaviours and lifestyle (action or maintenance stage).

Clients in the precontemplation stage are unaware of a need to change or are simply unwilling to change. These clients, who are in treatment only because they are being "pushed" by others to do something about their substance use, can be particularly challenging. Their resistance may take the form of reluctance, rebellion, resignation or rationalization (DiClemente & Velasquez, 2002).

When a person is *reluctant* to change, it may be due to inertia, lack of knowledge, fear or lack of comfort with the current situation. With these clients it is useful to listen carefully and gently provide feedback and information. It may take considerable time before they move on.

Rebellious clients are usually aware of the need to change their substance use, but are too invested in it to give it up. They can be very argumentative, and so the best approach is to roll with the resistance by letting them express their thoughts and suggesting a range of options to choose from.

Clients who are *resigned* typically feel overwhelmed by the thought of change, and have likely had many failed attempts. They can be low in energy and involvement. With these clients, the focus is on building confidence using reflections and affirmations.

Clients who *rationalize* typically take no ownership of the problem, blame others, have all the answers and get into debates. With these people, the counsellor avoids arguing and acknowledges the positives of the substance use. Reflections can be used to encourage reframing (seeing things in a new perspective).

DEALING WITH RESISTANCE

Generally it is helpful to join with resistant clients, letting them know that you understand their resistance. Talking about the resistance can help them to move forward. Some effective ways to deal with resistance include exploring ambivalence, identifying achievements and strengths, and offering choices and optimism that things can change.

The following types of reflection illustrate ways of dealing with resistance (Miller & Rollnick, 2002).

Simple reflection

Respond to resistance with nonresistance; your response may include a small shift in emphasis, but should acknowledge the client's perception or disagreement.

Client: "I couldn't change even if I wanted to."

Counsellor: "You can't see any way that you believe would work, and you might fail if you tried."

Amplified reflection

Reflect what the client has said in an amplified or exaggerated way (while avoiding a sarcastic tone) to elicit the other side of the client's ambivalence.

Client: "I can hold my liquor just fine. I'm still standing when others are under the table."

Counsellor: "So, you really have nothing to worry about—alcohol can't hurt you at all."

Double-sided reflection

Acknowledge what the client has said, and add to it the other side of his or her ambivalence, using material that the client has talked about previously.

Client: "I don't smoke any more than my friends. What's wrong with a joint now and then?"

Counsellor: "I can see how this is confusing. On the one hand you've told me you're concerned about how smoking affects you, but on the other hand you're not using more than your friends. Hard to figure out!"

Shifting the focus

Move the client's attention away from a stumbling block that is getting in the way of progress.

Client: "OK, maybe I have got some problems with drinking, but I'm not an alcoholic."

Counsellor: "I don't think whether you are an alcoholic is the issue. What's more important is some of the things happening in your life. Tell me more about . . ."

Reframing

Acknowledge the validity of the client's perspective, and offer a new meaning or interpretation.

Client: "I can't stand how my parents are always on my case, now that they know I use."

Counsellor: "Their control is hard to live with, they must care a lot about you and are worried about what could happen."

Emphasizing personal control

Assure the client that he or she is in control.

Client: "My wife wants me to talk to you about our marriage, but I don't see the point."

Counsellor: "She's concerned about the relationship, but you have your own reasons for coming today and that's what is important."

Agreement with a twist

Offer initial agreement but with a slight twist or change in direction.

Client: "I just can't see doing anything about my drinking. It's too tough."

Counsellor: "It's really difficult, and yet it's amazing how much you've been able to accomplish in your life."

Assessment and Motivational Interviewing

Although assessment is usually separate from actual therapy, it is an important initial part of the continuum of care. It sets the tone for what clients can expect from the treatment system. Many clients do not return after assessment; there is evidence that a brief MI session at the time of assessment can make follow-through with treatment more likely. It also gives clients who drop out a positive and informative experience to reflect on, and this may lead them to return to treatment at a later date.

Most clients feel anxious and uncomfortable at this first point of contact. Joining with the client by acknowledging these feelings can be effective, and makes clear that you are interested in the client. If you let the client know that he or she has the knowledge and information you are looking for, it sets up a partnership and empowers the client as the expert on his or her own life. The notion that the client is in control and has choices is also an important concept to introduce at this early stage.

Feeding back the results of the client's assessment can enhance the client's motivation. It is most respectful to give the client the feedback material to read and interpret on his or her own, to establish that the client "owns" this information. The assessor should always be willing to answer questions and help interpret the assessment findings. Letting clients compare their assessment results with societal norms is an effective way to bring objectivity into the interpretation. When clients compare themselves to others, it can create discrepancy in their perceptions of what they think is normal or usual (Mid-Atlantic Addiction Technology Transfer Center, 2003).

Most assessments explore the negative consequences of substance use. It is helpful to look at payoffs at the same time, and to talk about the client's ambivalence about change. If you make it clear that ambivalence is normal and acceptable, it can help the client feel understood.

When assessment leads to treatment planning and referral, it is necessary to match the treatment plan to the stage of change the client is in.

Motivational Interviewing and Concurrent Disorders

A number of recent studies have illustrated the efficacy of the MI approach with clients who have concurrent addiction and mental health problems (Swanson et al., 1999; Bellock & DiClemente, 1999). People with concurrent disorders may have disabling symptoms and poor functional adjustment, and are frequently demoralized by past failures, which often makes it hard for them to engage in treatment. The relationship-building aspect of MI can help people with concurrent disorders develop a lasting and therapeutic relationship with a counsellor.

In a groundbreaking article, Martino et al. (2002) describe a model called DDMI (Dual Diagnosis Motivational Interviewing). The model includes two types of modifications of MI: (1) the use of MI strategies in an integrated concurrent disorders approach, in which both mental health and substance use are addressed in a co-ordinated way, often simultaneously, and (2) the adaptation of MI techniques for this population.

In the integrated approach, MI is used to target three areas: substance use, medication compliance and attending treatment. All the counsellor's questions, reflections and other MI techniques attempt to integrate and explore the connections between these three areas. For example, the counsellor might ask such questions as: "When you get high, how does it affect your psychiatric symptoms?" This integration can have a positive effect on the final outcome of the treatment.

The adaptation of MI techniques for people with concurrent disorders focuses on the basic principles of MI: expressing empathy, developing discrepancy, rolling with resistance and supporting self-efficacy. All the MI techniques are carried out more simply and concisely, keeping in mind the suggestions listed below:

- Always be clear.
- Always be concise.
- Talk about or reflect one topic at a time.
- Avoid compound questions; address one area at a time.
- Reflect frequently.
- Reflect only on the positive, logical material (not on, for example, disordered thinking or flights of ideas).
- Give enough time for a response.
- Summarize frequently, referring to small pieces of information.
- Summarize concrete verbal or visual material.
- Use appropriate metaphors.
- Use affirmations as much as possible (generally these clients receive very little praise or positive feedback, so this can be a very valuable tool).
- Try to attain some current goals related to the three change areas.
- Have patience.
- Expect relapses and use them as learning experiences.
- When doing a decisional balance, work only on the positives and negatives associated with change.
- Movement from contemplation to action is most likely to occur after a very significant negative experience that the client does not want to repeat in the future (Martino, 2002).

MI's non-confrontational approach and open discussion are a welcome change to the sometimes more traditional didactic and hierarchical methods found in the mental health field. Clients are made to feel that their opinions have some validity, and their points of view are incorporated into decisions. MI can be especially powerful when exploring the good things about substance use and gaining an understanding that use of substances may actually make sense, given the "payoffs" clients experience.

Some of the challenges that need to be addressed when working with the severely mentally ill are decreased cognitive functioning, difficulty reflecting on and acting from the experience of past behaviours, deficits in abstract reasoning, failure (or inability) to follow through on planned intentions, and a general state of anhedonia (inability to experience pleasure), which some escape through the use of substances.

Applications of Motivational Interviewing

Although motivational interviewing was first developed for and applied to alcohol and other drug use, this approach is now increasingly used to counsel people to make health-related changes in other areas, such as diet, exercise and taking medication (Rollnick et al., 1999). The interpersonal style of motivational interviewing can be used by health care professionals in many different settings, and is not necessarily confined to formal counselling.

A number of interventions for substance use problems are derived from MI. The Drinker's Check-up (Miller & Sovereign, 1989) gives meaningful personalized feedback to people with alcohol problems, following a comprehensive assessment. The style in which the feedback is given is non-judgmental, and clients are invited to reflect on the information and come to their own conclusions. A brief motivational intervention at assessment can mobilize the client to contemplate change.

Motivational Enhancement Therapy (MET) is a four-session intervention that applies motivational principles and techniques (Miller et al., 1995), and was developed in Project MATCH, a very large treatment outcome study. (Project MATCH Research Group, 1993). Other brief interventions, such as Structured Relapse Prevention (Annis et al., 1996) and Guided Self Change (Sobell & Sobell, 1993), apply motivational interviewing to the treatment of people with problem drinking, while First Contact (Breslin et al., 1999) applies MI to young people with substance use problems. All these manualized brief treatments are used widely throughout Ontario.

Empirical Support for Motivational Interviewing

Clinical research on the efficacy of MI is continuously evolving. MI is generally integrated with other treatment techniques and usually serves as a brief preparatory intervention or as the primary treatment. The studies are of applications of MI (AMI) rather than evaluations of pure MI. A recent review of 26 controlled studies of AMI did an analysis using expert ratings of outcomes and methodologies to arrive at a cumulative evidence score (Burke et al., 2002). The results of the 11 AMI studies that focused on alcohol problems compared extremely favourably with the results of other studies of common treatments for alcohol problems. Two of the studies, which used AMI as a first step to prepare the client for further treatment, found positive outcomes regarding drinking levels at three months after treatment. Five of the six studies that examined AMI as a primary treatment showed clear differences in alcohol consumption between those treated with AMI and controls who received no treatment. Generally, compared with other interventions equal in duration and scope, AMI appears to be as good as, but not better than, other treatments for alcohol problems.

As a treatment for other substance use problems, there is evidence from the five studies that were reviewed that AMI is more effective as a first step to more intensive treatment than other credible approaches. As a stand-alone intervention, AMI can be as effective as more extensive group therapy and significantly more effective than no treatment. To date AMI has not been shown to be effective in smoking cessation or reducing HIV risk behaviours. There are some early indications that AMI increases treatment adherence, an important predictor of positive outcome (Zweben & Zuckoff, 2002). In particular, two studies of people with concurrent disorders suggest that AMI, when added to inpatient treatment, improves overall treatment adherence (Martino et al., 2002; Swanson et al., 1999).

While evidence suggests that MI works in the applications noted above, it is less clear how and why it works and with whom. One study found evidence that angry people responded better to MI than less angry people, but clearly more research is needed to help pinpoint when MI is most effective (Miller & Rollnick, 2002).

Conclusion

MI's non-confrontational, exploratory approach offers counsellors a more collaborative way of relating to their clients than do most other substance use therapies, and provides a welcome change from more didactic and hierarchal counselling methods. Clients are made to feel that their opinions are valid, and their points of view are incorporated into decision making. Therefore it is a good alternative for counsellors who aim to empower their clients to participate in their own treatment. The practical strategies of MI are designed to reduce the client's resistance and increase motivation for change—both major challenges in the treatment of substance use. The approach can be readily integrated with other treatments, and there are numerous resources available to help counsellors master its techniques.

REFERENCES

Annis, H., Herie, M. & Watkin Merrick, L. (1996). *Structured Relapse Prevention: An Outpatient Counselling Approach.* Toronto: Addiction Research Foundation.

Bandura, A. (1977). Self-efficacy: Toward a unifying theory of behavioral change. *Psychological Review, 84,* 191–215.

Bellock, A. & DiClemente, C. (1999). Treating substance abuse among patients with schizophrenia. *Psychiatric Services, 50*(1), 75–80.

Breslin, C., Sdao-Jarvie, K., Tupker, E. & Pearlman, S. (1999). *First Contact: A Brief Treatment for Young Substance Users.* Toronto: Centre for Addiction and Mental Health.

Burke, L., Arkowitz, H. & Dunn, C. (2002). The efficacy of motivational interviewing and its adaptations: What we know so far. In W.R. Miller & S. Rollnick (Eds.), *Motivational Interviewing: Preparing People for Change.* New York: Guilford Press.

DiClemente, C.C. & Velasquez, M.M. (2002). Motivational interviewing and the stages of change. In W.R. Miller & S. Rollnick (Eds.), *Motivational Interviewing: Preparing People for Change.* New York: Guilford Press.

Health Canada. (1999). *Best Practices—Substance Abuse Treatment and Rehabilitation.* Cat. No. H39-438/1998E. Ottawa: Minister of Public Works and Government Services.

Martino, S., Carroll, K., Kostas, D., Perkins, J. & Rounsaville, B. (2002). Dual Diagnosis Motivational Interviewing: A modification of Motivational Interviewing for substance-abusing patients with psychotic disorders. *Journal of Substance Abuse Treatment, 23*, 297–308.

Mid-Atlantic Addiction Technology Transfer Center. (2003). *MI Counseling Strategies.* Available: www.motivationalinterviewing.org.

Miller, W.R., Andrews, N.R., Wilbourne, P. & Bennett, M.E. (1998). A wealth of alternatives: Effective treatments for alcohol problems. In W.R. Miller & N. Heather (Eds.), *Treating Addictive Behaviours: Processes of Change* (2nd ed.; pp. 121–132). New York: Plenum Press.

Miller, W.R. & Rollnick, S. (1998). *Motivational Interviewing Video Series.* Albuquerque, NM: Horizon West Productions.

Miller, W.R. & Rollnick, S. (1999). *Teaching Motivational Interviewing: Materials for Trainers.* Albuquerque, NM: MINT-6.

Miller, W.R. & Rollnick, S. (2002). *Motivational Interviewing: Preparing People for Change.* New York: Guilford Press.

Miller, W.R. & Sovereign, R.G. (1989). The check-up: A model for early intervention in addictive behaviors. In T. Loberg, W.R. Miller, P.E. Nathan & G.A. Marlatt (Eds.), *Addictive Behaviors: Prevention and Early Intervention* (pp. 219–231). Amsterdam: Swets and Zeitlinger.

Miller, W.R., Zweben, A., DiClemente, C.C. & Rychtarik, R.G. (1995). *Motivational Enhancement Therapy.* Washington, DC: National Institute of Health.

Patterson, G.A. & Forgatch, M.S. (1985). Therapist behavior as a determinant for client non-compliance: A paradox for the behavior modifier. *Journal of Consulting and Clinical Psychology, 53*, 846–851.

Prochaska, J.O. & DiClemente, C.C. (1982). Transtheoretical therapy: Toward a more integrative model of change. *Psychotherapy: Theory, Research and Practice, 19*(3), 276–288.

Prochaska, J.O. & DiClemente, C.C. (1983). Stages and processes of self-change of smoking: Toward an integrative model of change. *Journal of Consulting and Clinical Psychology, 51*, 390–395.

Prochaska, J.O., DiClemente, C.C. & Norcross, J. (1994). *Changing for Good.* New York: William Morrow.

Project MATCH Research Group (1997). Project MATCH secondary a priori hypotheses. *Addiction, 92*, 1671–1698.

Rogers, C.R. (1965). *Client-Centered Therapy.* Boston: Houghton Mifflin.

Rollnick, S., Mason, P. & Butler, C. (1999). *Health Behavior Change: A Guide for Practitioners.* London: Churchill Livingstone.

Sobell, M. & Sobell, L. (1993). *Problem Drinkers: Guided Self-Change Treatment.* New York: Guilford Press.

Soden, T. & Murray, R. (1997). Motivational interviewing techniques. In S. Harrison & V. Carver (Eds.), *Alcohol and Drug Problems: A Practical Guide for Counsellors* (2nd ed.; pp. 19–59). Toronto: Addiction Research Foundation.

Swanson, A.J., Pantalon, M.V. & Cohen, K.R. (1999). Motivational interviewing and treatment adherence among psychiatric and dually diagnosed patients. *Journal of Nervous and Mental Disease, 187*, 630–635.

Zweben, A. & Zuckoff, A. (2002). Motivational interviewing and treatment adherence. In W.R. Miller & S. Rollnick (Eds.), *Motivational Interviewing: Preparing People for Change* (pp. 299–319). New York: Guilford Press.

Relapse Prevention

MARILYN A. HERIE AND LYN WATKIN-MEREK

Introduction

The chronic, relapsing nature of alcohol and other drug problems has been recognized since the early 1970s (Hunt et al., 1971). In the late 1970s and early 1980s, researchers began to focus on the factors that affect the process of relapse (Litman et al., 1979, 1984; Wilson, 1980) and on the development of "relapse prevention" treatment strategies (Marlatt & Gordon, 1985; Annis, 1986). Despite advances in substance use treatment, relapse prevention continues to be a major issue. For this reason, many researchers have come to regard addiction as a "chronic relapsingdisorder" (Dimeff & Marlatt, 1998). In other words, relapse prevention should be regarded as a series of small steps towards change rather than as a wholesale solution to the problem of relapse.

Relapse is defined as a failure to maintain behavioural change, rather than a failure to initiate it. Treatment approaches based on social learning theory, specifically Bandura's theory of self-efficacy, hold that the strategies that are effective in initiating a change in drinking or drug use behaviour may be ineffective at maintaining that change over time and avoiding relapse (Bandura, 1977, 1978, 1986). Definitions of relapse have evolved over time from "all or nothing" (relapse occurs at the time of first drink or drug use) to consider the nuances of quantity/frequency measures, lifestyle changes and progress in the direction of change (Dimeff & Marlatt, 1998).

This chapter examines the nature of relapse, along with some key questions: What is it? How do we define it? Are there problems with the term "relapse" itself? We then briefly review the major relapse prevention models developed by Terrence Gorski (1989) and Alan Marlatt (1985, 1996) and the Structured Relapse Prevention manual-based approach developed by Helen Annis and colleagues (1996). This review is followed by a discussion of research and practice implications of relapse prevention with diverse client populations.

Reprinted from S. Harrison and V. Carver (Eds.). (2004). *Alcohol and Drug Problems: A Practical Guide for Counsellors* (3rd ed.). Toronto: Centre for Addiction and Mental Health.

The chapter concludes with a brief discussion of empirical support for relapse prevention approaches.

Toward a Definition of Relapse

Addiction research and treatment has often been guided by binary thinking, where "alcoholism" can be compared to pregnancy: "either you have it or you don't, and there is nothing in between." (Miller, 1996, p. S15). This overly simplistic conceptualization of a complex problem has also been applied to treatment outcomes, judging them as either successful (abstinent) or relapsed (non-abstinent). But if treatment success were always judged solely on abstinence alone, almost all who complete treatment would be considered to have relapsed.

As Miller (1996) puts it:

> Treating addictive behaviors seems not so much like turning off a water faucet, but more like diminishing and altering the flow of . . . water. At a societal level, it is like trying to change the flowing course of a stream. Sometimes the change is slight, and sometimes it is dramatic. Sometimes it is long lasting, and sometimes the stream quickly flows back into its original course (p. S16).

Categorizing substance use treatment outcomes as either abstinent or non-abstinent ignores the behavioural changes that may occur post-treatment. For example, there may be changes in the number of drinks consumed, the number of drinking days and the frequency of binge use. There may also be changes in the use of other drugs, including prescription, over-the-counter and nicotine.

Defining and categorizing types of relapse is also problematic. Asking a client whether he or she had a relapse can be interpreted in a number of ways: Did you drink (at all)? Did you drink above a certain threshold? Or, did you drink more than the limit you had set for yourself?

Miller (1996) suggests that the term "relapse" itself imposes "binary decision" or "either/or" rules on a person's behaviour. Such rules, used to determine whether or not a person has relapsed, are based on a number of often arbitrarily applied criteria, such as:
- threshold (the amount of substance use)
- window (the period of time judged)
- reset (the period of abstinence required before a person can be considered to have relapsed)
- polydrugs (the types of substance use that constitute a relapse)
- consequences (behaviours/consequences associated with substance use required before a person can be considered to have relapsed)
- verification (self-report or collateral reports).

That there is no single empirically or theoretically ideal combination of these factors highlights the inherent ambiguity in the term "relapse." Miller (1996) further points out that the concept of relapse can, in itself, be harmful in its implicit imposition of a value judgment:

> Backsliding is an old synonym for sin, and few would fail to grasp which side of the relapse dichotomy is judged the more desirable. "Relapsed" has a connotation of failure, weakness and shame, of having fallen from a state of grace. Such overtones are likely to compromise self-regard and add needless affective meaning to what is a rather common behavioral event (p. S25).

Defining relapse—once thought to be straightforward—has proven to be more complex. Current definitions tend to be critical of the concept, and to take the person's movement in the direction of change into account.

Perspectives on Relapse Prevention

The theory and practice of the major perspectives in relapse prevention are summarized here, followed by an overview of a manual-based approach, Structured Relapse Prevention (Annis et al., 1996), which was developed from Marlatt's (1985) model.

THE GORSKI RELAPSE PREVENTION MODEL

Terrence Gorski's model focuses on relapse prevention in the context of an abstinence-based, 12-step approach. In Gorski's view, chemical dependence is a disease that can be remitted only through total abstinence from all substances. Abstinence, however, is only the first step towards sobriety, which is defined as "a lifestyle that promotes continued physical, psychological, social and spiritual health" (Gorski, 1989, p. 3).

Gorski divides recovery into a series of stages through which the "addicted" person must progress to achieve sobriety: (1) transition; (2) stabilization; (3) early recovery; (4) middle recovery; (5) late recovery; and (6) maintenance. Progression through these stages can take 18 months or longer. Gorski provides a framework of self-reflective and interpersonal exercises that are tailored to each of these recovery stages and complement the approach and teachings of the 12 steps of Alcoholics Anonymous (AA). These tasks are intended to be completed in parallel with attendance at AA meetings.

Many of the relapse prevention exercises introduced by Gorski reflect cognitive-behavioural principles and methods. For example, in the stage of "early recovery," Gorski encourages individuals to reflect on both the "drinking problem and the thinking problem" (as it is called in AA). The latter refers to the irrational thoughts, unmanageable feelings and self-defeating behaviours that can often lead to a relapse. Gorski asks individuals to write down what they think of their "addicted self" versus their "sober self," and to note the feelings they have about each "self." The object of the exercise is to challenge the belief and experience of alcohol or other drug use as positive or enjoyable.

Gorski's model is far-reaching and comprehensive in that it addresses physical and mental health, social support, family of origin issues and self-esteem. Although the model has not been well-researched, increasing attention is being given to the efficacy of AA approaches to addiction treatment (see www.niaaa.nih.gov/publications/aa49.htm for a summary of recent research findings).

Although Gorski's model has helped many people to recover from their addictions, his approach, which relies on 12-step principles and teachings, may alienate clients who do not find that approach congenial to their belief systems or preferences. For example, the self-help group Women for Sobriety was founded in response to the AA emphasis on powerlessness over alcohol or other drugs (step one of the 12 steps). These women believed that they had already surrendered their power to a great extent through their own past experiences of abuse and oppression and that they needed to focus on reclamation of their personal power. Not all clients want to address (or find relevant) the spiritual component in AA teachings, and the emphasis on total abstinence from all substances may not be suitable for some clients. Gorski's recent work, however, is less explicitly reliant on the spiritual components of AA. See his chapter on relapse prevention with adolescent offenders at www.treatment.org/Taps/Tap11/tap11chap9.html.

THE MARLATT RELAPSE PREVENTION MODEL

The work of Alan Marlatt has been enormously influential in addiction treatment and research. He provided a cognitive-behavioural framework with testable hypotheses and practical strategies for working with relapse.

Marlatt conceptualized relapse as a two-stage process, where the precipitants of substance use are distinct from the factors that prolong or sustain such use over time. Marlatt's research with people who experienced relapse (1980) led him to believe that relapse occurs as a result of a person's lack of coping skills to successfully avoid drinking or other drug use in certain challenging situations. Marlatt developed eight relapse determinants, or risk situations. These are:
• unpleasant emotions
• physical discomfort
• pleasant emotions
• tests of personal control
• urges and temptations
• conflict with others
• social pressure to use
• pleasant times with others.

Marlatt's approach to relapse prevention treatment focuses on providing coping skills training in the risk situations that are particular to each client.

Marlatt's taxonomy of risk situations is clinically useful in that it gives the therapist a "handle" on how to work with clients to prevent or discuss relapse. Relapse is therefore addressed

> in a pragmatic manner as an error, a lapse, a slip or temporary setback, and not an inevitable collapse on the road to recovery. Teaching people about high risk situations and how to cope with them more effectively is the essence of relapse prevention (Marlatt, 1996).

Marlatt's model, however, has some shortcomings. Saunders & Houghton (1996) point out that relapse precipitants may be multidimensional and highly complex. They note that additional variables, such as substandard housing, limited occupational opportunities, poor relationships and poverty can also impact behavioural change. Failure to cope may be evidence of a deficit in coping skills, but not necessarily. The person may choose not to employ coping skills because he or she is ambivalent about change. Saunders & Houghton (1996) also note that relapse can sometimes be helpful for clients who are ambivalent about change. The negative experience of a relapse can solidify intention to change. In addition, people with alcohol and other drug problems can have powerful attachments to their preferred substance, where giving up the substance can be compared to the ending of a love affair. Marlatt's taxonomy may not sufficiently capture the "magic" of the substance.

Marlatt (2002) has also conducted research and developed theory that applies Buddhist practices to relapse prevention. This groundbreaking work was inspired by his own experiences of the relaxing effects of transcendental meditation. Practices include the application of mindfulness to the internal monitoring of urges and cravings, accompanied by a lack of "attachment" to the urge to use. The efficacy of Buddhist practices such as mindfulness meditation in the prevention of relapse is supported by other research (Breslin et al., 2002), and interest in the compatibility of Buddhist teachings with cognitive-behavioural approaches is growing (see, for example, Campos, 2002, and Kumar, 2002). Buddhist thought and teachings, and related developments in relapse prevention theory and practice, are too complex to be done justice to here. Interested readers may wish to consult the articles cited. An on-line article by Parks & Marlatt (2000) on relapse prevention therapy can be found at http://nationalpsychologist.com/articles/art_v9n5_3.htm.

STRUCTURED RELAPSE PREVENTION: A MANUAL-BASED APPROACH

The Structured Relapse Prevention treatment approach (SRP) developed by Helen Annis is designed for people with moderate to severe levels of alcohol or other drug dependence. Based on social learning theory developed by Albert Bandura, as well as on the work of Alan Marlatt (Marlatt & Gordon, 1985; Marlatt, 1996) and Prochaska & DiClemente (1992), the model provides a highly structured, manual-based approach to treatment.

SRP is currently used in addiction treatment centres throughout Ontario and is applied as both a group and an individual modality. Many adaptations, based on the populations served, sociocultural and linguistic considerations, as well as counsellor preferences, have been made to the model originally outlined in the manual (Annis et al., 1996). Such various iterations of SRP tend to conform to the basic two-phase approach, in which initiation-of-change strategies, such as avoidance and reliance on the support of others, are gradually complemented or replaced by more internalized coping strategies. SRP is also used by residential treatment centres to help prepare clients for their return to the community, and as part of after-care programs.

Overview of Structured Relapse Prevention Counselling

SRP counselling considers client readiness for change as defined by Prochaska and DiClemente's (1984) transtheoretical model. SRP comprises five components (see Table 1), each of which is matched to a stage of change. Clients progress through each component, advancing to the next level when they are ready. As indicated by the dotted-line arrows in Table 1, some clients may not progress through the stages in a linear fashion due to setbacks in their level of readiness for change.

At intake to SRP counselling, all clients receive a comprehensive assessment (Component 1), followed by feedback of results during one or more motivational interviewing sessions (Component 2). Clients who are willing to change their substance use will collaborate with their counsellor to develop an individually tailored treatment plan (Component 3). Only clients in the action stage of change—those who decide to try to implement the treatment plan and work toward change—sign a formal treatment contract and enter SRP counselling. The first phase of SRP focuses on powerful techniques designed to initiate and stabilize change (Component 4), while the second phase focuses on reducing clients' reliance on initiation strategies and substituting strategies that have greater potential for long-term maintenance of change in substance use behaviour (Component 5).

Each component of the treatment process is described in greater detail below, beginning with a discussion of the type of client for whom this treatment approach is likely to be most effective.

TABLE 1

Components of the Outpatient Counselling Program in Relation to Five Stages of Change

PROGRAM COMPONENT	STAGE OF CHANGE				
	Precontemplation	Contemplation	Preparation	Action	Maintenance
1. Assessment					
2. Motivational Interviewing					
3. Individual Treatment Plan					
4. SRP "Initiation" Counselling					
5. SRP "Maintenance" Counselling					

Component 1: Assessment

During the assessment component of SRP counselling, two treatment planning tools are administered. The first tool, the Commitment to Change Algorithm for Alcohol (CCA-A) and Drugs (CCA-D) is a brief and easy-to-use tool developed to assess clients' readiness to change (Schober & Annis, 1996a). The CCA is based on the transtheoretical model (Prochaska & DiClemente, 1984) and classifies clients into one of five stages of change depending on recent drinking or other drug use, reported intention to change and recent quit/change attempts. Clients are placed in the highest stage for which they qualify. The second tool, the Inventory of Drug-Taking Situations (IDTS-50; Annis & Martin, 1985a) identifies any antecedents to alcohol and other drug use.

Examples of the CCA-A and CCA-D are shown in Table 2 on page 240, along with the definitions used for reduced drinking limits and quit attempts. Because the criteria for different stages are clear, a client's advancement to a higher stage, or regression to an earlier stage, can be readily tracked throughout treatment. High test-retest reliability for the CCA has been reported (Schober & Annis, 1996a).

The IDTS-50 is a 50-item assessment and treatment planning tool designed to provide a situational analysis of a client's substance use. This information is critical in understanding a client's motivation for substance use and in designing an individually tailored treatment program. The frequency of the client's past drinking or other drug use is assessed, following the classification system developed by Marlatt & Gordon (1980), across eight risk areas: unpleasant emotions, physical discomfort, pleasant emotions, tests of personal control, urges and temptations, conflict with others, social pressure to use and pleasant times with others.

The IDTS generates a personalized profile that provides a situational analysis of the client's substance use; Figure 1 on page 239 shows a sample IDTS profile of a person who uses cocaine. This client is at high risk when experiencing unpleasant emotions and urges and temptations; thus, treatment planning would emphasize strategies targeted to these risk areas. The IDTS may be administered either in writing or by using computer interactive software.

Component 2: Motivational Interviewing

The motivational interviewing approach is designed to help clients build commitment and readiness to change (Miller & Rollnick, 2002). Thus, motivation is not viewed as a static character trait, but rather as an expression of an individual's natural ambivalence toward change. In other words, motivation is a changeable state over which the counsellor can have considerable influence by actively engaging clients in changing their substance use. In SRP, the assessment process is conducted using techniques to build client motivation; for example, the personalized objective feedback of assessment results is excellent in building a client's commitment to change (Allsop, 1990; Saunders et al., 1991).

Component 3: Individual Treatment Plan

One of the most important components of SRP counselling is treatment planning. We have found the following tools and techniques to be helpful in encouraging client collaboration in the development of a treatment plan for SRP counselling: goal setting and self-monitoring, identifying problem drinking or other drug use situations, identifying coping strengths and weaknesses, and contracting for treatment. Each step is described in more detail below.

Goal setting and self-monitoring can be useful ways of facilitating client participation in the treatment planning process. Clients use self-monitoring forms to note their substance use goal each week—including their level of confidence in achieving this goal—and keep a daily record of any substance use that took place, the circumstances surrounding that use, risky situations encountered and coping strategies used. Clients then discuss the self-monitoring with their counsellor during subsequent treatment sessions.

A fundamental part of planning for SRP treatment involves agreeing on the client's most problematic drinking or other drug use situations. The IDTS, which is given at assessment, provides this information in a systematic way, based on the types of situations

TABLE 2

Commitment to Change Algorithm (CCA): Tool Used to Classify a Client into One of Five Stages of Change

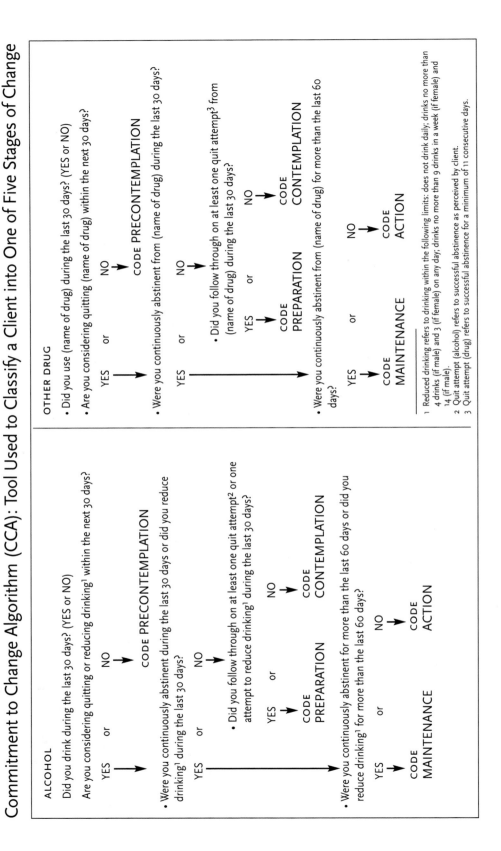

ALCOHOL

Did you drink during the last 30 days? (YES or NO)

Are you considering quitting or reducing drinking[1] within the next 30 days?

YES   or   NO → CODE PRECONTEMPLATION

- Were you continuously abstinent during the last 30 days or did you reduce drinking[1] during the last 30 days?

YES   or   NO

- Did you follow through on at least one quit attempt[2] or one attempt to reduce drinking[1] during the last 30 days?

YES   or   NO → CODE CONTEMPLATION

CODE PREPARATION

- Were you continuously abstinent for more than the last 60 days or did you reduce drinking[1] for more than the last 60 days?

YES   or   NO → CODE ACTION

CODE MAINTENANCE

OTHER DRUG

- Did you use (name of drug) during the last 30 days? (YES or NO)
- Are you considering quitting (name of drug) within the next 30 days?

YES   or   NO → CODE PRECONTEMPLATION

- Were you continuously abstinent from (name of drug) during the last 30 days?

YES   or   NO

- Did you follow through on at least one quit attempt[3] from (name of drug) during the last 30 days?

YES   or   NO → CODE CONTEMPLATION

CODE PREPARATION

- Were you continuously abstinent from (name of drug) for more than the last 60 days?

YES   or   NO → CODE ACTION

CODE MAINTENANCE

1 Reduced drinking refers to drinking within the following limits: does not drink daily; drinks no more than 4 drinks (if male) and 3 (if female) on any day; drinks no more than 9 drinks in a week (if female) and 14 (if male).
2 Quit attempt (alcohol) refers to successful abstinence as perceived by client.
3 Quit attempt (drug) refers to successful abstinence for a minimum of 11 consecutive days.

that triggered substance use over the past year. After discussing the IDTS results and the daily monitoring, clients are asked to rank the three most problematic triggers to substance use that they want to work on in treatment, and to give specific examples of past drinking or other drug use experiences for each situation. This exercise allows clients to analyze past situations in detail in order to identify what they might do differently in similar situations in the future. In addition, because the maintenance phase of SRP counselling focuses on planned exposure to high-risk situations for substance use (see below), it is important that both client and counsellor have a detailed overview of past drinking or other drug use scenarios.

FIGURE 1

Profile of a Cocaine Client on the Inventory of Drug-Taking Situations

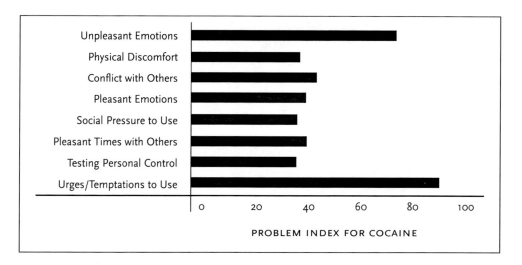

The strengths, supports and coping responses already available to a client are invaluable in preventing relapse, and they form the groundwork for developing successful homework assignments. The client must become more aware of his or her strengths and learn to use them effectively. Coping responses that the client may have used successfully in other areas may be quite effective, with only minor alterations, in addressing problematic drinking or other drug use situations. At this point in treatment planning, the therapist's task is to establish the client's existing repertoire of general coping behaviours, personal strengths and environmental resources. The process of reviewing the client's repertoire should provide a better appreciation of the possibilities open to the client, and should allow the client to focus on his or her strengths and successes rather than failures.

SRP treatment provides clients with a wide range of coping skills assignments, which are designed to help enhance and expand their coping repertoire. Clients select from a list of topics, which are then addressed during treatment sessions or provided as homework assignments. For example, during the early weeks of treatment clients often choose to work on coping with cravings or increasing social support. Later treatment sessions might address anger management, relaxation or healthy relationships.

Finally, the client is informed of the program's orientation, attendance requirements, the limits of client confidentiality and expectations for participation in planning and executing homework. Other possible treatment options are also presented. The client is then asked to decide whether he or she wishes to work toward change in substance use by entering SRP counselling. This decision is formalized with the signing of a treatment contract.

Component 4: Initiation Counselling

The "heart" of SRP counselling is divided into two major phases: initiation (Component 4) and maintenance (Component 5; Annis, 1990). The initiation phase focuses on counselling strategies suitable for clients in the action stage of change. That is, only clients who have decided to change and have signed a treatment contract enter this first phase of SRP counselling. This is because there is reason to believe that it can be detrimental to use action-oriented counselling procedures with clients who have not yet decided to change.

At the first treatment session and toward treatment discharge, the client should complete the Drug-Taking Confidence Questionnaire (DTCQ-50; Annis & Martin, 1985b), which is a 50-item self-report questionnaire designed to assess Bandura's concept of self-efficacy for alcohol- and other drug-related situations. Clients are asked to imagine themselves in a variety of situations derived from the work of Marlatt & Gordon (1980) and to indicate their level of confidence in their ability to resist the urge to drink or use other drugs in each situation. Levels of confidence are measured on the following six-point scale: zero (not at all confident), 20 (20 per cent confident), 40 (40 per cent confident), 60 (60 per cent confident), 80 (80 per cent confident), and 100 (very confident). A client's response on the DTCQ-50 allows the therapist to monitor the development of the client's self-efficacy in relation to coping with specific substance use situations over the course of treatment.

This initiation phase of SRP incorporates the substance use triggers identified by the client in the treatment plan. The focus is on assisting clients to anticipate substance use triggers for the coming week, and to identify and commit to alternative coping strategies that don't involve drinking or other drug use. Clients must begin to identify and plan for high-risk situations in advance, so that they can prepare alternative coping strategies.

Clients are encouraged to use coping plans that are known to be powerful strategies in initiating behavioural change. These strategies include avoiding risky situations (e.g., drug use settings and drug-using friends) and seeking out social support (e.g., from reliable friends or family members). Figure 2 shows the Weekly Plan (Initiation Phase) Form that clients complete to guide them in anticipating substance use triggers and using relatively safe initiation strategies, such as avoidance and social support, to cope.

For clients who have difficulty stabilizing abstinence while attending SRP outpatient sessions, the use of a protective drug or an anti-craving medication may be considered as part of the initiation phase of SRP counselling. An example of the integration of a pharmacological agent (calcium carbimide) with SRP homework assignments is given in Annis (1991); the results of a randomized controlled trial are presented in Annis & Peachey (1992).

FIGURE 2

Weekly Plan (Initiation Phase) Form

NAME: _____ SUBSTANCE: _____ DATE: _____

SRP WEEKLY PLAN — INITIATION PHASE

The early weeks of changing your alcohol or other drug use can be a challenging time. We call this early period of behaviour change the "Initiation Phase," which can last for anywhere from one month to much longer. Research has shown that "initiating" a change in your behaviour is easier and more effective when you use some of the following powerful strategies.

• Think about what you have to lose if you don't change. What are the factors "pushing" you to change your drinking or drug use at this time?
• Think about situations that could arise and present a risk for you. Plan ahead of time what you will do so that you aren't caught off guard.
• Avoid risky places and friends who use alcohol or other drugs.
• Involve your spouse, another family member, or a trusted friend or sponsor.
• During the first couple of weeks of changing your drinking or other drug use, living in a supportive environment can be especially helpful.
• If you want to stop drinking, consider discussing the use of alcohol-sensitizing or anti-craving medication (e.g., Antabuse®, Temposil® or Naltrexone®) with your doctor. These drugs can be a big help in getting you over those difficult first few weeks.
• Set a goal for your drinking or other drug use — make a commitment to yourself.

Below is some space for you to think about what you would like to accomplish in the coming week and how you will do so.

GOAL: _____

Confidence in achieving this goal: ❑ 0% ❑ 20% ❑ 40% ❑ 60% ❑ 80% ❑ 100%

Describe **two substance use triggers** that are likely to arise over the coming week: Indicate the following: Where will you be? What time of day? Who, if anyone, will be present? What will you be doing, thinking, feeling?	For each of the two triggers, describe **several coping strategies** that you will be prepared to use: You may want to use some of the strategies listed above, or plan other ways of coping that will work for you.

Component 5: Maintenance Counselling

This final phase of SRP counselling focuses on strategies suitable for clients in the maintenance stage of change. The Commitment to Change Algorithm identifies clients in the maintance stage as those who have successfully implemented a change in their substance use for a period of at least 60 days.

Although it can be argued that the term "relapse prevention" should be restricted to clients in the maintenance stage of change, in practice, clients do not progress from an exclusive use of initiation strategies (Component 4) to maintenance strategies (Component 5). Instead, clients tend to combine both action and maintenance strategies throughout treatment, coming to increasingly rely on maintenance phase strategies towards the end of treatment. The distinction between initiation and maintenance strategies is emphasized so that clients are aware of which strategies they are using. The objective is to encourage clients to rely less on initiation strategies and to gain confidence in the use of maintenance strategies before treatment ends. This last phase of treatment involves four stages: graduated real-life exposure to a client's high-risk situations for substance use; homework tasks within each type of risk situation; slowly reducing the client's reliance on initiation strategies (including reliance on pharmacological agents); and the design of homework tasks to promote self-attribution of control. These maintenance-of-change counselling strategies are discussed in greater detail in Annis (1990) and Annis & Davis (1989a; 1989b).

The Weekly Plan Form that is used to help clients to incorporate these maintenance strategies is shown in Figure 3. Several differences from the Weekly Plan (Figure 2) for initiation-phase sessions should be noted. While clients in the initiation phase are asked to focus on anticipating drug-use triggers that are likely to arise naturally over the coming week, clients in the maintenance stage are also asked to actually plan on entering self-identified high-risk situations.

Homework assignments must be designed so that clients experience success and begin to build confidence (self-efficacy) in their ability to cope in high-risk situations. Multiple homework assignments (i.e., three or more) should be agreed upon at each treatment session so that the client quickly learns that a high-risk situation does not automatically imply a relapse. These homework assignments should draw on a wide variety of the client's coping strengths and resources. As the client's confidence grows, he or she moves up the hierarchy to more difficult situations. At this later stage, a slip or lapse is unlikely to be the major setback it might have been early in treatment because the client has already begun a "snowball effect" in the growth of self-efficacy. By the end of treatment, the client should take most of the responsibility for designing his or her own homework assignments.

In summary, clients who are in the action stage or initiation phase are encouraged to use avoidance (e.g., avoidance of drug use settings, drug-using friends), social support (e.g., a reliable friend or family member) and perhaps a protective or anti-craving medication. Clients who are in the maintenance stage, however, are expected to use a greater variety of coping alternatives that will make them more self-reliant. Consistent with research on the relationship of coping repertoire to outcome (Bliss et al., 1989; Curry & Marlatt, 1985; Moser, 1993) and the superiority of many active coping strategies compared with simple avoidance (Moser, 1993; Shiffman, 1985), clients in the maintenance stage are encouraged to develop a broad repertoire of coping alternatives that include active as well as avoidant cognitive and behavioural coping responses.

Summary of the SRP Approach

Although SRP counselling has been presented as a highly structured, ordered sequence of five counselling components, in practice a dynamic interplay occurs between counselling components and a client's readiness to change. Counselling components are designed to

FIGURE 3

Weekly Plan (Maintenance Phase) Form

NAME: _____ SUBSTANCE: _____ DATE: _____

SRP WEEKLY PLAN — MAINTENANCE PHASE

Congratulations! You've successfully made some changes in your drinking or other drug use. The next step is to maintain those changes and prevent relapse. Research has shown that two of the most powerful strategies for maintaining behaviour change are to:

1. take stock of all of the high-risk situations that you are likely to encounter as a natural part of your lifestyle, and
2. gradually enter these situations, starting with a lower risk and working your way up.

The idea behind planning to enter situations in which you might be tempted to drink or use other drugs is that, if these situations are likely to arise at some point, it's better for you to be in control of where and when they do. The following are more tips for maintaining behaviour change.

• Experience each risk situation a few times before moving on to the next one.

• Make sure that you take the credit for success! For example, in the initiation phase of change, we encouraged you to seek the support of others. Now that you are learning to maintain change, it's important for you to know that you can "do it on your own" if you have to.

• Make sure that the situation you plan to enter is challenging, but not too challenging.

• If you are having difficulty with entering high-risk situations, you may be moving too quickly. Take your time! You can always go back to using some of the initiation strategies (like avoiding people, places and things, or relying on the support of others) until you feel more confident.

Two powerful strategies to help maintain changes in your drinking or other drug use are setting a goal and planning to enter risk situations. Below is space for you to plan what you would like to accomplish in the coming week.

GOAL: _____

Confidence in achieving this goal: ❑ 0% ❑ 20% ❑ 40% ❑ 60% ❑ 80% ❑ 100%

HOMEWORK ASSIGNMENT Planned Exposure to a Substance Use Trigger	OUTCOME REPORT
Describe triggering situation: _____ _____ _____ Planned experience: When? _____ Where?_____ Who present? _____ Coping plan (be specific, describe exactly what you will say and do, what you will be thinking, etc.): _____ _____ _____	Did you attempt this assignment? ❑ No ❑ Yes Were you successful? ❑ No ❑ Yes Comment: _____ _____ _____ Did you use? ❑ No ❑ Yes If Yes, how much? _____ What, if anything, might you try doing differently next time? _____ _____ _____

enhance client readiness to change and client stage of change affects the choice of counselling components. While some clients may proceed in a linear fashion through the stages of change and counselling components, others may not. For example, an action-stage client who experiences a lapse to substance use while receiving initiation-stage counselling may need earlier counselling components such as continued assessment and motivational interviewing. Similarly, a preparation-stage client may experience uncertainty regarding the decision to change when faced with signing an individual treatment contract. If this occurs, further exploration of the costs and benefits of change through motivational interviewing is required. Thus, the SRP treatment model takes into account clients' readiness to change—the SRP components can be individually tailored to fit clients' ongoing needs.

The purpose of treatment is to effect a rise in self-efficacy across all areas of perceived risk. If the client fails to show growth of confidence in coping with a particular risk situation, further work in this area should be considered before the client is discharged from treatment. The therapist must consider possible reasons for the lack of development of confidence in the identified area. For example, has the client successfully performed homework assignments involving entry into situations of this type? If so, what self-inferences is the client drawing from those experiences? Such an inquiry by the therapist should uncover the reason for the client's lack of confidence in relation to the particular risk area and identify any further work that needs to be done before treatment completion.

Research Findings for the SRP Model

The SRP counselling process focuses heavily on the conduct of homework assignments, particularly in the initiation (or action) and maintenance phases. An early study by Annis and Davis (1988) that evaluated the homework component of SRP counselling found that clients successfully completed the vast majority of homework assignments. Ninety per cent of assignments generated by the client were completed successfully compared with 73 per cent of those generated by the therapist, emphasizing the importance of active client participation. Although homework assignments involve entry into risk situations for substance use, particularly during the maintenance phase, most clients were successful in adhering to their treatment goal. Typically, any slips (lapses) occurred outside of homework assignments. Interestingly, negative mood states and interpersonal conflict increased the likelihood that a lapse would become a serious relapse.

Clinical trials evaluating the effectiveness of SRP counselling for people with alcohol problems have supported the following conclusions:

- In the year following SRP treatment, most clients dramatically reduce their substance use (Annis & Davis, 1988; Graham et al., 1996).
- Group-delivered SRP counselling can be equally effective as individual SRP counselling for clients with both alcohol and other drug problems (Graham et al., 1996).
- Clients with well-differentiated profiles on the Inventory of Drug-Taking Situations do better in SRP counselling than clients with undifferentiated profiles, while the reverse is true with more traditional counselling (Annis & Davis, 1991).
- Clients with good outcomes show high confidence (self-efficacy) and make good use of coping strategies when faced with high-risk situations (Moser & Annis, 1996).
- The greater the number and variety of coping strategies used by the client, the lower the likelihood of relapse (Moser & Annis, 1996).

Further research is needed to establish the relative effectiveness of SRP counselling for clients with problems resulting from use of other substances, such as cocaine and opioids, and to evaluate the SRP counselling components in relation to client readiness for change.

Relapse Prevention with Diverse Client Populations

In any treatment intervention, the needs of diverse client populations need to be considered and treatment strategies tailored accordingly. Although this is a major concern in the treatment of substance use problems, little research has been done with many special populations and marginalized groups. This section highlights a few key considerations from existing research and clinical practice implications of relapse prevention counselling, taking into account gender, age (youth and older adults), ethnocultural factors, sexual diversity and concurrent mental health disorders.

GENDER

Studies of treatment populations have shown that married men have a lower rate of relapse than unmarried men. For women, marriage is protective for some, and is related to relapse for others (for example, if the woman is returning to a partner who uses alcohol or other drugs; Walton et al., 2001). Research has also shown that men tend to report more negative social influences, greater exposure to substances and poorer coping skills than women (Walton et al., 2001). Some research has suggested that a depressed mood is the most frequent determinant of relapse (Strowig, 1999) for men and that Caucasian men report the poorest coping when compared with a matched sample of Caucasian women and African-American men and women (Walton et al., 2001).

In general, women tend to report better coping mechanisms than men (Walton et al., 2001). Women also tend to see their substance use as secondary to more general problems, such as anxiety and depression. As a result, women use medical and psychiatric services more frequently than men and perceive these services as more effective (Osorio et al., 2002).

YOUTH

Few relapse prevention models focus on youth. However, some research has explored ways of adapting these models to best fit the needs of younger clients.

Relapse prevention for young people needs to focus on issues of youth-parent relationships and peer group membership, as these are central to the lives and experiences of younger clients. Illicit substance use by youth is strongly related to parental support as well as parental awareness and monitoring of the whereabouts and activities of their child (Miller & Plant, 2003). Peer influences, delinquency and re-offending behaviour are also strongly associated with youth substance use (Roget et al., 1998). In some cases, relapse prevention for youth may need to include liaison with the juvenile justice system, or a contract with a specific substance use treatment provider.

Roget and colleagues (1998) suggest that a relapse prevention program for youth should include assessment, incentive building, contract development and evaluation. Assessment that combines theories of adolescent development with Marlatt & Gordon's (1985) eight high-risk situations discussed earlier in this chapter may be helpful. In this view, high-risk situations for relapse are connected to the drive to meet developmental needs (Roget et al., 1998). For example, social pressure to use substances can be linked with peer acceptance in young adults. Building a high-risk "profile" that is particular to each client and takes into account the developmental tasks unique to youth can facilitate work on relevant coping skills.

In facilitating change in youth, research shows that alcohol and other drug education is not enough. Elkind (1984, in Roget et al., 1998) suggests that adolescents think and behave with the notion that nothing bad will happen to them—talking about the consequences of substance use gets cognitively re-interpreted to mean "others become addicted, but not me."

Clinicians need to make feedback personally relevant to young clients, and to avoid confrontation. In addition, they need to encourage youth to actively prepare for relapse and to practise coping strategies.

An important component of relapse prevention strategies with youth is the develop-ment of a behavioural contract, in this case a "relapse contract." This contract is created by all parties involved and might include family rules, school or job requirements, probation requirements, treatment attendance, urinalysis, social supports and relapse consequences. It is important to keep in mind that any relapse episodes need to focus on what can be learned, as "learning by doing" is important in this stage of life.

OLDER ADULTS

Most research exploring relapse has focused across the adult age range rather than specifi-cally on older adults. However, a few differences in treatment outcomes for older adults have been noted (Barrick & Connors, 2002). For example, high-risk situations among older adults tend to involve intrapersonal issues more frequently than among younger adults (Barrick & Connors, 2002). In addition, several age-specific issues were found to be relevant to relapse prevention in older adults. Negative emotional states related to anxiety, interper-sonal conflict, depression, loneliness, loss and social isolation appear to be the highest-risk situations identified. Retirement, the death of a partner or child and the stressors of aging represent a risky time for alcohol or other drug use. Cognitive impairments associated with aging, no matter what the etiology, need to be assessed and taken into consideration in relapse plans for older adults (Barrick & Connors, 2002).

Schonfeld and his colleagues (2000) evaluated a 16-week relapse prevention program called "Get Smart" and found that cognitive-behavioural programs that focus on identify-ing high-risk situations, coping skills and relapse plans worked well with older clients with significant medical, social and substance use problems.

ETHNOCULTURAL FACTORS

Many treatment programs have difficulty attracting and retaining clients from diverse ethnocultural communities. Language, treatment philosophies and methods, clinician demographics, and lack of agency knowledge or awareness of cross-cultural counselling implications create systemic barriers for many clients. Increasingly, the literature indicates that clinicians need to develop competence in working with clients from diverse racial, cultural, ethnic and religious backgrounds (Straussner, 2002). Ethnocultural competence, defined as "the ability of a clinician to function effectively in the context of ethnocultural differences" (Straussner, 2002, p. 35) is a critical skill in the application of relapse preven-tion strategies and techniques.

Although some research has been carried out on substance use patterns and issues in different cultural groups, caution needs to be exercised in drawing particular clinical implications from this work given the heterogeneity of ethnocultural groups. In addition, more research is needed to help develop relapse prevention approaches specific to different populations.

For example, little research exists regarding relapse prevention applications for Aboriginal peoples. Clients who live on reserves may face geographical barriers to accessing treatment. In addition, Western models of treatment may not fit with traditional Native healing approaches. This was found in the development of the Inventory of Drinking Situations questionnaire (Annis & Davis, 1991) when Aboriginal reviewers suggested the addition of a Native spirituality component to reflect a high-risk situation relevant to this population.

SEXUAL DIVERSITY

Little has been written about relapse prevention specific to lesbian, gay, bisexual, trans-sexual or transgendered people. However, as with all counsellor-client interactions, mutual respect, unconditional positive regard, and attentiveness to the client's issues and goals should be paramount. Clients from sexually diverse groups will often have specific issues relating to discrimination (homophobia, biphobia, transphobia), coming out, openness about sexual orientation/gender identity, family issues, involvement in the community, body image and HIV/AIDS (Barbara et al., 2002). See Chapter 16 for specific suggestions on how to be intentionally inclusive with these client populations.

CONCURRENT MENTAL HEALTH DISORDERS

It is estimated that 50 to 65 per cent of people with substance use problems also experience a co-occurring mental health disorder (Bellack & DiClemente, 1999). Excessive substance use in people with mental illness has all of the same adverse health, social, legal and financial consequences that it does for others, along with the additional complications of decreased treatment compliance, increased risk of exacerbating the symptoms of mental illness, increased risk of relapse and compromised efficacy of neuroleptic medications (Bellack & DiClemente, 1999). Because non-adherence to treatment among psychiatric patients who use substances can lead to a number of adverse consequences ranging from poor clinical outcomes to violent behaviour, efforts to increase adherence have been attempted (Swanson et al., 1999). An integrated approach drawing from both the addiction and mental health domains attempts to address both problem areas at the same time, explore how they interact and examine how substances are used to treat the negative symptoms of mental illness or the side-effects of treatments.

One such integrated approach is an adaptation of the motivational interviewing model by Bellack & DiClemente (1999). Their approach attempts to minimize the impact of the cognitive, motivational and social skill deficits associated with severe mental illness. The treatment protocol contains four modules: the first focuses on social skills and problem-solving techniques to help people deal with peers and to refuse substances; the second focuses on education in triggers, cravings, the reasons for use and the risk of using for people with severe mental illness; the third consists of motivational interviewing, goal setting and contingency plans such as urine screens; and the fourth focuses on relapse prevention strategies. The 90-minute sessions are held twice a week for approximately six months. The sessions are highly structured, and the concepts are broken down into smaller learning units. There is an emphasis on behavioural rehearsal and the repetitive learning of a small number of specific skills to use in a few key high-risk situations. There is also an extensive use of learning aids and content repetition.

Empirical Support for Relapse Prevention Approaches

In general, relapse prevention approaches, including the SRP model, fall under the category of cognitive-behavioural coping-skills therapy (CBST). These approaches are based on social learning theory, and have been well-validated in the research literature (Longabaugh & Morgenstern, 1999). The two core components shared by these approaches include (1) a theoretical foundation that examines deficits in one's ability to cope with overall life stressors and alcohol-related stimuli; and (2) the use of individualized coping skills training. These types of therapies were among the first to demonstrate efficacy in reducing drinking in randomized clinical trials and are "among those [interventions] having the most evidence for clinical and cost effectiveness" (Longabaugh & Morgenstern, 1999, p. 79). In addition, other authors (Dimeff & Marlatt, 1998) have noted that:

> relapse prevention may be particularly promising in reducing the severity of relapses when they occur, in enhancing the durability of treatment effects, and for patients who demonstrate higher levels of impairment across multiple dimensions. . . . In essence, while relapse prevention does not provide full inoculation against relapse, it significantly reduces the negative consequences and harm resulting from the fall (p. 516).

A meta-analysis of 26 studies supported the overall efficacy of relapse prevention in reducing substance use and improving psychosocial adjustment (Irvin et al., 1999). Thus, the relapse prevention approaches discussed in this chapter are suitable for a range of individuals with moderate to severe levels of alcohol and other drug dependence. Indeed, these interventions have made a significant contribution to the growing body of evidence-based interventions in the addiction field.

Conclusion

This chapter has highlighted a few of the many approaches used to address relapse to substance use. These treatment approaches must be considered against a backdrop of research findings and theorizing that may contradict or challenge accepted models of care. Overall, cognitive-behavioural approaches such as the SRP model demonstrate empirical support and can be used effectively with a variety of clinical populations. In all cases, it is critical to ensure that relapse prevention strategies are tailored to the unique needs of clients and that the particular issues of diverse populations are considered.

ADDITIONAL INFORMATION

The following materials are available from Publication Services, Centre for Addiction and Mental Health, 33 Russell Street, Toronto, ON M5S 2S1 (Telephone: 1 800 661-1111):

Annis, H.M. & Martin, G. (1985). *Inventory of Drug-Taking Situations (IDTS-50)*. Computer interactive software is also available. Toronto: Addiction Research Foundation.

Annis, H.M. & Martin, G. (1985). *Drug-Taking Confidence Questionnaire (DTCQ-50)*. Computer interactive software is also available. Toronto: Addiction Research Foundation.

Annis, H.M., Turner, N.E. & Sklar, S.M. (1997). *Inventory of Drug-Taking Situations (IDTS-50) User's Guide*. Toronto: Addiction Research Foundation.

Annis, H.M., Sklar, S.M. & Turner, N.E. (1997). *Drug-Taking Confidence Questionnaire (DTCQ-50) User's Guide*. Toronto: Addiction Research Foundation.

REFERENCES

Addiction Research Foundation. (1993). *Core Client Interview: Behaviour Change and Relapse Prevention Unit*. Toronto: author.

Allsop, S. (1990). Relapse prevention and management. *Drug and Alcohol Review, 9,* 143–153.

Annis, H.M. (1986). A relapse prevention model for treatment of alcoholics. In Miller, W.R. & Heather, N. (Eds.), *Treating Addictive Behaviors: Processes of Change* (pp. 407–421). New York: Plenum.

Annis, H.M. (1990). Relapse to substance abuse: Empirical findings within a cognitive-social learning approach. *Journal of Psychoactive Drugs, 22*(2), 117–124.

Annis, H.M. (1991). A cognitive-social learning approach to relapse: Pharmacotherapy and relapse prevention counselling. *Alcohol and Alcoholism, Suppl. 1,* 527–530.

Annis, H.M. & Davis, C.S. (1988). Self-efficacy and the prevention of alcoholic relapse: Initial findings from a treatment trial. In Baker, T.B. & Cannon, D.S. (Eds.), *Assessment and Treatment of Addictive Disorders* (pp. 88–112). New York: Praeger.

Annis, H.M. & Davis, C.S. (1989a). Relapse prevention. In Hester, R.K. & Miller, W.R. (Eds.), *Handbook of Alcoholism Treatment Approaches* (pp. 170–182). New York: Pergamon Press.

Annis, H.M. & Davis, C.S. (1989b). Relapse prevention training: A cognitive-behavioral approach based on self-efficacy theory. *Journal of Chemical Dependency Treatment, 2*(2), 81–103.

Annis, H.M. & Davis, C.S. (1991). Relapse prevention. *Alcohol Health and Research World, 15*(3), 204–212.

Annis, H.M. & Martin, G. (1985a). *Inventory of Drug-Taking Situations (IDTS-50)*. Toronto: Addiction Research Foundation.

Annis, H.M. & Martin, G. (1985b). *Drug-Taking Confidence Questionnaire (DTCQ-50)*. Toronto: Addiction Research Foundation.

Annis, H.M. & Peachey, J.E. (1992). The use of calcium carbimide in relapse prevention counselling: Results of a randomized controlled trial. *British Journal of Addiction, 87*, 63–72.

Annis, H.M., Schober, R. & Kelly, E. (1996). Matching addiction outpatient counselling to client readiness for change: The role of structured relapse prevention counselling. *Experimental and Clinical Psychopharmacology, 4*, 37–45.

Bandura, A. (1977). Self-efficacy: Toward a unifying theory of behavioral change. *Psychological Review, 84*(2), 191–215.

Bandura, A. (1978). Reflections on self-efficacy. *Advances in Behaviour Research and Therapy, 1*, 237–269.

Bandura, A. (1986). *Social Foundations of Thought and Action*. Englewood Cliffs, NJ: Prentice Hall.

Barbara, A.M., Chaim, G. & Doctor, F. (2002). *Asking the Right Questions: Talking about Sexual Orientation and Gender Identity During Assessment for Drug and Alcohol Concerns*. Toronto: Centre for Addiction and Mental Health.

Barrick, C. & Connors, G.J. (2002). Relapse prevention and maintaining abstinence in older adults with alcohol-use disorders. *Drugs & Aging, 19*(8), 583–594.

Bellack, A. & DiClemente, C.C. (1999). Treating substance abuse among patients with schizophrenia. *Psychiatric Services, 50*(1), 75–80.

Bliss, P., Murphy, K. & Ricketts, T. (2002). Relapse prevention group-work: A clinical evaluation. *Journal of Substance Use, 7*, 78–84.

Bliss, R.E., Garvey, A.J., Heinhold, J. & Hitchcock, J.L. (1989). The influence of situation and coping on relapse crisis outcomes after smoking cessation. *Journal of Consulting and Clinical Psychology, 57*, 443–449.

Breslin, F.C., Zack, M. & McMain, S. (2002). An information-processing analysis of mindfulness: Implications for relapse prevention in the treatment of substance abuse. *Clinical Psychology: Science and Practice, 9*(3), 275–299.

Campos, P.E. (2002). Integrating Buddhist philosophy with cognitive and behavioral practice. *Cognitive and Behavioral Practice, 9*, 38–40.

Curry, S.G. & Marlatt, G.A. (1985). Unaided quitters' strategies for coping with temptations to smoke. In Shiffman, S. & Wills, T.A. (Eds.), *Coping and Substance Use* (pp. 243–265). New York: Academic Press.

Dimeff, L.A. & Marlatt, G.A. (1998). Preventing relapse and maintaining change in addictive behaviours. *Clinical Psychology: Science and Practice, 5*(4), 513–525.

Gorski, T.T. (1989). *Passages through Recovery: An Action Plan for Preventing Relapse.* Center City, MN: Hazelden.

Graham, K., Annis, H.M., Brett, P.J. & Venesoen, P. (1996). A controlled field trial of group versus individual cognitive-behavioral training for relapse prevention. *Addiction, 91*(8), 1127–1139.

Hunt, W.A., Barnett, L.W. & Brach, L.G. (1971). Relapse rates in addiction programs. *Journal of Clinical Psychology, 27*, 455–456.

Irvin, J.E., Bowers, C.A., Dunn, M.E. & Wang, M.C. (1999). Efficacy of relapse prevention: A meta-analytic review. *Journal of Consulting and Clinical Psychology, 6*(4), 563–570.

Kumar, S.M. (2002). An introduction to Buddhism for the cognitive-behavioral therapist. *Cognitive and Behavioral Practice, 9*, 40–43.

Litman, G.K., Eiser, J.R., Rawson, N.S.B. & Oppenheim, A.N. (1979). Differences in relapse precipitants and coping behaviors between alcohol relapsers and survivors. *Behaviour Research and Therapy, 17*, 89–94.

Litman, G.K., Stapleton, J., Oppenheim, A.N., Peleg, M. & Jackson, P. (1984). The relationship between coping behaviors, their effectiveness and alcoholism relapse and survival. *British Journal of Addiction, 79*(3), 283–291.

Longabough, R. & Morgenstern, J. (1999). Cognitive-behavioural coping-skills therapy for alcohol dependence. *Alcohol Research and Health, 23*(2), 78–85.

Marlatt, G.A. (1996). Taxonomy of high risk situations for alcohol relapse: Evolution and development of a cognitive-behavioral model. *Addiction, 91* (Supplement), S37–S49.

Marlatt, G.A. (2002). Buddhist philosophy and the treatment of addictive behavior. *Cognitive and Behavioral Practice, 9*, 44–50.

Marlatt, G.A. & Gordon, J.R. (1980). Determinants of relapse: Implications for the maintenance of behavior change. In Davidson, P. & Davidson, S. (Eds.), *Behavioral Medicine: Changing Health Lifestyles* (pp. 71–127). New York: Brunner/Mazel.

Marlatt, G.A. & Gordon, J.R. (1985). *Relapse Prevention: Maintenance Strategies in the Treatment of Addictive Behaviors.* New York: Guilford Press.

Miller, P. & Plant, M. (2003). The family, peer influences and substance use: Findings from a study of UK teenagers. *Journal of Substance Use, 8*, 19–26.

Miller, W.R. (1996). What is a relapse? Fifty ways to leave the wagon. *Addiction, 91* (Supplement), S15–S27.

Miller, W.R. & Rollnick, S. (2002). *Motivational Interviewing* (2nd ed.). New York: Guilford Press.

Miller, W.R., Tonigan, J.S., Montgomery, H.A., Abbott, P.J., Meyers, R.J., Hester, R.K. et al. (1990). *Assessment of Client Motivation for Change: Preliminary Validation of the Socrates (Rev.) Instrument.* Albuquerque, NM: Center for Research on Addictive Behaviors, University of New Mexico.

Moser, A.E. (1993). *Situational Antecedents, Self-efficacy and Coping in Relapse Crisis Outcome: A Prospective Study of Treated Alcoholics.* Toronto: York University.

Moser, A.E. & Annis, H.M. (1996). The role of coping in relapse crisis outcome: A prospective study of treated alcoholics. *Addiction, 91*(8), 1101–1113.

Osorio, R., McCusker, M. & Salazar, C. (2002). Evaluation of a women-only service for substance misusers. *Journal of Substance Use, 7,* 41–49.

Parks, G.A. & Marlatt, A. (2000, September/October). Relapse prevention therapy: a Cognitive-behavioral approach. *The National Psychologist, 9*(5). Available: http://nationalpsychologist.com/articles/art_v9n5_3.htm.

Prochaska, J.O. & DiClemente, C.C. (1984). *The Transtheoretical Approach: Crossing Traditional Boundaries of Therapy.* Homewood, IL: Dow Jones/Irwin.

Prochaska, J.O. & DiClemente, C.C. (1992). Stages of change in the modification of problem behaviors. In Hersen, M., Eisler, R. & Miller, P.M. (Eds.), *Progress in Behavior Modification Series, 28,* 184–218. Sycamore, IL: Sycamore Publishing Company.

Roget, N.A., Fisher, G.L. & Johnson, M.L. (1998). A protocol for reducing juvenile recidivism through relapse prevention. *Journal of Addictions and Offender Counselling, 19,* 33–43.

Saunders, B. & Houghton, M. (1996). Relapse revisited: A critique of current concepts and clinical practice in the management of alcohol problems. *Addictive Behaviors, 21*(6), 843–855.

Saunders, B., Wilkinson C. & Allsop, S. (1991). Motivational interviewing with heroin users attending a methadone clinic. In Miller, W.R. & Rollnick, S. (Eds.), *Motivational Interviewing* (pp. 279–292). New York: Guilford Press.

Schober, R. & Annis, H.M. (1996a). Commitment to change in individuals seeking treatment for excessive drinking. Manuscript submitted for publication.

Schober, R. & Annis, H.M. (1996b). Stages and processes of change in individuals seeking treatment for excessive drinking. Manuscript in preparation.

Schonfeld, L., Dupree, L.W., Dickson-Fuhrmann, E., McKean Royer, C., McDermott, C.H., Rosansky et al. (2000). Cognitive-behavioural treatment of older veterans with substance abuse problems. *Journal of Geriatric Psychiatry Neurology, 13,* 124–129.

Shiffman, S. (1985). Preventing relapse in ex-smokers: A self-management approach. In Marlatt, G.A. & Gordon, J.R. (Eds.), *Relapse Prevention.* New York: Guilford Press.

Straussner, S.L. (2002). Ethnic cultures and substance abuse. *Counselor,* December 2002, 34–38.

Strowig, A.B. (1999). Relapse determinants reported by men treated for alcohol addiction: The prominence of depressed mood. *Journal of Substance Use Treatment, 19,* 469–474.

Swanson, A.J., Pantalon, M.V. & Cohen, K.R. (1999). Motivational interviewing and treatment adherence among psychiatric and dually diagnosed patients. *The Journal of Nervous and Mental Disease, 187*(10), 630–635.

Walton, M.A., Blow, F.C. & Booth, B.M. (2001). Diversity in relapse prevention needs: Gender and race comparisons among substance abuse treatment patients. *American Journal of Drug Alcohol Abuse, 27*(2), 225–240.

Wilson, G.T. (1980). Cognitive factors in lifestyle changes: A social learning perspective. In Davidson, P.O. & Davidson, S.M. (Eds.), *Behavioral Medicine: Changing Health Lifestyles* (pp. 3–37). New York: Brunner/Mazel.

Dual Diagnosis Motivational Interviewing: A Modification of Motivational Interviewing for Substance-Abusing Patients with Psychotic Disorders

STEVE MARTINO, PHD, KATHLEEN CARROLL, PHD, DEMETRIOS KOSTAS, MSW, JENNIFER PERKINS, BA, BRUCE ROUNSAVILLE, MD

1. Introduction

Motivational Interviewing (MI) is a brief psychotherapeutic intervention for helping patients change addictive behaviors. Over the past two decades William Miller and his colleagues have detailed the principles, practices, and research supporting this treatment approach. *Motivational Interviewing: Preparing People for Change Addictive Behavior* by Miller and Rollnick (2002) provides the most comprehensive singular and updated presentation of MI techniques and strategies. In addition, there are several comprehensive research reviews of the efficacy of MI (Dunn, Deroo, & Rivara, 2001; Miller, 1983; 1985; 1996; 1998).

Conceptually, MI is a blend of principles drawn from motivational psychology, Rogerian therapy, and the stages of change model of recovery. MI aims to facilitate and enhance the patient's intrinsic motivation to change substance use or other problem behaviors by engaging the patient in an empathetically supportive but strategically directed conversation about the patient's use of substances and related life events. Typically, the MI therapist uses a variety of techniques to help increase intrinsic motivation for change. These techniques can be divided into two categories: microskills and strategies (Rollnick, Heather, & Bell, 1992).

Reprinted from *Journal of Substance Abuse Treatment*, 23(4), 297–308, copyright 2002, with permission from Elsevier.

Microskills function to initiate and facilitate an open discussion with the patient about problem areas. These skills include the use of open-ended questioning, reflective listening, using affirmations, and summarizing the patient's comments in a balanced manner. The therapist uses these skills to accurately understand the patient's perceptions about a problem, heighten the patient's problem recognition, and resolve ambivalence about changing it. The therapist's consistent and competent use of microskills is essential for the creation of MI's highly empathic and collaborative style.

Motivational Interviewing strategies involve increasingly directive techniques for building intrinsic motivation for change, particularly when the microskills alone have not achieved this aim. These techniques involve asking direct open-ended questions to increase problem awareness, concern, or intention and optimism to change. Therapists may construct decisional balance matrices to elicit the patient's perceptions of the costs and benefits of remaining the same or trying to change. Additionally, therapists may attempt to create discrepancies between the patient's current behavior and his or her goals, values, or self-perceptions. Therapists also commonly use supportive feedback of selected objective assessment results within the body of an overall MI style to promote problem recognition and desire to change. Through the skillful use of these skill sets, the therapist attempts to move the patient from a position of establishing the patient's motivation for change to strengthening the patient's commitment to attempt the change. If the patient's resistance to change arises during any phase of the interview, the therapist avoids argumentation and encourages the patient to conversationally explore his or her resistance using one or more of the microskills or MI strategies.

Support for the efficacy of MI has come from many sources. It has been effective in reducing alcohol consumption in nontreatment community samples of drinkers (Miller, Benefield, & Tonigan, 1993; Miller, Sovereign, & Krege, 1988), in patients participating in an inpatient alcohol treatment facility (Brown & Miller, 1993), and among outpatients seeking traditional substance abuse treatment services (Bien, Miller, & Boroughs, 1993) or receiving MI as the sole intervention (Project MATCH Research Group, 1997). Across these studies positive treatment outcomes persisted during follow-up periods ranging from 3 to 15 months.

As a consequence of Miller's compelling rationale for MI, its potential for wider application, and research supporting its clinical utility and efficacy for alcoholism treatment, investigators have begun to systematically apply MI to additional problem areas. Some of these areas have included heroin dependence (Saunders et al., 1995), cocaine dependence (Stotts, Schmitz, Rhoades, & Grabowski, 2001), nicotine dependence (Butler et al., 1999) and adolescent smoking (Lawendowski, 1998), HIV risk behavior (Carey et al., 1997), obesity (Smith, Heckemeyer, Kratt, & Mason, 1997), diabetes care (Stott, Rollnick, Pill, & Rees, 1995), and bulimia nervosa (Treasure et al., 1999). Recently, the use of motivational techniques with patients who have cooccurring substance abuse and psychiatric problems or dual disorders has begun to be explored (Carey, 1996; Daley & Zuckoff, 1998; Van Horn and Bux, 2001; Ziedonis & Fischer, 1996; Ziedonis & Trudeau, 1997).

1.1. RATIONALE FOR MI WITH DUALLY DIAGNOSED PATIENTS

As a therapeutic approach MI seems very well suited for dually diagnosed patients. The severe and disabling symptoms, frequent failed treatment episodes, and poor functional adjustments often contribute to the patient's demoralization and lack of intrinsic motivation for alcohol and drug abstinence or sustained efforts to productively manage their dual disorders (Brady et al., 1996; Carey, 1996; Ziedonis & Fischer, 1996). References to these patients' low motivation for change occur throughout the literature (Drake & Wallach, 1989; Minkoff, 1989) and have led many who specialize in dual diagnosis treatment to emphasize the primary importance of engagement and motivational enhancement strategies (Carey, 1996; Kofoed & Keyes, 1988; Ziedonis & Fischer; 1996; Ziedonis & Trudeau, 1997). Given these observations and recommendations, MI's emphasis on building motivation for change and strategies for handling resistance to the change process have made MI a very appealing approach in the dual diagnosis field.

Very few studies, however, have been conducted to examine MI's efficacy with dually diagnosed patients. In one pilot study (Swanson, Pantalon, & Cohen, 1999), the effect of MI on outpatient treatment adherence among psychiatric and dually diagnosed inpatients was investigated. The results suggested that the proportion of dually diagnosed patients who attended their first outpatient appointment was significantly higher for patients who had received the MI (42%) than for those in standard treatment alone (16%). Substance use treatment outcomes were not evaluated in this study.

In a pilot study conducted by our group (Martino, Carroll, O'Malley, & Rounsaville, 2000), we randomly assigned patients with co-occurring psychotic or mood disorders and alcohol or drug abuse or dependence to either a one-session 45–60 minutes MI or equivalently long standard preadmission session. The session occurred immediately before the patients started a dual diagnosis partial hospital program. We found that MI, in comparison to the standard preadmission interview, yielded better patient program attendance patterns (less program tardiness and early departures and greater number of days attended). While we did not find significant differences in substance use between the conditions, the MI group had lower substance use indices than the standard interviewing condition using a small pilot study sample size ($n = 23$).

Despite these encouraging initial pilot study results and the consensus about the probable utility of MI for patients who have dual disorders, few professionals have written about how to modify MI for this population. Published reports of motivation-based interventions for patients with dual disorders typically imply a direct application of MI. Namely, these reports state that many patients who have dual disorders have little motivation to change their substance abuse problems or have recurrent wavering commitments to alcohol or drug abstinence. Additionally, the reports uphold the nonconfrontational MI approach as preferable to the traditionally confrontational substance abuse treatment strategies when working with dually diagnosed patients (Beeder & Millman, 1992; Bellack & DiClemente, 1999; Carey, 1996). Beyond summarizing the now familiar MI strategies, the reports do not describe modifications needed to effectively use MI as an interviewing strategy within this population or detail how to use MI with specific psychiatric diagnostic groups of substance abusing patients within the larger rubric of dually diagnosed patients. Moreover, the numerous clinical challenges posed by dually diagnosed patients, such as active psychotic symptoms, treatment and medication noncompliance, cognitive impairments and disordered thinking, and social stigma suggest that a direct application of MI may be ill advised and ineffective. To address this shortcoming, this article describes our experience in using MI with patients who have psychotic disorders (Schizophrenia, Schizoaffective Disorder, Schizophreniform Disorder, and Psychotic Disorder NOS) and co-occurring drug or alcohol use problems (henceforth referred to as dually diagnosed patients). We call our approach Dual Diagnosis Motivational Interviewing or DDMI.

2. Methods

2.1. SUBJECTS

Two groups of dually diagnosed patients participated in the development of DDMI. The first group consisted of 12 patients with psychotic disorders who had been subjects in our initial pilot study (Martino et al., 2000). Clinical experience with these patients provided the basis for the first draft of a two-session manualized DDMI. The second group included 7 patients who received this initial version of DDMI. In both groups the patients had been referred to a dual diagnosis ambulatory program (see Martino, McCance-Katz, Workman, & Boozang, 1995, for program description) by clinicians from inpatient and outpatient facilities. Prior to entering the program, we approached patients who met eligibility criteria to request their participation in the respective phases of DDMI's development. Eligible subjects had to have co-occurring DSM-IV psychotic and substance use disorders based upon the clinical consensus of the referring treatment team. In addition, they had to report abuse of at least one substance in the past two months, take at least one psychotropic medication for their psychiatric condition, not have active symptoms necessitating inpatient psychiatric or detoxification treatment, and have basic reading and comprehension skills. All subjects provided written informed consent.

Table 1 describes the demographic and diagnostic characteristics of both participant groups. Across the groups, the subjects typically were in the 25–45 age range, single, unemployed, experiencing severe psychiatric symptoms, and abusing alcohol, cocaine, or cannabis. Most subjects abused more than one substance. The number of male and female participants was similar. The first group, however, had a higher percentage of ethnic minorities, a somewhat lower level of educational attainment, and a more even distribution of types of psychotic disorders than the second group.

TABLE 1

Demographic and Diagnostic Characteristics of Participant Groups

	Group 1 (n = 12)[a]		Group 2 (n = 7)[b]	
	M	(SD)	M	(SD)
Age	35.08	(7.12)	33.57	(10.20)
Years of Education Completed	10.58	(2.81)	12.71	(1.50)
Current Global Assessment of Functioning[c]	45.92	(6.47)	39.86	(4.10)
	n	(%)	n	(%)
Gender				
Males	6	(50.0)	4	(57.1)
Females	6	(50.0)	3	(42.9)
Ethnicity				
Caucasian	4	(33.3)	5	(71.4)
African American	6	(50.0)	1	(14.3)
Hispanic American	2	(16.7)	0	(0.0)
Asian American	0	(0.0)	1	(14.3)
Marital Status				
Single	11	(91.7)	6	(85.7)
Divorced	1	(8.3)	1	(14.3)
Unemployment	12	(100)	7	(100)
DSM-IV Substance use disorders				
Alcohol	7	(58.3)	4	(57.1)
Cocaine	8	(66.7)	4	(57.1)
Cannabis	8	(66.7)	3	(42.9)
Opiates	1	(8.3)	1	(14.3)
Sedatives	0	(0.0)	1	(14.3)
> 1 disorder[d]	9	(75.0)	6	(85.7)
DSM-IV Psychotic disorders				
Schizophrenia	5	(41.7)	1	(14.3)
Schizoaffective Disorder	5	(41.7)	5	(71.4)
Schizophreniform Disorder	1	(8.3)	0	(0.0)
Psychotic Disorder NOS[e]	1	(8.3)	1	(14.3)

[a] Group 1 consisted of patients who had participated in a MI pilot study (Martino et al., 2000).

[b] Group 2 consisted of patients who received a two-session manualized working version of DDMI based upon the experiences of using MI with Group 1 participants.

[c] Global Assessment of Functioning (American Psychiatric Association, 1994) level reflects overall psychological functioning on a scale of 0–100, with lower scores indicating more severe symptomatic and functional impairment and higher scores representing improved mental health.

[d] Patients in this cohort had heterogeneous combinations of substance use disorders. Combinations of alcohol, cocaine, and cannabis accounted for most multiple disorders in both groups (Group 1 = 66.7%; Group 2 = 57.1%).

[e] Patients who had received a Psychotic Disorder NOS diagnosis had historical and presenting evidence of psychotic symptoms that were consistent with Schizophrenia, but their active substance use confounded a conclusive diagnostic determination at the point of their participation.

2.2. PROCEDURES FOR DEVELOPING DDMI

We developed DDMI using a Stage I Model of Behavior Therapy research (Rounsaville, Carroll, & Onken, 2001). Initially, we used standard MI techniques within a one session, 45–60 minute ambulatory program preadmission interview for the first group of subjects who had participated in our pilot study. Within the overall MI therapeutic style, common techniques used in the session included querying patients to elicit self-motivational statements, providing feedback from preadmission questionnaires, and completing a decisional balance activity.

Based on this experience, we isolated MI principles and practices that we believed required modification to better accommodate the clinical challenges posed by dually diagnosed patients. We organized these modifications into a two-session manualized working version of DDMI following the procedures outlined by Carroll and Nuro (1997). The second group of subjects received this initial version of DDMI. We videotaped all sessions. Using informal subject feedback, review of videotaped sessions, and our clinical judgment, we further refined the DDMI approach and made final modifications to recommended guidelines and techniques. The Human Investigation Committee of the institution where we conducted this project approved all the procedures.

3. Dual Diagnosis Motivational Interviewing

While the DDMI approach adheres to the basic tenets of MI and relies upon many of its fundamental strategies, we have found that specific emphases and technical modifications of MI make it more clinically amenable for substance abusing patients who have psychotic disorders. We have organized our discussion of applying MI to dually diagnosed patients into four areas: (a) supplemental guidelines to MI basic principles; (b) MI microskill modifications; (c) modifications to MI strategies and (d) other clinical considerations. Table 2 (page 262) provides an overview of how we have modified the standard practices of MI to address the clinical challenges posed by dually diagnosed patients. We detail each area of modification below.

3.1. SUPPLEMENTAL GUIDELINES TO MI BASIC PRINCIPLES

The foundation of DDMI lies in its adoption of the four MI basic principles that guide all therapists' interactions with patients, namely: (a) expressing empathy; (b) developing discrepancy; (c) rolling with resistance and avoiding argumentation; and (d) supporting self-efficacy. The therapist upholds these principles throughout the interview to create and sustain an environment that promotes the patient's comfortable exploration of problem areas, resolution of ambivalence toward change, and planning and initiation of change efforts. In this regard DDMI is no different than MI. However, we have found two supplemental guidelines to MI's basic principles helpful to increase the chance that DDMI achieves similar aims as MI when working with dually diagnosed patients who have psychotic disorders. The two supplements are: (a) adopting an integrated dual diagnosis interview approach that targets more than substance use; and (b) accommodating cognitive impairments and disordered thinking.

3.1.1. Adopting an Integrated Dual Diagnosis Approach That Targets More Than Substance Use

Adopting an integrated approach to substance abuse and psychiatric treatment is the sine qua non of the dual diagnosis field (Drake, Bartels, Teague, Noordsy, & Clark, 1993; Drake,

Mercer-McFadden, Mueser, McHugo, & Bond, 1998; Drake et al., 2001; Minkoff, 2001; Minkoff & Drake, 1991; Rosenthal, Hellerstein, & Miner, 1992). In this regard, dual diagnosis interventions attempt to address both problem areas equally and with an understanding of how the dual disorders and related life events interact with one another. For example, dually diagnosed patients may use substances to lessen negative psychotic symptoms such as blunted affect, depersonalization, or social inhibition or to reduce discomfort caused by positive psychotic symptoms such as auditory hallucinations or paranoid delusions. In other instances, patients might not acknowledge psychotic difficulties and prefer to see their psychiatric symptoms as substance-induced. As applied to DDMI, therapists remain mindful of these types of potential interactions, so they can strategically explore with the patient both the problem areas and their effects on one another using the microskills and MI strategies. For example, the therapist may query the patient with general open-ended questions such as, "How does your drug use affect your psychiatric symptoms?" or use more evocative questions that pull for specific self-motivational statements, such as, "How does your use of drugs cause problems for you psychiatrically?" Failure to discern how both areas inform the patient's motivational base may reduce the therapist's effectiveness in building and strengthening the patient's motivation and capacity to prepare for change.

As a corollary to this integrated approach, DDMI targets a wider array of behavior than is typical in MI. Though several investigators have begun to apply MI to behavioral domains other than addiction problems (Dunn, DeRoo, & Rivara, 2001), MI's traditional primary target for change has been on substance use. This focus is insufficient to meet the complex change challenges confronted by substance abusing patients with psychotic disorders. Thus, DDMI includes two other domains as additional targets for change, treatment and medication compliance.

Enhancing motivation for treatment compliance is crucial for several reasons. First, dually diagnosed patients are notorious for treatment program noncompliance (Drake & Wallach, 1989; Richardson, Craig, & Haugland, 1985) if they participate in treatment at all (Drake, McLaughlin, Pepper, & Minkoff, 1991). Second, noncompliance with treatment can lead to numerous adverse consequences such as poorer clinical outcomes (Eisenthal, Emery, Lazare, & Udin, 1978), violent behavior (Zitrin, Hardesty, Burdock, & Drossman, 1976), and increased rates of rehospitalization (Drake, Osher, & Wallach, 1989; Lyons & McGovern, 1989) and utilization of emergency services and jails (Bartels et al., 1993). DDMI attempts to enhance the patient's motivation for treatment compliance by building and strengthening the patient's commitment to participate in dual diagnosis specialty ambulatory programs and other related outpatient services.

Regarding medication compliance, adherence to appropriate pharmacotherapy is essential to the successful treatment of dually diagnosed psychotic disordered patients (Drake et al., 1989; Osher & Kofoed, 1989; Owen, Fischer, Booth, & Cuffel, 1996; Zweben & Smith, 1989). DDMI tries to promote the patient's motivation for medication compliance by exploring the patient's view about taking prescribed medications and to attend to obstacles that may have diminished the patient's adherence to medication regimens in the past.

TABLE 2

Overview of Recommended Modifications for Motivational Interviewing with Dually Diagnosed Patients

MI Standard Practices	Dual Diagnosis Clinical Challenge	DDMI Modifications
MI BASIC PRINCIPLES Targets substance use.	Psychiatric condition is primary problem area that interacts with substance use. Noncompliance with treatment and psychotropic medications is common.	Addresses substance use, psychiatric condition, and their interaction. Targets behavioral change for treatment and medication compliance, in addition to substance use.
Presumes patients are cognitively intact and logically organized.	Cognitive impairments, such as inattention, poor concentration, illogical reasoning, and diminished mental flexibility are common. Disordered thinking (e.g., tangentiality) or pervasive psychotic symptoms (e.g., paranoia) may be present.	Incorporates strategies of repetition, simple verbal and visual materials, and breaks within sessions. Emphasizes strategic nature of guiding conversation to promote logical organization and improved reality testing.
MI MICROSKILLS Uses open-ended questioning.	Patients may have difficulty tracking or organizing responses to complex questions.	Avoids compound open-ended questions and queries in clear and concise terms.
Uses reflective listening	Psychotically organized statements and information processing deficits complicate reflective listening process.	Uses reflections and summaries often in simply stated terms; reduces reflection on disturbing life experiences; incorporates metaphors to anchor statements in reality; provides sufficient time for patient's response to reflections.
Affirms patients' personal qualities and efforts that promote change.	Invalidating experiences of social stigma from dual disorders and being misfit to treatment programs that do not integrate care leave patients unaccustomed to affirming support.	Heightens emphasis on affirming patients.
MI STRATEGIES Provides personalized feedback from objective substance-related assessment results.	Psychiatric problems that interact with substance use should be part of the personalized feedback. Feedback needs to be simple and compelling to accommodate potential information processing impediments.	Uses comparisons of interviewer- and patient- rated severity items across Addiction Severity Index problem areas, with emphasis on substance use and psychiatric condition; uses Positive and Negative Syndrome Scale for feedback about psychotic symptoms. Uses color-coded bar charts, analogies, metaphors, and demonstration models.
Uses decisional balance activity to discuss the positive and negative aspects of continuing to use substances in comparison to those aspects expected from changing patterns of use, resulting in a 2 x 2 matrix.	Decisions to change dual disorder outcomes often involve reluctance or ambivalence about seeking treatment as part of the change plan strategy. Constructing a 2 x 2 decisional balance matrix can be confusing to patients.	Uses decisional balance techniques to explore patient's ambivalence about getting dual diagnosis treatment and for examining the positives and negatives of not using alcohol and drugs. Focuses only on the positive and negative aspects of changing behavior.
OTHER CLINICAL CONSIDERATIONS Developed for use with patients who have primary substance use problems without complications posed by severe psychiatric conditions.	Psychotic exacerbations and acute suicidality and homicidality occur.	Determines if the patient needs other interventions that promote psychiatric stability, logical reasoning, and safety; requires special professional qualifications and supervision.

3.1.2. Accommodating Cognitive Impairments and Disordered Thinking

The second supplemental guideline to MI's basic principles is the need to accommodate cognitive impairments and disordered thinking resulting from the patient's psychotic disorder, prolonged substance abuse, preoccupation with present crisis or combinations of these factors (Bellack & DiClemente, 1999). Cognitive impairments among dually diagnosed patients may include problems with attention and concentration, short-term and working memory, organizing and abstracting information, and mental flexibility (Bell, Lysaker, Milstein, & Beam-Goulet, 1994; Green, 1996; Lysaker, Bell, Zito, & Bioty, 1995; Seidman et al., 1993). To address these information processing impediments, DDMI incorporates strategies of repetition, use of simple and concrete verbal and visual materials, and breaks within sessions. Disordered thinking may include circumstantiality, tangentiality, thought blocking, or other pervasive psychotic symptoms such as paranoia or grandiosity that may impede the motivational enhancement process. In particular, interviews that have insufficient structure or that excessively delve into emotionally laden material or psychotic belief systems may heighten the patient's psychotic symptoms and reduce the effectiveness of the therapist to motivate the patient for change. Likewise, trying to follow the patient's conversational lead when the patient continues to veer from a logical pathway may be very difficult for the therapist and patient and result in the therapist becoming confused and uncertainty about what part of the patient's discourse to reflect. To navigate these occurrences, the DDMI therapist places more emphasis on the strategic nature of guiding the conversation with the patient in a manner that promotes the patient's logical organization and reality testing without sacrificing the collaborative and respectful tenor of MI. This article's subsections that describe recommended modifications to MI microskills and strategies provide specific examples of how DDMI accommodates cognitive impairments and disordered thinking processes common to dually diagnosed patients.

3.2. MI MICROSKILL MODIFICATIONS

The core MI microskills are asking open-ended questions, listening reflectively (including summarizing), and affirming the patient. These microskills also are fundamental to the DDMI approach. We have found, however, that each microskill requires slight modification or unique emphasis to be most effective when used with dually diagnosed patients. We also have found that the general supportive and collaborative MI style of interaction established by the therapist's use of microskills often is unfamiliar to patients with dual disorders who may have become accustomed to a more directive and authoritarian style of traditional psychiatric interviewing. In traditional interviewing, the therapist most often controls the immediate direction of the interview by using numerous closed-ended questions to determine diagnoses, obtain biopsychosocial information, and prescribe treatments. Because many dually diagnosed patients expect a traditional interviewing framework, the DDMI therapist first provides the patient with a brief and simple introduction to DDMI before asking openended questions and beginning the reflective listening process. For example:

> "Before we begin, I would like to explain what we will do in this meeting.
> I recognize that you may have talked with many professionals in the past
> about your use of substances and psychiatric issues. We also will talk

about these areas today and any other areas that are important to you but perhaps in a slightly different way. My main interest is in understanding how you view your problems and get to know you better. I would like to talk with you about how alcohol or drug use and psychiatric issues have affected your life from your point of view. I may ask you a few questions along the way, but mostly I want to listen to what you have to say and make sure I have correctly understood what you have told me."

3.2.1. Simplifying Open-ended Questions

After the opening remarks, the therapist typically begins with an open-ended question (e.g., What brings you here today?). Asking open-ended questions is a primary MI strategy, particularly at the early stages of the interview when a therapist encourages the patient to talk about his or her perception of specific problem areas. Open-ended questions (e.g., What type of psychiatric issues have you been grappling with in your life?) are questions that result in more than a "yes/no" response and that encourage the patient to elaborate on a topic rather than to provide a terse answer or very specific information. These types of questions generally provide the patient with ample opportunities to express his or her viewpoint uninterrupted by the therapist. While fairly straightforward, we have found that open-ended questions are most effective with dually diagnosed patients when the therapist asks them in very clear and concise terms and avoids compound questions that may be difficult for psychotic patients to track. For example, the question, "What types of psychiatric symptoms do you experience and how does your use of cocaine affect your symptoms in the short term and long term?" is complex and may overwhelm the patient's organizational capacity to respond to it. DDMI therapists try to avoid these types of open-ended questions and strive to simplify them at all times.

3.2.2. Refining Reflective Listening Skills

Listening reflectively to patients is a vital MI microskill that infuses the entire interviewing process. Reflective listening means that the therapist takes time to carefully understand what the patient has said and confirms this understanding with the patient by repeating it back to him or her in similar (simple reflection) or somewhat transformed ways (restatement, paraphrasing, double-sided reflection). By using this microskill, the therapist unveils the structure of the patient's motivational base and uses this structure as a foundation from which to establish and resolve ambivalence toward change. In MI, competent reflective listening is a difficult task that requires keen therapist attention and capacity to organize and rephrase what the patient has said.

Yet in DDMI, by comparison, reflective listening is an even more challenging microskill for a therapist to implement effectively. Patients with psychotic disorders may exhibit some degree of disordered thinking and poor reality testing that might unravel further in the absence of a sufficiently structured interview or in the face of a therapist's repeated reflection of fundamentally psychotic material. Beyond requiring therapists to heighten their active attention to meaningful and logically organized elements of the patient's discourse, we have found several other recommendations useful for how to most effectively listen reflectively with psychotic disordered substance abusing patients. These recommendations are: (a) using simple and concise language; (b) reflecting often; (c) using metaphors;

(d) avoiding excessive focus on despairing patients' statements and negative life events; (e) logically organizing patients' statements with summaries; and (f) giving patients enough time to respond to reflections. We summarize these recommendations with examples in Table 3 (pages 265–266).

3.2.3. Heightening Emphasis on Affirmations

The last MI microskill is affirming the patient. The therapist affirms the patient by acknowledging the patient's personal qualities and efforts that promote change. The execution of this microskill is the same in DDMI as it is in MI. The caveat to its use in DDMI is in the heightened emphasis placed upon affirming patients during the interview process. Dually diagnosed patients often have had the personally invalidating experience of combined social stigma associated with their substance use and psychotic disorders (Evans & Sullivan, 1989) and feeling misfit to treatment systems that do not have integrated dual diagnosis care (Ridgely, Goldman, & Willenbring, 1990). In DDMI, the therapist strives to affirm patients who may not be accustomed to receiving such support. For example, a therapist might express appreciation for a patient's candor and ability to talk about what the patient sees as problematic after the patient has criticized several prior treatment experiences. Likewise, a therapist might express appreciation to a patient who has had a history of treatment noncompliance for attending a session or taking medications as prescribed. We have found that dually diagnosed patients experience a therapist's frequent complimenting of their personal qualities and initial change efforts inspiring and very helpful in establishing a supportive and collaborative interviewing tone.

TABLE 3

Recommendations for Effective Reflective Listening with Substance Abusing Patients with Psychotic Disorders

1. Reflect in simple and concise terms to reduce the information processing demands placed upon the patients.
   Patient: My medications are drugs that don't work, drugs that make me feel worse—not better.
   Therapist: You don't like the way your medications make you feel.
2. Reflect often to assist in structuring the interview and maintaining a logical organization to the conversation.
   Patient: What's wrong with me is that my mind and body go in old directions any time I confront new situations of substance with people.
   Therapist: You find yourself using again when people who use drugs are around you.
   P: Yeah, like I wasn't planning on it, but it was put before me somehow, like they are setting me up again.
   T: Your intention is to not use drugs, but it is hard to not use when you are around people who do.
   P: I can't say I don't try not to use. But these people are evil, bad. I know what they are thinking. But they won't get the best of me.
   T: They are of no help to you, and you really want to stay way from them to be the best you can be without using drugs.
   P: That's right.
3. Reflect metaphors often embedded in the patient's psychotically driven statements and nonverbal communication to promote empathic listening while trying to anchor the patient's statements in a reality base from which motivational interviewing may proceed.

Patient: I don't have a problem with cocaine. I stopped using it. It's tucked under and out. I've seen the light, and now I've turned it over and off never to witness such events again. (*Patient lies down on the floor.*)

Therapist: You've put your cocaine use to rest.

P: Completely to rest. I ain't using it no more.

T: How will you pick yourself up now that you no longer want to use cocaine? (*Patient sits down in the chair again.*)

4. Avoid repeatedly reflecting patients' despairing statements or negative current or past life events; this reflective listening pitfall can diminish motivation for change and heighten further psychotic symptoms expressed by the patient.

Patient: You know I was hit a lot by my mother growing up. Sometimes she was a vicious, angry woman—very strict. I remember she slapped me so hard I heard my brains rattle. "Don't hit me again," my mind would say or I'll hit you back. Now I'm told to hit back if someone isn't treating me right.

Therapist: Told to hit back.

P: I hear voices that tell me to hit people when I don't like them.

T: Then what happens?

P: I try not to do it. You know my brother used to treat me badly too. That son-of-a-bi. . .

T: So even though many people have treated you badly, you don't want to hurt others.

P: Usually, that's when I get high.

T: Getting high helps you not do what the voices are telling you to do.

P: In the moment, but then it messes up my mind more.

T: So getting high is good in the moment, but over the long haul it makes matters worse for you.

5. Summarize often to promote meaningful relationships among the patient's statements and to juxtaposition them in a strategic manner that promotes the motivational enhancement process.

A patient has acknowledged abusing cocaine but does not believe she has a psychotic disorder. The patient thinks her many prior experiences in which she heard voices and spoke in disorganized ways were cocaine-induced. She believes that as long as she does not use cocaine, she will be mentally stable and will not need antipsychotic medication in the future. At present, however, she is unsure if she should stop taking her medications out of concern that she has not been abstinent from cocaine for a long enough period, thus far for two weeks.

Therapist: You know very clearly that you do not want to use cocaine anymore. It messes up how you think and causes you to hear voices. You see staying drug-free as the best way to feel better. The medication may have been helpful in getting past the worst part of what cocaine does to you. You just are not sure how long you may need it as a part of your treatment. At the same time, you have some concern that you might have some problems with your mind again if you stop taking your medications now.

6. For patients with a slow response time and other negative psychotic symptoms, pause sufficiently after reflecting the patient's statement to provide the patient with a sufficient opportunity to consider and respond to the reflection.

Therapist: You seem very tired (*pause*).

Patient: (*no response*)

T: So tired it's hard to talk about what's going on (*pause*).

P: Yeah, I'm tired.

T: It's hard to have a conversation about what you are going through when you are so tired (*pause*).

P: It takes me awhile to get going in the morning and this is early for me.

T: If we were to meet later in the day, what would be some of the things you would want to talk about?

3.3. MODIFICATIONS TO MI STRATEGIES

DDMI incorporates many of the commonly used MI strategies. These strategies include the use of evocative open-ended questions to elicit self-motivational statements (e.g., What concerns you about how your drug use affects your psychiatric condition?). They also include a variety of MI techniques for handling resistance skillfully. Mastery of this skill set is very important for DDMI therapists because dually diagnosed patients often express resistance in reaction to perceived coercive forces (therapists or case managers, psychiatrists, residential or vocational counselors, probation officers, child protective services personnel) compelling them to make changes. Dually diagnosed patients also may have paranoid proclivities that heighten their baseline levels of resistance irrespective of external contingencies on them. An area of significant modification to standard MI practice is in the DDMI therapist's efforts to develop discrepancy in the patient's perceptions of his or her problems. Specifically, in DDMI we have revised the methods of providing personalized feedback and constructing decisional balance matrices as a means to alter the patient's view that substance use or psychiatric issues are not problematic. We describe these modifications to MI strategies below.

3.3.1. Providing Personalized and Engaging Feedback That Addresses Dual Diagnosis Concerns

In MI, feedback typically involves a therapist providing a structured review of objective assessment results in an empathetic and collaborative style. The therapist explores with patients their reaction to the feedback and the possible relationships between the patients' use of substances, their problems or concerns, and their intention to change their behavior. In DDMI, feedback also must include information about psychiatric symptoms and contain mechanisms for exploring the interaction of these symptoms with the patients' use of substances and the impact on their functioning overall. In addition, the feedback needs to be simple in presentation, flexible to accommodate different areas relevant to dual diagnosis recovery, and capable of compelling patients to look at their long-standing problem areas in a renewed light.

To accommodate these requirements, we prepared a pamphlet for patients to organize the presentation of feedback into areas relevant for dual diagnosis recovery. These areas include feedback about the patient's substance use from the Addiction Severity Index or ASI (McLellan, Luborsky, Woody, & O'Brien, 1980; McLellan et al., 1985), the patient's psychotic symptoms from the Positive and Negative Syndrome Scale or PANSS (Kay, Fizbein, & Opler, 1987), how substance use and psychotic-related problems interact, and a model of dual diagnosis recovery. Both the ASI and PANSS are structured clinical interviews administered to patients, scored and compiled into feedback forms prior to the DDMI sessions. The ASI is designed to provide problem severity ratings (lifetime and past 30 days) in areas commonly affected in people who abuse alcohol and drugs (alcohol and drug use, medical condition, employment, legal status, family relations, and psychiatric condition). For each problem area, patients also provide subjective ratings of their recent (past 30 days) problem severity by indicating the importance they attach to seeking treatment for it. Using a color-coded bar chart comparing the recent ASI and patient-rated severity items per problem area, the DDMI therapist compares and contrasts the ratings, notes rating discrepancies, and promotes the patients' exploration of their substance use in relationship to other areas, particularly in interaction with the psychiatric condition.

The PANSS is designed to evaluate positive, negative, and other symptom dimensions of schizophrenia phenomenon. The PANSS provides a score for how much a patient experiences symptoms that are in excess of what most people experience (positive symptoms), such as delusions or hallucinations. It also provides a score for how much a patient experiences symptoms that involve the absence of thoughts and feelings that most people experience (negative symptoms), such as feeling emotionally flat or having slowed thinking. As in the ASI feedback, we present these two dimensions in a color-coded bar chart format. Based on patient input, we renamed the positive symptoms "hot" symptoms (i.e., symptoms that make patients feel like they are boiling inside) and color-coded the bar in red. Similarly, we renamed the negative symptoms "cold" symptoms (i.e., symptoms that make patients feel like they are frozen inside) and color-coded the bar in blue. We found this metaphor helped the patients understand and relate to the scores better and made the feedback activity more engaging. As with the ASI, the DDMI therapist reviews and explores the patient-specific information with the patient to promote psychiatric problem recognition and related motivation for change.

The pamphlet ends with a discussion of the interaction of substance use and psychotic disorders and presents a metaphor of a three-legged stool model of dual diagnosis recovery (see Figure 1). In brief, the therapist describes how many dually diagnosed patients have found that their ability to make productive change in their lives has rested upon three principles: staying clean and sober, taking medications as prescribed, and participating in a dual diagnosis treatment program. Using a demonstration model, the therapist notes how these principles represent three legs of the stool supporting the seat of dual diagnosis recovery. Beginning with an open-ended question, the therapist asks the patient what happens when an individual does not use or strengthen one or more legs of the stool. Next, the therapist unscrews one of the stool's legs and demonstrates how the stool falls in the absence of a critical area of support. While this feedback strategy contains elements that are not unique to MI (e.g., Socratic questioning), we have found that this simple and interactive model is very engaging for patients and helpful in garnering and organizing their motivation for productively addressing their dual disorders.

FIGURE 1

Dual Diagnosis Recovery

| Staying Clean and Sober | Taking Your Medications | Participating in a Dual Diagnosis Specialty Program |

3.3.2. Constructing Decisional Balance Matrices Appropriate for Dually Diagnosed Patients

Another frequently used technique in MI is the construction of a decisional balance matrix. In this technique, the therapist tries to normalize ambivalence by having the patient discuss the positive and negative aspects of continuing a behavior (e.g., drinking alcohol) and trying to change it (e.g., not drinking alcohol). The therapist typically records what the patient enumerates into a 2 × 2 matrix and then explores with the patient the array of underlying attitudes that make up the competing dimensions of the patient's motivation for change. Beyond applying this technique to the patient's substance use, DDMI also uses the decisional balance technique to explore the patient's ambivalence about getting treatment for his or her dual disorders. Here, we defined treatment as participation in a dual diagnosis specialty program and taking prescribed medications. The consolidation of two treatment areas into one decisional balance activity reduces the task demands placed on the patients without neglecting the primary targets of DDMI. We also determined that many dually diagnosed patients found completion of a 2 × 2 matrix confusing and redundant. For example, the negative expectancies for not using a substance ("I won't feel good") often are inversely related to the positive expectancies for continuing to use a substance ("I will feel good."). To simplify the task, DDMI focuses only on the patient's anticipation of positive and negative aspects of changing a behavior and the relative balance of these two areas in promoting or hindering a patient's motivation for change. Examples of items that comprise the decisional balance activities used in DDMI (Positives and Negatives of Staying Clean and Sober and Getting Treatment for My Dual Disorders) are presented in Table 4.

3.4. OTHER CLINICAL CONSIDERATIONS

We believe that the modifications described above help therapists use MI more effectively with dually diagnosed patients. Nevertheless, we qualify our recommendation of MI for use with this population by emphasizing how patients must have sufficient psychiatric stability to benefit from MI's ample use of verbal persuasion and logical reasoning, albeit in the overall MI style. When patients are too psychotically disorganized to logically attend to the content of the interview or consistently remain based in reality, they are not appropriate for DDMI and may require other types of interventions (e.g., crisis intervention, pharmacotherapy) first. If patients' psychotic symptoms are so severe that patients cannot make informed decisions or properly take care of their basic needs, DDMI therapists must be prepared to arrange for the patients' hospitalization.

TABLE 4
Example Items in DDMI Decisional Balance Activities

Staying Clean and Sober

POSITIVES

- I will focus better on my psychiatric treatment.
- I will take my medication the way I should.
- I will have more money.
- I won't be sick all of the time.
- I will feel like I finally am accomplishing something good for me.

NEGATIVES

- I will feel miserable.
- I will have to deal with people pressuring me to use.
- I will not know how to spend my time.
- I will not have anyone to hang out with.
- It will be more difficult to be around people and to deal with them.

Getting Treatment for My Dual Disorders

POSITIVES

- I might learn how to deal with my dual disorders better.
- If I start to get into trouble, I have somewhere to go before I get too deep into it.
- I can meet people who may be positive for me.
- If I am in the program, I may be able to get into the vocational training program.
- I need the structure; I have nothing to do during the day.

NEGATIVES

- I will have to follow the program's rules.
- I do not like talking about my personal business with other people.
- I will not have time to do the things I like to do.
- I do not like the way my medications make me feel.
- I do not like feeling that people are looking over me.

In addition to psychotic exacerbation, dually diagnosed patients have higher rates of suicidality and homicidality (Craig, Linm, El-Defrawi, & Goldman, 1985; Drake et al., 1989; Lyons & McGovern, 1989; Turner & Tsuang, 1990) than substance abusing patients without co-occurring psychiatric conditions. Therefore, DDMI requires that therapists are capable of performing risk assessments of patients' dangerousness to self and others and are knowledgeable about the policies and procedures for handling patients who the therapists deem are at imminent risk for self- and other destructive behavior. As with grave disability caused by psychosis, when patients pose clear threats to themselves and others, therapists must alter their style of intervention away from DDMI where collaboration and patients' freedom of choice operate, to crisis intervention where therapists' decision making and direction, even if coercive, matter most. Under these circumstances, safeguarding the patient and the public through immediate protective measures supersedes the basic principles underlying DDMI. To anticipate these events and to be clear about the related clinical dilemmas posed by them, we routinely review with patients in the interview the circumstances that necessitate involuntary protective measures.

These issues and the general clinical complexity of most dually diagnosed patients dictate that DDMI therapists have special professional qualifications. We have found that beyond supporting the highly empathic and collaborative MI style, therapists should have at least one year of supervised work experience with dually diagnosed patients to demonstrate familiarity with psychotic phenomenon and to adequately appreciate the possible interactions of substance use and psychotic functioning. In addition, therapists must have familiarity with psychotropic medications and potential side effects, given that most of these patients receive prescribed antipsychotic and mood stabilizing medications for their psychiatric conditions. Finally, DDMI requires consistently scheduled and ad hoc therapist supervision to continuously refine the therapist's skills in applying MI to dually diagnosed patients and to aptly handle crisis situations.

4. Conclusions

Motivational Interviewing is a promising treatment approach to use with dually diagnosed patients. Within this promise, we have found that MI requires modifications to accommodate the special needs of substance abusing patients who have psychotic disorders. DDMI is our initial attempt to systematically develop and describe how MI might be altered for this patient population and be most effective in promoting the patients' productive efforts to change previously problematic behaviors. We recognize that the complex and severe problems experienced by dually diagnosed patients may limit the ultimate capacity of a brief two-session intervention like DDMI to render beneficial impact. Nonetheless, studies of brief motivational interventions have shown their effectiveness in reducing substance use outcomes with high-average effect sizes comparable to more extensive treatments (Bien, Miller, & Tonigan, 1993), particularly when they are used to enhance engagement in intensive treatment-as-usual (Dunn et al., 2001). If our initial pilot study (Martino et al., 2000) showing some benefit of a one-session motivational interview for dually diagnosed patients is any indication, a two-session and carefully developed DDMI may have the potential for greater merit as a brief intervention. Our current effort to examine the feasibility and effectiveness of DDMI in a randomized controlled trial will address this issue directly and will be the subject of future reports. Finally, while we have presented DDMI as an independent clinical intervention, we recognize that DDMI might best function as a complement to the many recommended health service system approaches described by Drake and others (Drake et al., 1993, 1998, 2001; Minkoff, 2001) to improve treatment outcomes for dually diagnosed patients. In this regard, DDMI may be viewed as a guideline for how service providers might best interact with dually diagnosed patients on an individual level while they work with these patients in the context of the broader service system.

REFERENCES

American Psychiatric Association. (1994). *Diagnostic and statistical manual of mental disorders* (4th ed.).Washington, DC: American Psychiatric Association.

Bartels, S. J., Teague, G. B., Drake, R. E., Clark, R. E., Bush, P., & Noordsy, D. L. (1993). Service utilization and costs associated with substance abuse among rural schizophrenic patients. *Journal of Nervous and Mental Disease, 181,* 227–276.

Beeder, A. B., & Millman, R. B. (1992). Treatment of patients with psychopathology and substance abuse. In J. Lowinson, P. Ruiz, & R. Millman (Eds.), *Substance abuse: A comprehensive textbook* (3rd ed., pp. 675–690). Baltimore: Williams & Wilkins.

Bien, T. H., Miller, W. R., & Boroughs, J. M. (1993). Motivational interviewing with alcohol outpatients. *Behavioural and Cognitive Psychotherapy, 21,* 347–356.

Bien, T. H., Miller, W. R., & Tonigan, J. S. (1993). Brief interventions for alcohol problems: A review. *Addictions, 88,* 305–325.

Bell, M. D., Lysaker, P. H., Milstein, R. M., & Beam-Goulet, J. L. (1994). Concurrent validity of the cognitive component of schizophrenia: Relationship of PANSS scores to neuropsychological assessments. *Psychiatry Research, 54,* 51–58.

Bellack, A. C., & DiClemente, C. C. (1999). Treating substance use among patients with schizophrenia. *Psychiatric Services, 50,* 75–80.

Brady, S., Hiam, C. M., Saemann, R., Humbert, L., Fleming, M. Z., & Dawkins-Brickhaus, K. (1996). Dual diagnosis: A treatment model for substance abuse and major mental illness. *Community Mental Health Journal, 32,* 573–578.

Brown, J. M., & Miller, W. R. (1993). Impact of motivational interviewing on participation and outcome in residential alcoholism treatment. *Psychology of Addictive Behaviors, 7,* 211–218.

Butler, C. C., Rollnick, S., Cohen, D., Russell, I., Bachmann, M., & Stott, N. (1999). Motivational consulting versus brief advice for smokers in general practice: A randomised trial. *British Journal of General Practice, 49,* 611–616.

Carey, K. B. (1996). Substance use reduction in the context of outpatient psychiatric treatment: A collaborative, motivational, harm reduction approach. *Community Mental Health Journal, 32,* 291–306.

Carey, M. P., Maisto, S. A., Kalichman, S. C., Forsyth, A. D., Wright, E. M., & Johnson, B. (1997). Enhancing motivation to reduce the risk of HIV infection for economically disadvantaged urban women. *Journal of Consulting and Clinical Psychology, 65,* 531–541.

Carroll, K. M., & Nuro, K. F. (1997). The use and development of manuals. In K. M. Carroll (Ed.), *Improving compliance with alcoholism treatment. Project MATCH Monograph Series, Volume 6* (pp. 53–72). Bethesda, MD: NIAAA.

Craig, T. J., Linm, S. P., El-Defrawi, M. H., & Goldman, A. B. (1985). Clinical correlates of readmission in a schizophrenic cohort. *Psychiatric Quarterly, 57,* 243–249.

Daley, D. C., & Zuckoff, A. (1998). Improving compliance with the initial outpatient session among discharged inpatient dual diagnosis clients. *Social Work, 43,* 470–473.

Drake, R. E., Bartels, S. J., Teague, G. B., Noordsy, D. L., & Clark, R. E. (1993). Treatment of substance abuse in severely mentally ill patients. *Journal of Nervous and Mental Disease, 181,* 606–611.

Drake, R. E., Essock, S. M., Shaner, A., Carey, K. B., Minkoff, K., Kola, L., Lynde, D., Osher, F. C., Clark, R. E., & Rickards, L. (2001). Implementing dual diagnosis services for clients with severe mental illness. *Psychiatric Services, 52,* 469–476.

Drake, R. E., McLaughlin, P., Pepper, B., & Minkoff, K. (1991). Dual diagnosis of major mental illness and substance disorder: An overview. *New Directions for Mental Health Services, 50,* 3—12.

Drake, R. E., Mercer-McFadden, C., Mueser, K. T., McHugo, G. J., & Bond, G. R. (1998). Review of integrated mental health and substance abuse treatment for patients with dual disorders. *Schizophrenia Bulletin, 24,* 589–608.

Drake, R. E., Osher, F. C., & Wallach, M. A. (1989). Alcohol use and abuse in schizophrenia: A perspective community study. *Journal of Nervous and Mental Disease, 177,* 408–413.

Drake, R. E., & Wallach, M. A. (1989). Substance abuse among the chronically mentally ill. *Hospital and Community Psychiatry, 40,* 1041–1046.

Dunn, C., Deroo, L., & Rivara, F. P. (2001). The use of brief interventions adapted from motivational interviewing across behavioral domains: A systematic review. *Addiction, 96,* 1725–1742.

Eisenthal, S., Emery, R., Lazare, A., & Udin, H. (1978). Adherence and the negotiated approach to patienthood. *Archives of General Psychiatry, 36,* 393–398.

Evans, K., & Sullivan, J. M. (1989). *Dual diagnosis: Counseling the mentally ill substance abuser.* New York: Guilford Press.

Green, M. F. (1996). What are the functional consequences of neurocognitive deficits in schizophrenia? *American Journal of Psychiatry, 153,* 321–330.

Kay, S. R., Fizbein, A., & Opler, L. A. (1987). The Positive and Negative Syndrome Scale (PANSS) for schizophrenia. *Schizophrenia Bulletin, 13,* 261–276.

Kofoed, L. L., & Keyes, A. (1988). Using group therapy to persuade dual-diagnosis patients to seek treatment. *Hospital and Community Psychiatry, 39,* 1209–1211.

Lawendowski, L. A. (1998). A motivational intervention for adolescent smokers. *Preventive Medicine, 27,* A39–A46.

Lyons, J. S., & McGovern, M. P. (1989). Use of mental health services by dually diagnosed patients. *Hospital and Community Psychiatry, 40,* 1067–1069.

Lysaker, P. H., Bell, M. D., Zito, W. S., & Bioty, S. M. (1995). Cognitive deficits in schizophrenia. Prediction of symptom change for participators in work rehabilitation. *Journal of Nervous and Mental Disease, 183,* 332–336.

Martino, S., McCance-Katz, E., Workman, J., & Boozang, J. (1995). The development of a dual diagnosis partial hospital program. *Continuum, 2,* 145–165.

Martino, S., Carroll, K. M., O'Malley, S. O., & Rounsaville, B. J. (2000). Motivational interviewing with psychiatrically ill substance abusing patients. *The American Journal on Addictions, 9,* 88–91.

McLellan, A. T., Luborsky, L., Cacciola, J., Griffith, J., Evans, H. L., & O'Brien, C. P. (1985). New data from the Addiction Severity Index: Reliability and validity in three centers. *Journal of Nervous and Mental Disease, 173,* 412–423.

McLellan, A. T., Luborsky, L., Woody, G. E., & O'Brien, C. P. (1980). An improved diagnostic evaluation instrument for substance abuse patients: The Addiction Severity Index. *Journal of Nervous and Mental Disease, 168,* 26–33.

Miller, W. R. (1983). Motivational interviewing with problem drinkers. *Behavioural Psychotherapy, 11,* 147–172.

Miller, W. R. (1985). Motivation for treatment: A review with a special emphasis on alcoholism. *Psychological Bulletin, 98*, 84–107.

Miller, W. R. (1996). Motivational interviewing: Research, practice, and puzzles. *Addictive Behaviors, 21*, 835–842.

Miller, W. R. (1998). Why do people change addictive behavior? The 1996 H. David Archibald Lecture. *Addiction, 93*, 163–172.

Miller, W. R., Benefield, B., & Tonigan, J. S. (1993). Enhancing motivation for change in problem drinking: A controlled comparison of two therapist styles. *Journal of Consulting and Clinical Psychology, 61*, 455–461.

Miller, W. R., & Rollnick, S. (2002). *Motivational interviewing: Preparing people for change.* New York: Guilford Press.

Miller, W. R., Sovereign, R. G., & Krege, B. (1988). Motivational interviewing with problem drinkers: II. The drinker's check-up as a preventive intervention. *Behavioural Psychotherapy, 16*, 251–268.

Minkoff, K. (1989). An integrated treatment model for dual diagnosis of psychosis and addiction. *Hospital and Community Psychiatry, 40*, 1031–1036.

Minkoff, K. (2001). Developing standards of care for individuals with cooccurring psychiatric and substance use disorders. *Psychiatric Services, 52*, 597–599.

Minkoff, K., & Drake, R. (Eds.) (1991). *Dual diagnosis of major mental illness and substance disorder* (New Directions for Mental Health Services No. 50). San Francisco: Jossey-Bass.

Osher, F. C., & Kofoed, L. L. (1989). Treatment of patients with psychiatric and psychoactive substance abuse disorders. *Hospital and Community Psychiatry, 40*, 1025–1030.

Owen, R. R., Fischer, E. P., Booth, B. M., & Cuffel, B. J. (1996). Medication noncompliance and substance abuse among patients with schizophrenia. *Psychiatric Services, 47*, 853–858.

Project MATCH Research Group. (1997). Matching alcoholism treatment to client heterogeneity: Project MATCH posttreatment drinking outcomes. *Journal of Studies on Alcohol, 58*, 7–29.

Richardson, M. A., Craig, T. J., & Haugland, C. (1985). Treatment patterns of young chronic schizophrenic patients in the era of deinstitutionalization. *Psychiatric Quarterly, 57*, 104–110.

Ridgely, M. S., Goldman, H. H., & Willenbring, M. (1990). Barriers to care of persons with dual diagnoses. *Schizophrenia Bulletin, 16*, 123–132.

Rollnick, S., Heather, N., & Bell, A. (1992). Negotiating behaviour change in medical settings: The development of brief motivational interviewing. *Journal of Mental Health, 1*, 25–37.

Rosenthal, R. N., Hellerstein, D. J., & Miner, C. R. (1992). A model of integrated services for outpatient treatment of patients with comorbid schizophrenia and substance abuse patterns. *Psychiatric Quarterly, 63*, 2–26.

Rounsaville, B. J., Carroll, K. M., & Onken, L. S. (2001). NIDA's stage model of behavioral therapies research: Getting started and moving on from Stage I. Clinical *Psychology: Science and Practice, 8*, 133–142.

Saunders, B., Wilkinson, C., & Phillips, M. (1995). The impact of a brief motivational intervention with opiate users attending a methadone programme. *Addiction, 90*, 415–424.

Seidman, L. J., Pepple, J. R., Farone, S. V., Kremen, W. S., Green, A. I., Brown, W. A., & Tsuang, M. T. (1993). Neuropsychological performance in chronic schizophrenia in response to neuroleptic dose reduction. *Biological Psychiatry, 33*, 575–584.

Smith, D. E., Heckemeyer, C. M., Kratt, P. P., & Mason, D. A. (1997). Motivational interviewing to improve adherence to a behavioral weight-control program for older obese women with NIDDM: A pilot study. *Diabetes Care, 20*, 53–54.

Stott II, N. C., Rollnick, S., Pill, R., & Rees, M. (1995). Innovation in clinical method: Diabetes care and negotiating skills. *Family Practice, 12*, 413–418.

Stotts, A. L., Schmitz, J. M., Rhoades, H. M., & Grabowski, J. (2001). Motivational interviewing with cocaine-dependent patients: A pilot study. *Journal of Consulting and Clinical Psychology, 69*, 858–862.

Swanson, A. J., Pantalon, M. V., & Cohen, K. R. (1999). Motivational interviewing and treatment adherence among psychiatric and dually diagnosed patients. *Journal of Nervous and Mental Disorders, 187*, 630–635.

Treasure, J. L., Katzman, M., Schmidt, U., Troop, N., Todd, G., & DeSilva, P. (1999). Engagement and outcome in the treatment of bulimia nervosa: First phase of a sequential design comparing motivation enhancement therapy and cognitive behavioural therapy. *Behaviour Research and Therapy, 37*, 405–418.

Turner, W. M., & Tsuang, M. R. (1990). Impact of substance abuse on the course and outcome of schizophrenia. *Schizophrenia Bulletin, 16*, 87–95.

Van Horn, D. H. A., & Bux, D. A. (2001). A pilot test of motivational interviewing groups for dually diagnosed inpatients. *Journal of Substance Abuse Treatment, 20*, 191–195.

Zweben, J. E., & Smith, D. E. (1989). Considerations in using psychotropic medication with dual diagnosis patients in recovery. *Journal of Psychoactive Drugs, 21*, 221–228.

Ziedonis, D., & Fischer, W. (1996). Motivation-based assessment and treatment of substance abuse in patients with schizophrenia. *Directions in Psychiatry, 16*, 1–7.

Ziedonis, D., & Trudeau, K. (1997). Motivation to quit using substances among individuals with schizophrenia: Implications for a motivation-based treatment model. *Schizophrenia Bulletin, 23*, 229–238.

Zitrin, A., Hardesty, A. S., Burdock, E. I., & Drossman, A. K. (1976). Crime and violence among mental patients. *American Journal of Psychiatry, 13*, 142–149.